W9-CXW-943

TOUGH CALLS

OTHER BOOKS BY DICK IRVIN

Now Back to You, Dick

*The Habs: An Oral History of the
Montreal Canadiens*

*Behind the Bench: Coaches Talk About
Life in the NHL*

*In the Crease: Goaltenders Look at
Life in the NHL*

01/05 Don 21.99

TOUGH CALLS

NHL Referees and Linesmen
Tell Their Story

DICK IRVIN

0105

Copyright © 1997 by Dick Irvin Enterprises Ltd.

Cloth edition published 1997
Trade paperback edition published 1998

All rights reserved. The use of any part of this publication,
reproduced, transmitted in any form or by any means, electronic,
mechanical, photocopying, recording, or otherwise, or stored in a
retrieval system, without the prior written consent of the
publisher – or, in case of photocopying or other reprographic
copying, a licence from the Canadian Copyright Licensing
Agency – is an infringement of the copyright law.

Canadian Cataloguing in Publication Data

Irvin, Dick, 1932–
Tough Calls : NHL referees and linesmen tell their story

Includes index.
ISBN 0-7710-4366-X (bound)   ISBN 0-7710-4368-6 (pbk.)

1. Hockey referees – Anecdotes.
2. National Hockey League – Anecdotes.   I. Title.

GV847.8.N3178 1997   796.962   C97-931472-0

We acknowledge the financial support of the Government of
Canada through the Book Publishing Industry Development
Program for our publishing activities. We further acknowledge
the support of the Canada Council for the Arts and the Ontario
Arts Council for our publishing program.

Set in Trump Mediaeval by M&S, Toronto
Printed and bound in Canada

McClelland & Stewart Inc.
The Canadian Publishers
481 University Avenue
Toronto, Ontario
M5G 2E9

2 3 4 5 6   05 04 03 02 01 00

Contents

Introduction

In the mid-1960s *Toronto Star* sports columnist Jim Proudfoot mailed a questionnaire to the coaches in the then six-team National Hockey League. They were asked to pick their "bests" in hockey: best skater, best shooter, best stick-handler, best bodychecker, and so on. The final category was best referee.

The coaches diligently listed their choices, with one exception. When he came to best referee Toe Blake of the Montreal Canadiens wrote, "None. All bad." Blake's answer perhaps echoed the thoughts of coaches past, present, and future, but such is life for the men who wear striped jerseys and blow whistles in the game of hockey.

There is no question that while the majority of games in the NHL are well handled by the officials, some are not. I have seen clear-cut examples of great, good, bad, and ugly officiating in the more than two thousand games I have attended. Yet because their imperfections are so visible, referees and linesmen are subjected to an incredible amount of public scrutiny and abuse. Media types, many of whom likely haven't read past the first few pages of the rule book, if that, write, and broadcast in judgement. And of course there are the fans, who feel their team always plays against nine men: six players, the referee, and the two linesmen.

A favourite topic for the critics is inconsistency. Another is non-calls in the areas of holding, hooking, and interference. At times complaints about any or all of these are warranted, but this is nothing new. In the late 1940s the Toronto Maple Leafs won three straight Stanley Cups while their opponents loudly accused the referees of letting them get away with what was termed "clutch-and-grab hockey."

A referee once said, "If we called a penalty every time there was hooking, holding, or interference, you'd have thirty-five to forty penalties a game on those infractions alone." Was it somebody like Bill McCreary or Rob Shick refereeing in the 1990s? It could have been, but it wasn't. It was Frank "King" Clancy, when he was refereeing in the 1940s.

I conducted most of the interviews for this book during the 1996–97 season, the toughest season officials had experienced in a long time. Television viewers with only a rudimentary knowledge of lip-reading could tell several times during a game how upset the coaches and players were at the officials. Hardly a game went by when a coach, whose team had just lost or tied, didn't blame the referee for everything from a missed holding call in the first period to the latest increase in the federal deficit. To my knowledge, no losing or tying coach ever admitted he may have made a mistake or two himself that evening.

A mid-season hockey story in the *New York Times* carried the headline "REFEREES BECOMING THE NATIONAL LEAGUE'S BELEAGUERED MEN." In it, retired referee Andy van Hellemond, who left the league amidst bitterness on both sides, said officials are "the bottom rung" of the ladder of league authority, adding, "You're only as strong as the support from above." Those who are above were also quoted. Brian Burke, the NHL's senior vice-president for hockey operations, said "referees have never received the backing at league level that they've gotten from Commissioner Gary Bettman," and that "we've tried to upgrade their image. We've backed them vociferously and aggressively." The official who has worked the most games in NHL history, linesman Ray Scapinello, told me, "Gary Bettman has brought us out of the stone age."

Hockey referees are not the only beleaguered officials these days in the sometimes not-so-wonderful world of sports. In 1996 baseball had the bizarre case of Roberto Alomar of the Baltimore Orioles spitting at umpire John Hirschbeck. Almost as bizarre were remarks a few weeks later by the Orioles' owner, who said Hirschbeck owed Alomar an apology. The chief of Hirschbeck's umpiring crew that day was Jim McKean, a Montreal native, who once did some hockey refereeing. McKean, a twenty-five-year veteran of major league baseball, says he is fearful that someday there will be a fistfight between a player and an umpire on the field. In recent years in pro basketball, Nick Van Exel of the Los Angeles Lakers shoved an official into a table, while the ever-popular Dennis Rodman was suspended for head-butting a referee. In the 1996 Canadian Football League season, five players, more than ever before, were ejected from games for "physical abuse of an official."

During the 1996–97 NHL campaign, Kelly Chase, a forward with the Hartford Whalers, was fined the maximum thousand dollars for blasting the work of referee Kerry Fraser after a game in Montreal. At the time Chase had a record of 19 games played, no goals, 1 assist, and 86 minutes in penalties. At the other end of the talent scale, Mario

Lemieux threatened to boycott the 1997 All-Star Game to protest the work of the officials. Mario relented and found his way to San Jose to be part of the festivities, but one week later he used *Hockey Night in Canada* to vent his feelings anew during a post-game interview with Ron MacLean. Lemieux told the million-or-so people watching that the referees weren't allowing great players to play great. Mario belongs amongst the greats and he had just scored four goals in the third period. It made you wonder: If the refereeing had been stronger would he have scored eight?

Another great player, Mark Messier, was fined a thousand dollars for launching a verbal attack on referee Don Van Massenhoven. Anaheim defenceman Jean-Jacques Daignault was suspended for ten games for hitting referee Don Koharski with his stick. Hockey's all-time winningest coach, the always innovative Scotty Bowman, claimed some of his Detroit Red Wings were being discriminated against by referee Terry Gregson because they were Russian. The NHL promptly fined Bowman ten thousand dollars. Scotty then suggested that since the maximum fine for a player criticizing an official is only a thousand, in the future he'd give ten of them each that amount to put his message across with more frequency.

And then there was the in-the-crease call, which was at first controversial and then, because of its frequency, an embarrassment. With the ability to use video replays the league decided on zero tolerance when it came to a foot, a toe, or a sliver of a skate blade in the crease when a goal was scored. Any of the above meant no goal. This led to one of the most frequently uttered phrases of the season after a puck went into a net: "They're going upstairs for this one." A referee on the telephone with the video goal judge became a familiar and much-maligned sight. One night, in Montreal, referee Don Koharski was on the phone for almost four minutes while the video goal judge determined if a goal had actually been scored. Coaches and players ranted and raved, fans and the media scoffed, but the league didn't budge. Following a meeting of the top brass during the 1997 Stanley Cup finals it was announced that, like it or not, folks, zero tolerance in the goal crease is here to stay.

Through it all the officials soldiered on, suffering in silence, unable to answer their critics publicly. However, I must say that during my interviews with current officials, in what must have been a long season of discontent for them, every one appeared upbeat, positive, and, as far as I could see, very happy to be doing what he was doing.

So why do they do it? As I worked my way through the interviews the answer to that often-asked question became clear. They do it because they love it. When they are on the ice standing for the national anthem just before the opening faceoff, the referee and the linesmen are exactly where they want to be. They are thrilled when their career begins in the NHL and they are sad when it is over. Many hate to give it up, and leave with a bitter taste if their career ends before they think it should.

This book is written mainly in the words of men who have worked as on-ice officials in the National Hockey League, past and present. My game plan was to ask them where they came from, how they got there, and to tell my tape recorder some of their most memorable experiences. We begin *Tough Calls* with the story of the toughest, and most regrettable, call ever made by the man who refereed more games than anyone in the history of the National Hockey League.

I

Andy

ANDY VAN HELLEMOND

On May 12, 1995, the New York Rangers and the Quebec Nordiques played the fourth game of their Eastern Conference playoff series at Madison Square Garden, in New York, with the Rangers leading the series two games to one.

In the first period, with his team holding an early 2–0 lead, Quebec captain Joe Sakic intercepted a pass near his team's blueline during a New York power play. As Sakic rushed up the right wing, his teammate, defenceman Craig Wolanin, took a one-handed swipe with his stick at New York forward Alexei Kovalev and struck him across the back. When I later asked Wolanin how he would describe the force of the blow he replied, "I hit him with a one-hander and he was skating away from me. On a scale of one to ten, I'd give it about a five." Nevertheless, Kovalev dropped to the ice as though he had been shot. And once he dropped, Kovalev didn't get back up – he didn't even move.

Kovalev was still down and out along the boards back at the Quebec blueline when Sakic reached the faceoff circle in the New York zone and took a shot but partially fanned on it. Sakic kept going and took another swipe at the puck. That time it went into the net but as it did the referee, who had alternately been looking ahead at Sakic's rush and over his shoulder at the possibly deceased Rangers forward, blew his whistle.

Rule 18(f) in the NHL rule book reads: "When a player is injured so that he cannot continue play or go to his bench, the play shall not be stopped until the injured player's team has secured possession of the puck."

A footnote to the rule reads: "In the case where it is obvious that a player has sustained a serious injury, the Referee . . . may stop the play immediately."

The referee that night was Andy van Hellemond, who knew exactly what rule 18(f) was all about. What Andy didn't know was if Kovalev was really seriously injured or acting to get a whistle to stop a potential scoring play by the Nordiques. He also didn't know that Sakic's shot had gone in the net.

The Rangers came back to win the game 3–2 on an overtime goal by Steve Larmer, and went on to win the series in six games. After game four the big story was van Hellemond's call on that confusing first-period play, a call he now says was the toughest in the 1,702 league and playoff games he worked. His ruling was no goal, no penalty.

Because of his call on the play, the NHL kept van Hellemond out of that year's Stanley Cup final series, the only time that happened to him between 1977 and his retirement in 1996.

ANDY VAN HELLEMOND

What happened was, the Rangers were on a power play and the puck had gone back to the point. I thought Brian Leetch was gonna shoot it on the net and I was watching for high sticks with the players jostling for position and driving for the net. Most teams, when they kill penalties, set up in a box and don't go out to challenge, so as a referee you've got time to see where everybody is. All of a sudden Quebec has the puck and there's a roar from the crowd and I look and this guy [Kovalev] is lying down by the boards and he's not moving.

I didn't know what happened to him and there isn't anybody close to him who might have cross-checked or speared him. The only guy close is maybe ten or fifteen feet away. So what happened? Did he lose his balance and crash into the boards? I don't know and I haven't put my arm up because I don't know who to give a penalty to.

Now Quebec's got the puck and I'm gonna let them finish their play. I was in the corner, on the goal line, on the same side of the ice as the guy lying down. So I start to skate up the ice and I'm lucky enough to be going by the guy and I said, "Get up," figuring I'd get a response from him like "I'm hurt" or "Somebody speared me." But there was no response, no movement, no nothing.

I looked ahead and Sakic looked to me like he was gonna shoot the puck and then he seemed to have fanned on it. The puck moved away from him and went past the defence-man who was between him and the goalie and it was sliding away. That's the last time I saw it. I figured it's either going to the goalie or the end boards so I took one more look back and the guy still wasn't moving. So I just turned and blew the whistle. What I didn't know was that Sakic got to the puck as it was sliding towards the goal line and whacked it with a backhand. It went between Glenn Healy's leg and the goal post. I saw that on the tape afterwards. When I blow the whistle Sakic is behind the net with his arms up and he's looking back at me. I don't know if it went in before or after I blew my whistle.

I was stopping the play for the injured player but I can't phone upstairs to the video judge on that, and I can't check the audio whether I blew it before or after because that's not one of our criteria.

Now I go to the linesman who went in and covered the goal line and I ask him if he could tell me if the whistle went before or after the puck went in, and he says, "Andy, I never heard your whistle." The people were all screaming about the guy lying on the ice and in fairness to him I blew the whistle near the Rangers' blueline and Kovalev was down on the other blueline. So I had no way of verifying when it went in.

Suddenly the Rangers are complaining to me that there should be a major penalty to Quebec for slashing and I had to turn again to the linesmen. I felt so empty because it's my job to see things like that. I didn't see it so I asked them if there should be a major penalty because, if so, then the goal doesn't count because the major would override it. They said, "No major. At best it's a minor. In fact, he just one-handed swung at him and hit him on the back." I said, "Are you serious? Look at him. He's still lying there. He looks like he's dead." They told me the stick hit him either on the pants or just above the pants, and I kept saying, "Look at him. He hasn't moved yet." I mean, it looked like he was really speared, or hurt.

We agreed, no penalty. Now I've got to say to myself that if I allowed the goal and the replay shows it went in after I blew my whistle, why did I count it as a goal? You blew your whistle, then the puck went in, and now you're counting it?

So here I am in never-never land having to make a decision. I just felt, I can't count it. I blew the whistle to stop the play and I was killing the play because of the injured player.

Quebec is all upset, of course, and their coach Marc Crawford called me over and asked me what happened. I said I wasn't sure when the puck went in but I felt I blew my whistle before it did. I told him I blew it because of the injured player, that I couldn't leave him lying there. I told him, "Marc, you guys took the puck all the way up the ice and I let you finish your play." He said, "Yeah, but the puck went into the net." I said, "Look, when I last saw the puck nobody had it. Your guy lost control of it and that's probably when I should have blown the whistle. But I took one more look back. So I was two seconds too slow." He finally said, "Okay. That's fine." And we started the game again.

I never, ever, said to him that I blew the whistle before it went in. I couldn't say that because I didn't know. [*The audio on the tape picked up the whistle blowing 2.1 seconds after the puck crossed the goal line.*] I had to make a decision and it was that I had killed the play because of the injured player. That's exactly how I told it to Gary Bettman and Brian Burke but they wouldn't let me go public and explain it. Now it has to look like somebody's gotta take the hit. I said, Well, the only person taking the hit is me. I'm the one who was on the ice.

It was the hardest decision, or non-decision, I ever had to make, especially when the outcome two and half hours later is a defeat for Quebec. But you would figure that after explaining, after all your years of experience and drawing on your resources, when you came up with a conclusion and explained it properly that somebody would support you. Maybe somebody would say, listen, it was a human error. He made a mistake, that's plain to see, but in fairness to him he couldn't confirm when it went in. But I got none of that. It was just "glaring error, glaring this, glaring that." Sure, it's glaring when you watch it on the replay and slow it down and follow the puck and know exactly what to watch. Anybody can referee that way.

The people that were there to support me, that I thought would be on my side, weren't. So I have to ask the question: Why? Was it because of my involvement with our association? You can just speculate on things like that. Instead of saying that I made a mistake and we don't feel very good about it, but let's go forward, they put out a press release. They knew the Nordiques were being sold and leaving Quebec and they made sure the release came out before the sale was announced so it could look like they were doing something about the situation because Quebec complained.

After I had a meeting with Gary Bettman and Bryan Lewis I said I knew what was gonna happen, that I probably wouldn't get to work in the finals. I've done them for eighteen years and that'll probably be my punishment. And it was. The next year was my last year and I worked game three in the finals. So it would have been twenty straight years.

One other thing about that game in New York. In overtime Wendel Clark had a great chance to win it for Quebec. For a split second I found myself talking to the puck, saying, "Go in!" It didn't.

Harry Neale, the esteemed commentator on Hockey Night in Canada, *likes to tell an Andy van Hellemond story from the time Harry was coaching the Vancouver Canucks.*

"Referees from the East would take a Western swing that would keep them on the road for several days and Vancouver was often their last stop," Harry says. "When Andy would come to Vancouver I'd ask him before the game if he was heading home on the red-eye that night. If

he said he was I'd go back to the team and tell them, 'Boys, there won't be too many penalties called because Andy wants to get the game over in a hurry. He doesn't want to miss the red-eye.'"

On a more serious note Harry adds, "I always felt good whenever we had an important game and Andy van Hellemond was working because I knew it would be well refereed, for both teams." Harry might not get universal agreement on that, but it would be close.

When he retired in 1996 at the age of forty-eight, Andy van Hellemond had worked 1,475 regular-season games, 227 playoff games, and nineteen years in the Stanley Cup finals, all records for referees. And it began on a community-centre baseball field in his native Winnipeg for the man many feel was hockey's best-ever referee.

ANDY VAN HELLEMOND

When I was young I started umpiring baseball games. It seemed they always needed an umpire, especially the younger kids. They'd play after our games and I would be hanging around so they put me to work. One of the parents would call balls and strikes and I'd umpire at first base. I liked it. I used to help out at the Isaac Brock Community Centre and there was a lot of pick-up hockey in the winter. On the weekends some good players, like Art Stratton, who had started there and were playing junior, would come back and get into the games. They needed somebody to control the scrimmage. I was younger than they were and they knew I'd umpired baseball so they got me to blow the whistle. It was nothing serious but I grew to enjoy the challenge of it.

I played junior hockey for the Winnipeg Braves but I didn't feel there was a career for me in professional hockey.

Gordie Kerr was a good amateur official in Manitoba and I asked him if I could do some refereeing. He said they'd love to have me and told me there were lots of games in rural Manitoba I could work and make twenty dollars a game. They used a two-referee system so it gave me a chance to call penalties right away. I was never a linesman.

I went to Bruce Hood's referee school in Haliburton, Ontario. After that I was asked if I'd be interested in working full time in the Western Junior League. I'd been going to university but I quit after my first year and became a referee.

Right from the start there was a lot of travel. I'd leave home in Winnipeg and drive to Brandon, then to Estevan, Regina, Saskatoon, Swift Current, Medicine Hat, Calgary. There were plenty of times I did sixteen games in sixteen nights working with local linesmen.

I was getting fifty dollars a game and they'd pay me after the second period. Jackie McLeod was coaching in Saskatoon and one night he didn't like some of the things I did. So after the second period I didn't get any money. The intermission was over but I didn't leave the room. The timekeeper came in and I told him I was supposed to get paid, fifty dollars plus my mileage. The teams were out on the ice and the fans were stomping their feet but I didn't move. I told him I'd sit there until the game was over unless they found somebody to pay me. They owed me about a hundred. So he went out and told McLeod and pretty soon some guy came in and he threw about a hundred one-dollar bills at me. They were all over the floor. I said, "Tell them I'll be right out," and then I picked up every one of them. The fans were booing because I was late coming out but you had to stick to your guns. That's the way it was then. There were a lot of old pros running that league and they tested you early.

Like Bill Hunter, who was running the team in Edmonton. They played in the old Edmonton Gardens and before a game Hunter came into the room and said, "Andy, we've got a big crowd tonight so we're not going to start the game on time. We're going to wait ten or fifteen minutes so that everybody can get in." So I sit there, twenty or twenty-one years old and still wet behind the ears, and all of a sudden there's a knock on the door. It's Jimmy Watson, who was playing for the Calgary Centennials, and he wanted to know what was going on. When I told him we were holding up the game to let the fans get in he said, "Nobody told us. We've been on the ice skating around for fifteen minutes." I got myself in trouble with the league over that one. Hunter had no right to tell me to hold up the game. But it was a great lesson. You're in charge, you're running the game. Don't let them hoodwink you.

Flin Flon was always a tough place. Patty Ginnell was running the team there and we might have a lunch or two together and shoot the breeze, but he'd warn me that once the game started he'd look for an edge. Sure enough, one Sunday afternoon there's a wild game there and I've got eight players in the penalty box at the same time. I've got a picture of it from the newspaper with the caption, "Not the player's bench . . . The penalty box." Ginnell always wore a hat. When the period ended I was skating off and I stumbled on something on the ice and it was his goddam hat. He'd thrown it on the ice just to see what I would do. I learned then and there that if you don't see somebody throw something on the ice you can't assume he did it. Like when there's a water bottle on the ice. If you don't see somebody actually throw it you can't give him a penalty. A fan sitting six rows up can throw a hat, or a water bottle. So Ginnell was testing me. I picked up the hat, crumpled it all up, took it over to the penalty box and told the guy not to give it back to anybody. He was used to getting it back when there were local referees working, and everybody knows everybody else in a town like Flin Flon. A local referee has to live there. But I came from Winnipeg. It didn't matter to me who won or lost. I just wanted to have a fair game.

Flin Flon was tough but it gave me great experience. When I was a junior in Winnipeg I played up there against Bobby Clarke, and if he and his teammates weren't beating the other guy on the scoreboard they'd bump and push and punch, anything to get an edge. He took the same kind of thinking to the Philadelphia Flyers when he was captain there, so when I was refereeing their games I knew exactly where he was coming from because I'd gone through it with him in junior. I earned my spurs in that league.

Travelling through the Western Junior League by car was really something. I mean, we're talking winter on the prairies. Bloody miserable. I used to play cards in the hotels with the scouts from the NHL and sometimes they'd ride with me. Men like Clare Rothermel, Del Wilson, Gerry McNamara, Phil Maloney. They'd watch me work and then they'd go over things with me. They were great for a young referee. They were sort of my mentors.

Claude Ruel would show up once in a while scouting for the Canadiens. He was playing hearts with us one day and I threw the queen of spades down on him and he got bent right out of shape. A few years later I'm in the NHL and he's coaching Montreal. We're in Minnesota and he didn't like a call or two I had made. All of a sudden he starts in at one of the linesmen, Leon Stickle, and I hear him muttering something about the queen of spades. Leon came over to me and I asked him what Ruel was talking about, and Leon says, "I'm not sure. All I know is he says you don't know how to play cards, and you don't know how to referee." [Laughs]

I got hired by the NHL out of Winnipeg the year before the WHA started and they sent me to the old Western Pro League. My wife and I moved to Vancouver. There were some tough games and some tough guys. One was Ted McCaskill, whose son became a big-league baseball pitcher. He'd use his stick pretty good, and one night in San Diego, in one of my first games refereeing the pros, McCaskill got into a stick fight with Willie O'Ree. They were swinging like crazy and one of them busted the end of his stick off. I said to one of the linesmen, "You better go in now and stop it." He said to me, "For thirty bucks you want me to go in and stop it? You stop it, because I don't get paid enough for something like this." And that's what a local linesman got in those days. Thirty bucks. Finally the other players went in and separated them. That was my baptism into pro hockey.

Not long after that I had a game in Portland and called a lot of penalties, too many, I guess, against the home team, the Buckaroos. I'm coming off the ice and there's a guy standing on the rubber mat that's always on the floor for the officials to walk on to and from their dressing room. This guy starts yelling at me that I'd never referee another game in that building if he had anything to do with it, so I told him to get out of my way or else I'd kick him. I got to the room and all of a sudden the door flies open and in comes Dutch van Deelen, who was a supervisor for the NHL working in the West. He says, "Do you know who you just threatened to kick?" I told him I didn't and Dutch says, "It just happens to be Harry Glickman and he just happens to be the owner of the Portland Buckaroos." I said, "How was I supposed to know that? Would you know the owner in Denver? Would you know the owner in Phoenix?" To me he was just a guy in a sailing jacket yelling at me and blocking my way. I thought I was in big trouble.

I worked in that league for one year and then it lost some teams to the WHA and ended up playing an interlocking schedule with the Central League. We moved back east to Mississauga and I got a chance to work twenty NHL games. Officials like Bill Friday, Bob Sloane, and Ron Ego had all jumped to the WHA, so it opened up a chance for a young guy working in the minors. I was only twenty-two years old.

I did my first NHL game in Chicago, in November. They were playing Vancouver and I ended up doing 1,474 more regular-season games after that. I just hoped I'd get through the games I did that season. I did, and then I was into the next season, full time. Then you get the playoffs and, after a few years, the finals, and you wonder when it's gonna end.

It ended for Andy van Hellemond the night of June 8, 1996, at the Miami Arena when he skated off the ice after refereeing the third game of the Stanley Cup finals between the Florida Panthers and the Colorado Avalanche. If, as the NHL claims, referees skate an average of seven miles per game, Andy had skated 11,914 miles refereeing in the big leagues. A lot of miles. A lot of memories.

ANDY VAN HELLEMOND

I was struck by a player twice in '81–82. The first was in the regular season when Paul Holmgren went after Paul Baxter. There was bad blood between the Flyers and the Penguins at the time and the game was in Pittsburgh. There was an assignment change for that game and I got it instead of the referee originally booked. I was gonna go in there and be the steadying influence.

Baxter had punched Behn Wilson about two weeks earlier, suckered him from the side and broke his jaw. So the Flyers were all gonna get Paul Baxter. The first couple of shifts, not bad, but then on the third or fourth shift Holmgren got a chance to come at Baxter. He sort of jumped him from behind and because Baxter knew he was coming he turned and they started beating on each other. I blew the whistle and jumped in and so did a linesman, Bob Hodges. We had it broken up.

Holmgren went off to the side and wouldn't leave. I'd given him a game misconduct for being the aggressor in the fight but he wouldn't leave. So the people started throwing stuff over the glass at him, pop and beer and all that. I went over to him and said, "Listen, Paul, you're in enough trouble right now so why don't you go to the room. Get out of here because they're gonna keep throwin' shit at you." He never answered me. He just put his head down and started taking deep breaths, like he had the heaves. Bob Hodges was between us and holding him and I told Holmgren again to get out or I'd give him another game misconduct. Bob was watching him and then I looked back and Holmgren was throwing a punch. Hodges had seen it coming so he ducked and it hit me right in the chest. Bob let go of him and Holmgren went flying over to where Baxter was. The other linesman, Will Norris, had Baxter up against the boards. He sees Baxter looking over his shoulder and Baxter's eyes are like, here comes Holmgren again. So Willie looked around, saw Holmgren, and that was the end of Willie. He got out of there. It was a bad scene.

Afterwards Holmgren was apologetic. Brian O'Neill was in charge of discipline in the league office and he had a tough decision to make. He suspended Holmgren for five games. It was really the first time a referee had been struck. It wasn't over a call I had made or didn't make. It was just the type of game it was and the environment we were in. It was get-even time for the Flyers and I was a victim of those circumstances.

We wanted a change in the rules for abuse of officials after that. There was a meeting in early December. I was there with Dave Newell, the president of our group, along with John Ziegler and Brian O'Neill. They said they couldn't change rules in the middle of the season but they would at the end of the year. We decided that day to put in a twenty-five-game suspension for anyone who abused an official. The next year the first time it was called was against Tom Lysiak for tripping a linesman, Ron Foyt. He got twenty-five games. The league thought that was too strong so they lowered it to twenty. Then they brought in other categories so we had a twenty, a ten, and a three, and that's the way it still is today.

That same year, in the playoffs, I had Quebec at Boston in the seventh game of their series. Dan Bouchard played great in goal for Quebec and they won the game 2–1. Dale Hunter was in his second year in the league and the Bruins were after him the whole series. In that game, in the second period, Terry O'Reilly cross-checked Hunter into the boards. I gave him a penalty and Quebec scored on the power play to go ahead 1–0. Now it's 2–1 and we're down to two seconds to go after an icing. There were lots of skirmishes when they were lined up for the faceoff and we couldn't get the puck dropped. Wayne Cashman and Wilf Paiement were chopping at each other with their sticks and there were little brushfires all over the place. Finally O'Reilly came running at Hunter to get him. He told him he was gonna take him on. I got between them and told Terry to take it easy. I just sort of grabbed him with one arm. His momentum took him past me and I grabbed him again and took him right off his feet. I told Hunter to get over to the penalty box before somebody did get him. He went. He didn't have a penalty but that was sort of the safest place to put him.

O'Reilly got up and told me, "If you don't get out of my way I'll go right through you." I said, "You're not going anywhere." That's when he reached out and cuffed me. I ducked, but he caught me on the side of my head. It was an open-handed swat. He took right off for the dressing room because he knew he wasn't gonna make any more of an issue of it than he had already. It was at that point I thought that this was probably worse than having O'Reilly get to Hunter and have the benches empty. [*O'Reilly was suspended for ten games at the beginning of the following season.*]

You always think you can prevent things like that, keep it from getting too silly. We're talking about the days when they would leave the benches and they didn't have instigator penalties. Now times have changed and that's what I found difficult the last couple of years I worked.

In the '70s I would do a game in Philadelphia when Schultz and Saleski and Dornhoefer played, the Broad Street Bullies. If you got out of there with maybe eight majors, that's four fights, a major for slashing, a major for high-sticking, maybe a head-butting and a gross misconduct, plus a bunch of minor penalties, that would be a normal night's work. They would go after teams and intimidate the daylights out of them and everybody accepted it as part of the game.

In the last couple of years of my career, what I'd be hearing would be, "Andy, he's holding my stick," "Andy, he pushed me offside." It wasn't the hockey I knew. The mindset was so different. The game has got to the point where it's not the always-in-your-face style. Not the take-a-punch-in-the-nose-and-get-up-and-keep-playing kind of hockey we used to have. Now, they get hooked on the arm and they're mouthing off about it. It's nauseating sometimes, it really is. It's sickening. As a referee you feel like saying something, but if you do they run right to management and the coach and tell them that the referee said this, the referee said that.

I think it's the European influence. I really blame it. They come over here and soon find out that you make two million dollars for playing 82 games and sixty thousand for playing 21 or 25 playoff games. What are you gonna do? I mean, they're not stupid. Playoffs are tough, man-to-man hockey. You go out there and get bumped and hit and pounded. And what does the Stanley Cup mean to a kid from across the ocean? He knows he'll make another two million next year if he stays healthy. That's why they score a hundred points in the regular season but they're not as productive in the playoffs.

In my years in hockey that's been the biggest change. A Canadian kid, or an American, will take a bump, a hit, a smack in the mouth, and keep playing. Now they see these guys from Europe fall down and grab their mouth and get a five-minute power play and a few of them start to do it too. Big money and too many Europeans.

One thing I'll always remember happened in the first game of the 1980 finals between Philly and the Islanders. It was in Philly and I called a penalty in overtime against Jimmy Watson for grabbing John Tonelli around the neck. The Islanders scored on the power play to win the game. It was a tense situation for me. The next game I worked in the series it was close, down to the short strokes again, and I see Bobby Clarke coming over to talk to me. He has that famous pose where he takes the tape off his stick and he's gliding over to talk to me and I say, "Bobby, get away from me. I can't talk to you." He says, "Good. I don't want you to talk to me. I just want you to listen." I was tense and uptight, but I had to smile. He mumbled something, and that was the end of it. But it's the scene there that's important. You've got seventeen thousand people screaming at you for something and here comes the captain of the home team gliding over to you, looking for an edge in front of his home fans. You know you're not giving him a penalty, and he knows you're not giving him a penalty, and all you want is to get that conversation done with as quick as you can. You can't back up and turn away and make it look like he's running the show. You've got to stand your ground. I thought I was being quite firm, and then he says, "I just want you to listen." That sort of thing paints quite a picture for a referee.

When it came to the players during a game I felt I could handle anybody on any given night. But what really scares you is the guy who is always quiet and then out of the blue he explodes. I'll use Jean Pronovost as an example. He had some good scoring years in Pittsburgh when they had a pretty decent team with guys like Lowell MacDonald and Syl Apps. He didn't get many penalties. One year Pronovost was having a tough time and hadn't scored in about twelve games. On a Saturday night they had been whacked in Atlanta and I've got them the next night. On one of the first shifts I gave him a penalty, and it *was* a penalty. When I made the call he smashed his stick and called me every name under the sun. It was totally out of character and took me by surprise. I had to give him a misconduct and I ended up throwing him out of the game. Why did he act that way? Who knows? He hadn't been scoring or maybe he had personal problems. We don't know that as officials. All of a sudden you're dealing with a man who has never acted like that before. That's scarier than dealing with a hardnosed type who's coming at you all the time. He's predictable.

Another one was Rene Robert, one night in Buffalo when they were playing Montreal. Don Awrey had him tied up at the side of the net and the puck came loose. Kenny Dryden was out of position and the net was open and Robert tried to swipe at the puck. He couldn't quite reach it because Awrey had him. Dryden finally grabbed it and I blew the whistle just as Robert got loose. Right away he started in on me about no penalty. I told him Awrey was just doing his job and he came back at me complaining about being held. Then, in my minute of wisdom, I said, "Listen, did I come over and give you shit when you missed that breakaway in the first period?" Well, Robert went nuts. He screamed that I didn't have any business talking to him like that and he kept getting madder and madder and he was all over me. Buffalo–Montreal games were very competitive in those days and the crowd was hootin' and hollerin' and here was one of their better players running after me. It was a wild scene and I had to give him a misconduct.

Joe Crozier was coaching Buffalo then and Punch Imlach was the manager. As soon as the game was over they were at the door of our room in a heartbeat. It so happened our referee-in-chief, Scotty Morrison, was at the game and I had to explain to everybody what I did. The moral of that story was that I shouldn't get personal with anyone. What did I gain by it? All I did was cause myself far more aggravation than I ever wanted.

You have to reason with players. They mill around and cuff people and start a brushfire here, another one there. You say, Okay, stop it right now or else somebody's gonna sit for ten minutes, and some guys do stop. Others don't care and they keep doing it. I was told by a lot of senior, competent officials who were in the league before me never to say something you don't mean. Perhaps that's why I could break those things up quicker than most guys. When I told them I was gonna start handing out tens, the guys knew I meant it.

I had a playoff game in Toronto when St. Louis was there and Gary Leeman scored for Toronto. Right afterwards they were milling around and everybody was piled into the corner. I blew my whistle a couple of times. Nobody was really fighting so I waded right into the thing and told them if they didn't stop everybody was going off for ten. It didn't seem to work so I ended up putting all ten skaters who were on the ice into the box. Five guys from each team got ten minutes. What was funny about that was they said to me that there was only room for four guys on each side of the box. I told them to take turns, each guy standing up for two minutes. I told them, "You guys are in here for a while, so try to get along." [Laughs] When they came out I told them if there was another scrum they were through for the night, and that was it.

I'd ask a player who seemed agitated if everything was all right and he'd say no, that somebody had just slashed him. I'd ask who it was, and they'd tell me, and I'd say that I'd watch for it. You give them the impression you're working with them and they can talk to you, use you as a bit of a sounding board. But you've also got to know when to break it off.

Some guys get so involved, so wound up in the game. One night in Philly, Dave Schultz put a good licking on somebody and then he wouldn't leave. I said, "C'mon, Dave, you've had your fight. You've won it. Get in the box." He kept looking for more and I told him again to get to the box before I threw him out. I said, "Let's go, Dave. Your team needs you out there tonight." He looked at me and said, "This team needs me? Who the hell are you kidding?" [Laughs] He had a role to play, his thing to do.

People always thought games with the Flyers in those years would be tough, an assignment a referee could do without. But I always looked forward to it, and I think the other officials did too. They were the best games to do because they played the same way all the time. They were rough, they were tough, and you knew you had to be on your toes. You wanted to catch the first good penalty and they didn't care. You'd say something like, "Keep your stick down, Ed" to Ed Van Impe and he'd yell back, "If it's a penalty, call the goddam thing, or leave me alone." That was their attitude. They defied you. If you called two penalties in a row on them somebody would run at somebody to see if you'd call three. They won a lot of games on intimidation.

A moment I'll never forget happened overseas, in London, when I was there to work an exhibition series between Chicago and Montreal in September 1993. I had taken our oldest daughter, Susan, over with me. She had been following the Royal Family since she was yea high and she loved being my tour guide. The first game was on a Saturday night. The next morning I got up early to go to the airport to meet my wife and her mother. I went to Wembley Station to get the first train at 6:30 and I'm sitting there reading the paper. I'm the only one there, and I hear somebody coming down the steps and into the subway. All of a sudden I heard a *snap*. It was a knife and the guy's got his hand and the knife under my collar and he says, "I want your money." I made a mistake, I guess, because I looked at him and when I did beads of sweat started rolling down my back. Instantaneous sweat.

I went into my pocket and gave him all the coins I had and then he stuck the knife through my jacket and said, "I want your paper money." I told him to relax, that I was from Canada, I was going to the airport to meet my wife. I just kept babbling. I had about two hundred pounds and I gave it to him. After I did that I thought he was either gonna cut my face, or jab me. Then I heard his feet running away. I just sat there and I couldn't believe it. I thought I was dreaming, but I wasn't. It was for real.

When I got on the train the girl taking the tickets believed my story when I told her why I didn't have any money and she let me ride to the airport for free. I guess she could see it in my face. My wife had to pay on the way back. I told her I had left my money at the hotel because I didn't want to upset her right away. I told her after the game was over that afternoon.

That turned out to be a tough September. The NHL was involved in negotiations at the time with both the players and the officials. Gil Stein was the interim president of the league. When we were in England I was talking with Red Fisher, the Montreal hockey writer, and I said that Gil Stein must be a great negotiator if he can do both our groups in one year. Red wrote that and when I got back to Toronto I was in big trouble. They were all over me for what I said in the paper.

I was on the executive of our association for twenty-two years and I got involved in the negotiations that year. That's when we went on strike. We had to challenge them on certain issues to make things better. I think we did. I believe we won. I don't think that will ever happen again because I think the National Hockey League will be better prepared and it won't come to that.

They used replacement officials and they were our best advertisement. I mean, we were more than willing to drive them to work. They weren't capable of doing that level of hockey and we knew it would just be a matter of time before they showed it. It might be all right for a game or two but you do it three or four nights a week on a regular basis, well, not everybody can do that.

For most of my career Brian O'Neill was in charge of league discipline and he was very fair. I was involved in a lot of hearings and he did a very thorough job. He tried to be consistent and get all the information he could. As you get a little older you realize it is a tough job to do, to be fair to everyone concerned, the players, the officials, and the fans.

When I first came into the league Clarence Campbell, the president, handled discipline. My first contact with him came after a game I did between Minnesota and Los Angeles. Bill Lesuk of L.A. and Bill Goldsworthy got into a scuffle and Goldsworthy kicked Lesuk. Before the linesman got to him he kicked him twice and when he started to haul him away, Goldsworthy kicked him again. I threw him out of the game with a match penalty for attempt to injure.

The next day my phone rings and the first words I hear are "Campbell here." His tone of voice was always so stern and official-sounding and I thought I was in trouble. He said, "Is it correct that Mr. Goldsworthy kicked Mr. Lesuk three times?" I said it was. "Are you sure there weren't four?" I said no, there were only three. He said, "That's fine. That's all I want to know. I am giving Mr. Goldsworthy a three-game suspension." I hung up the phone and I thought, boy, that player is really going to hate me for having said three kicks, because that's why he got three games.

A lot of nice things happened to me in my final season. I refereed the last game in the Montreal Forum [March 11, 1996] and the last league game in my home town at the Winnipeg Arena [April 12, 1996]. A couple of years before I worked the last game at the Chicago Stadium. That was in a 1994 playoff series between the Blackhawks and Toronto.

The first year I worked the Stanley Cup finals was 1977, Montreal against Boston, so it was a thrill to be on the ice for the last game played at the Forum. Before the game started there was a faceoff ceremony with Rocket Richard, Jean Béliveau, and Guy Lafleur at centre ice. I brought a camera with me so someone could take a picture of the three officials, Gérard Gauthier, Leon Stickle, and myself. I wanted pictures of the opening ceremony too so I had the camera around my neck and was taking pictures of these great stars walking onto the ice.

After the second period a representative of the league came into our room and wanted to know who I was taking pictures for. I told him for myself. He said it didn't look very good, the referee on the ice with a camera around his neck taking pictures. I said, "Well, is somebody from the league taking pictures so I can buy some copies?" I found out a long time ago that in the NHL, if you don't do it yourself, it doesn't get done.

I played my first hockey game at the Winnipeg Arena in a peewee tournament. I was nine years old and our team won the championship. Then, thirty-nine years later, I was standing at centre ice dropping the puck in the NHL's last league game there. The Jets made the playoffs and I didn't do the very last game but I did the regular-season finale. The Jets played the L.A. Kings. I had a lot of family there and I knew I'd never be back on that ice again. A lot of years had passed, a lot of things had happened. It was an emotional evening.

Hockey is a great game; you shouldn't tinker with it. Everybody is trying to make it different. You know, this isn't a penalty, or that is but this isn't. Referees miss hooks, referees miss slashes. If they tell you one year, call this, and the next year they say back off – I mean, all we are is the messenger. We're calling the rules we work under. If I don't like the rules, then I should quit. There are too many changes now. It seems whoever barks the loudest gets listened to and they start changing things.

When I started refereeing as a kid in Winnipeg I liked it because I enjoyed the challenge of the job. You always strive for that perfect game but you never have it. There's always something you could have done differently. The only thing you can ask is that one team wins, one team loses, you do your job and, hopefully, they go home saying what a good game it was.

A few days following his final game Andy van Hellemond officially retired from the NHL *to become senior vice-president and director of operations for the East Coast Hockey League. At the time Andy said all the right things and so did* NHL *commissioner Gary Bettman. But the parting was far from amicable. The ghost of Andy's toughest call, in the 1995 playoff game in New York, was still haunting him.*

A few days later when van Hellemond received his final paycheque from the league it was short two hundred and fifty dollars. The league had, more than a year after the fact, fined van Hellemond because of his mistake in disallowing the goal Joe Sakic scored against the Rangers. Van Hellemond didn't just shrug it off. Instead, he told a lot of people and Andy's fine was a hot topic for a few days. Many hockey people agreed it was sad to see his career end the way it did.

William Wirtz, the owner of the Chicago Blackhawks, wrote the league stating that instead of fining Andy van Hellemond a lousy two hundred and fifty they should have given him a testimonial dinner. Wirtz is an old-school owner. As an old-school broadcaster, I had to agree.

2

Setting the Standard

RED STOREY FRANK UDVARI

The history books give conflicting information about the exact place where hockey began. Halifax, Montreal, and Kingston all lay claim to being the birthplace of the game. Wherever, it seems there has always been a referee on the ice in organized hockey. The founding fathers apparently realized that someone was needed to control the exuberant young pioneers who were enthusiastically and combatively playing the new game.

In 1873 a native of Halifax, James George Aylwin Creighton, drafted the first rules of the game while attending McGill University in Montreal. Creighton called his work "Halifax Hockey Club Rules," and they were used when the first-ever indoor game was played in Montreal's Victoria Arena, March 3, 1875, between two nine-man teams composed of McGill students. Reports of the earliest games mention the referee and two goal umpires. Photographs and drawings from that era show referees, on skates, wearing overcoats over their normal business suits and using a bell rather than a whistle. The umpires, now known as goal judges, stood on the ice behind the goalkeepers to signal when a goal was scored.

In the mid-1880s J.G.A. Creighton moved to Ottawa where he became the law clerk of the Senate. There he met Arthur and Edward Stanley, recent arrivals from England who were sons of the Governor General, Lord Stanley of Preston. Creighton introduced the boys to hockey. His sons' immediate enthusiasm for the game prompted the Governor General to purchase a silver rose bowl to be used as the top prize for amateur competition. The bowl cost $48.66 and was christened the Stanley Cup.

In the 1960s the National Hockey League commissioned a three-volume history of hockey entitled **The Trail of the Stanley Cup.** Compiled by the late Charles L. Coleman, it records every game played in the first seventy-four years of competition leading to the winning of the Stanley Cup. The trilogy begins January 7, 1893, when the Montreal Victorias defeated Ottawa 4–3 in Montreal's Victoria Arena. It ends May 2, 1967, when the Toronto Maple Leafs defeated the Montreal Canadiens 4–2 at Maple Leaf Gardens in the last game played before the NHL expanded to twelve teams the following season.

There are several incidents mentioned involving the officials, some of them very early in the game's history. Some examples:

FEBRUARY 23, 1895 – OTTAWA 3 AT QUEBEC 2
At the conclusion of the match the crowd pursued referee Hamilton and umpire Findlay. The officials were seized as they were about to enter a rig for the station and dragged back to the arena where an attempt was made to declare the game a draw. Police eventually broke

up the demonstration and the officials retired with what dignity they could muster after a rough handling.

FEBRUARY 12, 1898 – MONTREAL VICTORIAS 9 AT OTTAWA 5

Referee Hamilton [again] came in for considerable abuse. It was reported that one young man left his seat and told umpire W. Baker of Montreal that he was crooked. The Ottawa club considered that the imputation was uncalled for and in regretting the incident believed that Mr. Baker had simply made a mistake.

FEBRUARY 18, 1899 – WINNIPEG 2 AT MONTREAL VICTORIAS 3

Gingras, the Winnipeg rover, received a blow across the back of one leg from Bob McDougall, went down, and was carried from the ice. When referee J.A. Findlay awarded McDougall a penalty of two minutes the Winnipeg team refused to continue, arguing that McDougall should be put off for the match. The referee went to the dressing room to debate the matter with the Winnipeg team and in the meanwhile 8,000 people staged a continuous uproar. The referee reappeared, announced he had been insulted, and left for home.

After further delay, during which a conference was held by officials of both teams, Messrs. H. Wilson and W. Barlow took a sleigh to Mr. Findlay's home and coaxed him to return to the arena. Upon the referee's arrival back at the game, one hour and five minutes after play had stopped, he gave Winnipeg fifteen minutes to return to the ice. On their failure to do so he then awarded the game to the Victorias.

That same year, 1899, on January 21, the regular Ottawa goaltender, Fred Chittick, was pressed into service as the referee in a game between Montreal and Quebec. With twelve minutes left to play the Montreal team refused to continue because of Chittick's work. It was reported that "Chittick may have been doing some celebrating before the game. Several Montreal players were alleged to have stated that Chittick was not in fit condition to handle the game." However, Chittick did become a regular official in later years and refereed two games in the 1904 Stanley Cup final series between Ottawa and Brandon. Presumably by then he was in "fit condition."

Andy van Hellemond was not the first referee to be the target of a player's punch, and in the old days the referees punched back. Cooper Smeaton was the referee in a game played in Ottawa January 13, 1917, between the Senators and the 228th Battalion. As reported in The Trail of the Stanley Cup:

Just before the end of the game Howard McNamara slashed Frank Nighbor and was again waved off. He accused Smeaton of robbing the 228th whereupon he was awarded another major penalty and a $5 fine. The Dynamite Boy, as he was called, found this too much and attacked Smeaton with his fists and the referee retaliated. The players were finally able to intervene and separate the combatants.

Cooper Smeaton refereed hockey through to the 1930s and for a time was the referee-in-chief of the NHL. In 1961, Smeaton, along with Chaucer Elliott and Mickey Ion, made up the first group of officials inducted into the Hockey Hall of Fame. Elliott was a referee in the early 1900s. Ion became a referee in 1913 and, by the time he retired from the NHL in 1941, had become the game's first high-profile official.

Mickey Ion grew up in Ontario but went west as a young man to play professional lacrosse. He began refereeing amateur hockey in Vancouver in 1911. Two years later he

West Nipissing Public Library

was hired by Frank and Lester Patrick, who were running a four-team professional league on the West Coast. Ion's first professional game, between New Westminster and Victoria, was a tough test. A playoff spot was at stake. If New Westminster won the game the Vancouver team would be in the playoffs. If Victoria won, Vancouver was out. With the score tied 1–1, Ion called back a New Westminster goal because of an offside. Victoria went on to win the game and Vancouver was out of the playoffs. A two-referee system was used then. Ion's partner, Didier Pitre, said to him after the game, "Mickey, if I had been you I wouldn't have called that goal back." Ion replied, "Pete, in the refereeing business you call them, or you don't." It would be his motto throughout his long career.

During a game in Vancouver a fan sitting along the boards was giving Ion a very rough time. Ion manoeuvred a faceoff near where his detractor was sitting, dropped the puck, then wheeled, drilled him with a solid right hand to the face, then skated away as though nothing had happened. Afterwards Ion's explanation was, "If you're refereeing and a guy keeps calling you this, that, and says you're blind, and you get a swell chance to let him have one, what are you supposed to do?" Another time Ion went into the stands and KO'd a tormentor who had been hitting him with pellets blown through a peashooter.

Ion continued to work for the Patricks until their league folded in 1926. Most of the players moved east to the National Hockey League, and so did Ion. For the next fifteen years he was considered the best referee in the game.

An oft-told Mickey Ion story involved Toe Blake, who was a great left winger for the Montreal Canadiens before his coaching days with that team. During a Saturday night game in Toronto Blake let loose an obscenity-laced tirade at Ion, who then threw him out of the game. The next night the Canadiens played in Chicago. Ion was the referee and early in the game he gave Blake a penalty for slashing. When Blake looked at him with fire in his eyes Ion said, "You say one word, just one word, and you're out of the game." Blake replied, "I'm not going to say anything, but you know what I'm thinking." Whereupon Ion said, "You're damned right I do and you're gone. You can do your thinking in the dressing room." And Blake was gone, out of the game for thinking.

Mickey Ion coined a phrase that young referees today should take note of. Whenever he worked with a newcomer Ion would tell him, "Remember, once that puck drops and the game starts, you and I are the only two sane people in the rink."

The legendary King Clancy said of Ion: "He used his own rules. He could run a game better than anyone I ever saw. If the game got draggy he let just enough rough stuff in to pep things up. But he knew when to pull the string. There were some tough babies in those days but Mickey Ion could handle them like little kids."

Clancy himself was a tough baby, or at least tried to be one. Clancy played defence in the NHL for fifteen seasons, weighing no more than 155 pounds at his heaviest. His pals from those days would kid him that he started a hundred fights, and lost a hundred fights. After retiring as a player Clancy had a brief stint as coach of the Montreal Maroons. When the Maroons fired him he went home to Ottawa to work with his uncles in a construction business. Later that same hockey season NHL president Frank Calder hired him as a "local linesman" for games played at the Montreal Forum. Clancy would drive to Montreal from Ottawa, work the game, then drive home. He began the following season, 1938–39, doing the same thing. One night Calder walked into the officials' room before a game and changed *assignments. The referee would be a linesman and Clancy, who had never refereed a game in his life, would be the referee. He liked it, and the league liked him, and he worked as a referee for the next eleven years.*

King Clancy often claimed he never read the rule book, that he refereed a game the way he knew the players wanted it to be done. King was never one to let facts stand in the way of a good story, but there is no doubt he was a player's referee. When Clancy was set to drop the puck to start a game, he'd say to the players, "All right, you guys, any way you want to play, you play, and any way I want to call it, I'll call it." He'd skate up and down the ice yelling, "Look out for the trip. Look out for the hold."

In the early 1970s I interviewed King on the radio between periods of a game in Montreal. I asked him to reminisce about his refereeing days and he began with a story about a game between the Canadiens and the Blackhawks at the Chicago Stadium.

"I gave Chicago some penalties in the third period," King said, "and the Rocket [Maurice Richard] scored a couple of goals to put the game out of reach. The fans were really on me. Near the and of the game I was standing by the Chicago bench and a guy came down from his seat, leaned over the boards, and punched me right in the kisser. Then he took off. He ran behind the Chicago bench and they just sat there and watched him. The Canadiens had some tough guys, like Murph Chamberlain and Kenny Reardon, and when this guy ran past them they clipped him with their sticks. By the time he got to the end of their bench he was bleeding like a stuck pig. For the rest of the night all I did was give Chicago penalties. If a guy was breathing hard I threw him off. The Canadiens scored a couple more and I didn't mind it a bit."

I then asked him for a memory about refereeing at the Montreal Forum.

"There was a game between Montreal and Toronto," King began, *"and the teams were fighting all night. It was a rough one, and when the Canadiens started to lose in the third period the fans threw everything at me. Rubbers, galoshes, programs, everything. After the game I changed and went outside and got on the streetcar to go back to the Mount Royal Hotel, where we stayed. I sat down beside a guy and I guess he didn't recognize me because I was wearing a hat. He asked me if I had seen the game. I said I had, and then he started in about the lousy referee. That's all he talked about and I agreed with everything he said. When the streetcar got to Peel Street I said good night, and got off. The guy had no idea I was the referee we both agreed had done such a lousy job."*

Clancy had problems with the ladies in the crowds. One night in Chicago he jumped up on the boards to avoid a traffic jam of players, something referees could do in the days before Plexiglas. King's posterior was hanging over the edge, right in front of a lady seated along the rail who promptly jabbed him with her hat pin. Clancy stopped the game and refused to resume play until the lady was thrown out of the building.

On another occasion, so he claimed, a lady in Boston was yelling at him, "Clancy, if you were my husband I'd give you poison!" Clancy hollered right back, "Lady, if I was your husband, I'd take it!"

When I started watching NHL games regularly, in the early 1950s, Bill Chadwick was considered the best referee. Chadwick was the first referee to use hand signals to identify the penalties he was calling. I was young and impressionable in those days and I remember being very impressed when Chadwick gave Ken Mosdell two penalties on the same play. Mosdell, a centre for the Canadiens, hauled down a Toronto player and Chadwick immediately signalled a penalty. When Mosdell saw that he got mad and promptly chopped the feet out from under another Toronto player. When that happened Chadwick yelled at the top of his voice. "And that's another one!"

Bill Chadwick was born in New York and was playing hockey in that city's Metropolitan Junior League when he was struck by a puck just above his right eye. He has been partially blind in that eye ever since, a fact that no doubt prompted a lot of comments from players and coaches during his officiating career. With his playing days over, Chadwick turned to officiating and at twenty-five joined the NHL as a linesman for the 1940–41 season. He was a referee from the following year until he retired in 1955. He says the rule book is only a small part of refereeing a hockey game. His credo was "common sense," something he says he learned from King Clancy. He was also a firm believer in establishing his presence from the opening faceoff. A typical Bill Chadwick game would have a lot of penalties in the first period, not as many in the second, and hardly any in the third. By that time the players had got the message.

Bill Chadwick's first game as a linesman gave him a taste of what the NHL was all about. The Montreal Canadiens played the New York Americans at Madison Square Garden and the referee was another American, Bill Stewart. (More about him later from his grandson, current NHL referee Paul Stewart.) The Canadiens rode Stewart unmercifully all night. When the game ended, Stewart told Chadwick, "Stay right with me. We're going into the Montreal dressing room." A terrified rookie linesman obeyed his referee and was very relieved when the Garden security blocked their way.

At the end of Chadwick's first season as a referee he was on the officiating crew for the 1942 Stanley Cup finals *between Toronto and Detroit. Detroit won the first three games. After Toronto stayed alive by winning the fourth game, which ended in a near-riot, Detroit coach and general manager Jack Adams rushed onto the ice and started a fight with the referee, Mel Harwood. Adams was suspended for the rest of the series. Chadwick, never a fan of Adams, wrote in his autobiography, "I would have thrown the bum out of hockey, if I'd had my way."*

The Maple Leafs won the next two games, setting up a seventh game at Maple Leaf Gardens. Chadwick, who had worked the second game of the series, naturally thought the job of doing the big one would be handled by either King Clancy or Norm Lamport, two of the league's senior referees. So he was stunned when Frank Calder told him he was working the game. The Maple Leafs won 3–1 before 16,218 fans, which at that time was the largest crowd ever to see a game in Canada. That year marked the only time a team has come from three games behind to win a Stanley Cup final, and the only time in the modern era of the NHL a rookie referee was chosen to work the seventh game of a final series.

Bill Chadwick ended his career after working the seventh game of the 1955 Stanley Cup finals. In later years he sounded a trifle bitter when he claimed the only time anyone ever told him he had done a good job was in 1964 when he was inducted into the Hockey Hall of Fame. But he was a great one. Chadwick was working when the referees began wearing numbers and he always wore number 1. I think they were trying to tell him something.

Old-time referees were a talented and busy bunch. Mike Rodden, by his own count, refereed 2,864 hockey games, including 1,187 in the NHL. Over the same time, Rodden coached twenty-seven championship football teams, three of which won the Grey Cup, the University of Toronto in 1920 and the Hamilton Tigers in 1928 and 1929. The versatile Mr. Rodden was also a sportswriter and was sports editor of the Toronto Globe *from 1928 to 1936 while he was refereeing in the NHL. After he retired as an official, Rodden was sports editor of the Kingston* Whig-Standard *for fifteen years. Two other NHL referees in the 1930s, Lou Marsh and Bobby Hewitson, were also full-time sportswriters. You wonder if these men ever critiqued their own on-ice work, or that of their fellow officials, in print.*

The oldest active referee today is Roy Alvin "Red" Storey. At times during the early 1950s the legendary "Old Redhead" would be a member of the officiating crew at a Canadian Football League game on a Saturday afternoon, and referee a National Hockey League game that same night. Early in 1997 Storey was injured while refereeing a charity hockey game in Stephenville, Newfoundland, suffering a couple of cracked ribs, torn stomach muscles, and a bruised kidney. But he was on the ice the next night refereeing another game for charity. So what, you say. Referees get hurt all the time. Yes, they do, but we're talking here about a guy who was seventy-nine years old at the time.

Since he refereed his last game in the NHL in 1959, Red Storey has never stopped putting on his striped jersey and blowing his whistle. He refereed eighty games in 1996–97 when he was in his eightieth year. He began that season by accompanying a team of NHL oldtimers on a trip that started in Alaska, and continued on to the Yukon, British Columbia and Alberta. The team played sixteen charity games in seventeen nights, and Storey refereed every one of them. When Red isn't on the ice he's on the banquet circuit regaling audiences from coast to coast with his large repertoire of stories, a few of which are even true.

My father was a coach in the NHL *in Montreal and Chicago during most of Red's career as a referee. They didn't like each other much, but that doesn't stop Red from using him as the source of one of his favourite anecdotes. As Red tells it, he was working a game in Montreal and got the worst of it in a collision with a couple of players in front of the Canadiens' bench. Down he went and as he lay on the ice battered and bruised my father leaned over the boards and hollered at him, "I hope it's nothing trivial!"*

Red may not have wanted to be at the same party as Irvin, Sr., but he and Irvin, Jr., have always been compatible. I've played a lot of golf and been at a lot of banquets with Red all over the country and, if I get the chance, when he's in the room, I always use this one. I'll say, "My father claimed the excitement level of a hockey game was determined by the incompetence of the referee and therefore Red Storey refereed some of the most exciting games in hockey history."

A native of Barrie, Ontario, Red Storey burst onto the Canadian sports scene as a twenty-year-old rookie for the Toronto Argonauts when he came off the bench to score three touchdowns in the final thirteen minutes of the Argos' 30–7 win over Winnipeg in the 1938 Grey Cup game. In those years he was also one of Canada's top lacrosse players and a pretty fair competitor at the senior level in hockey and baseball. He's always described as "colourful," and people in my business are very thankful that the Old Redhead has never met a microphone he didn't like.

RED STOREY

To tell you the truth, I never made up my mind to be a referee. I got hurt so badly playing sports I couldn't compete any more. I was in Montreal then and was sitting at home when I got a call from a fellow running a lacrosse league and he said, Would you like to referee lacrosse? I told him I'd never refereed anything. He said, I didn't ask you that, I asked would you like to referee lacrosse. I said I'd take a whack at it and so I went and the first game I ever refereed was top-level senior lacrosse. I don't know how good I was but I do know I found out it was something I liked. I could control people playing the game, so I continued. That was in the summer.

Now it's the fall. I get a call from the school board and they said, Would you like to referee football? And I said I'd never refereed football. They said they knew that but would I like to try it. I tried it and I liked it because football was in my butt anyway. And then, before the football season was over, I get a call from the junior hockey league and they asked me if I would referee and again I said I'd never done it. They said, try it, and I did. My first game was a Quebec Major Junior game at the Forum and I didn't even know what a referee wore. I didn't have a tie, just an old sweater, and I must have looked like a refugee coming out on the ice. But again something seemed to tell me that I could do that and I kept plugging away.

I never turned down a game. I did games for fifty cents, I did games for a buck. I did everything I could to continue to learn. I never had any intention of becoming an official but thank God somebody asked me. Whether I knew it or not, it was going to be a big part of my life. I think a lot of people in hockey were born to be in the entertainment world, as I call it. My part of the entertainment world started with me as a player. Fortunately – and I say that now – fortunately, injuries turned me to something else, which was refereeing. When it was over I left the NHL under controversial circumstances and that kept my name front and centre for a while and I was able to get onto the banquet circuit. Like a lot of people, my whole life unfolded into the thing I was born to do.

When I was starting out and moved into higher leagues I got a lot of help from a chap named Kenny Mullins. He was a powerful guy on the ice, really controlled a game, and he showed me a lot of things. While we were at it we had a lot of fun and had some wild moments.

One of the roughest nights I ever had was when Mullins and I were working a Senior League game in Quebec City between the Quebec Aces and Sherbrooke. Things didn't go good for the home team and, naturally, we were blamed. When the game was over we had to fight our way through the fans to get to our dressing room. We showered and we were drying off and we could hear the bedlam outside our room because the fans were still after us. I looked at the brick wall and it was moving and I said, "Kenny, I think we're in trouble." He asked what I meant and I told him to take a look at the wall because it was moving and looked like it was gonna cave in. He grabbed a chair and so did I and he's saying that the first guy who breaks through is in for a surprise.

Well, the wall did cave in and as it did the police came through the door at the other side of the room with their guns drawn. So there we were standing in the middle of the room stark naked and we've got a mob of crazy fans one side of us and the police with their guns drawn on the other side. Now that was a tender-tootsie moment, let me tell you.

The police got us out of the building and put us in their police car to drive us to the train station. But then the people rushed to the car and started rocking it, trying to turn it over with us inside. So again the cops pull out their guns and the people started to scatter. We're sitting in the back seat and by then we're thinking all this is pretty funny.

We always carried a little libation with us for after the game, and Kenny has a twenty-five-ounce bottle of V.O. That's for the train ride home. He asked me if he should offer the cops a drink and I told him, "Are you kidding? Think what would have happened to us if they hadn't shown up." So he asks the driver, and he says, "Don't mind if I do." Kenny hands him the bottle and he takes a couple of swigs and hands it back. Then Kenny asks the other cop in the front seat if he would like a drink and of course he did and he takes the bottle and starts to chug-a-lug the thing right down. Kenny grabs the bottle from him and yells, "You don't have to make a pig of yourself!" and I said, "Hey, Kenny, relax. These guys just saved our lives." [Laughs]

I was in the American League one night in Cleveland when they were playing Springfield. Eddie Shore owned the Springfield team and he was coaching too in those days. Late in the game it was tied and Springfield comes down into the Cleveland end and a guy takes a shot and it hits the goalie, Paul Bibeault, right between the eyes. The puck bounces straight up in the air, his eyes cross, and he's out like a light. I blow my whistle before he hits the ice, but as he's on the way down the puck hits him on the back of the head and goes into the net. I'm standing there waving off the goal and, oh boy, did all hell break loose. At the end of the game Shore came out on the ice after me and I said to him, "Eddie, as long as I'm refereeing nobody is ever gonna win a game with an unconscious goalkeeper in the net." He blasted me all over the papers and as he was a powerful guy in the league they had me up on the carpet. The next summer, at the June meetings, I gave him hell about it and he said, "What's wrong with that? I almost made you famous," and I said, "Famous? You almost cost me my job!"

I signed my first contract with the National Hockey

League for the 1950–51 season. It was for $4,500 base pay plus extra if you did over a minimum number of games. You could also pick up extra money by doing games in the American League and at playoff time. They also gave you ten dollars a day for expenses on the road.

At first they took me around the league a couple of times as a linesman to get the feel of things and I remember the first time I did a game at Maple Leaf Gardens. George Gravel was the referee, and after the first period we're sitting in our room and the door flies open, almost comes off its hinges, and Conn Smythe, the boss of the Maple Leafs, comes charging in. It's like there's flames coming out of his nostrils, and he's all over Gravel for a call that upset him. I'm sitting there listening to this and said to myself, "Son of a gun. I was the guy who made that call." So I said, "Mr. Smythe, may I interject here?" I'm the rookie and he says in that gruff voice of his, "What do you want?" I said, "You're going after the wrong guy. I was the one who blew the whistle on that play, and you wanna know something, Mr. Smythe? I was wrong. Now, you've got eighteen players in your dressing room across the hall. Why don't you go and ask them if they made any mistakes in that period? I made one, and I admit it. You find out if they made any." He said, "That's fair enough with me," and he walked out of the room.

From that day on I never had a problem with Conn Smythe. Oh, we had our verbal disputes and all that. He always fought hard for his team but he was always honest with me and I give him credit for that.

I never minded the crowds when they'd get on me. There's a chance that sort of thing could intimidate some referees but I was not one of those. But you might say I could be intimidated when it got quiet in the building. I'd wonder what was wrong. We had a product to sell, and as long as the public was yelling and screaming and hollering it meant they were interested in the product. If they quieted down I used to think something was wrong.

There was a guy in Boston I like to talk about. I'd skate out on the ice and he'd yell, "Hey, Storey, we've named a town after you. Marblehead." [Laughs] In New York, as soon as they announced my name when they were introducing the officials the crowd would go absolutely bananas. Then they'd introduce the linesmen and the noise was so loud nobody would ever hear their names. The linesmen protested to the league and they had them change it at Madison Square Garden so that when I was working the game there they would introduce the linesmen first. As soon as they'd introduce me eighteen thousand people would stand up and they'd all be chanting, "Storey is a bum! Storey is a bum!" I loved it. It was great.

The guy who gave me the most trouble on any given night, verbally, was Ted Lindsay. Ted knew more swear words than a marine on a tough night. He was always snarly, always on your back, but he was the leader of the Detroit Red Wings. He only weighed about 165 pounds but he might have been the most complete left winger who ever played the game and one of the best team leaders ever. He was really bad to me but he could be funny too. One night it was really noisy in the Olympia and I'm facing off in the corner. Ted's yelling at me from the edge of the circle, the usual stuff with lots of cuss words, so I leaned over, cupped my hand to my ear, and said, "What's that? I can't hear you." And he puts his hands over his eyes and says, "You can't see me either."

That whole Detroit team was bad in the '50s. First you had the boss, Jack Adams, who couldn't see across the rink but was always screaming at you. The coach was Tommy Ivan and he hated anything that didn't have on a Detroit uniform, especially the officials. Also behind the bench was their trainer, Lefty Wilson, and he was screaming all the time. He got more bench penalties than any trainer in history. They'd be giving it to me and I'd be facing off with my back to their bench and I'd put my hand behind my fanny and give them a sign. They had me up before the league because of that. They thought they should have total power over everybody and they hated it when you went back at them and they couldn't intimidate you. I figured that the worst thing they could do was have me fired but I knew none of them had the guts to come after me face to face.

Then you had a guy like big Butch Bouchard of the Canadiens who would make you laugh, except that referees aren't supposed to laugh. One night in Montreal the fans were after me, throwing all kinds of stuff on the ice, and somebody threw a bag of peas. It broke open when it hit the ice and the peas were rolling all over the place. Butch was in his last year, not playing much, but he was still the captain and Toe Blake sent him out to give me the business. I said, "Don't open your mouth or I'll throw you out of the game." Butch says, "Hey, Red, I'm not mad at you. The guy who threw all those peas is mad at you. If you pick them up and give them to me I'll make you a good pea soup for dinner." [Laughs]

There were also guys like Gump Worsley in my day. I called only one penalty shot in my whole career in the NHL and the Gumper was the goalie. He was playing for the Rangers against Detroit and Gordie Howe took the shot. Howe gets to about fifteen feet in front of Gump, gives a flick of his wrist, and the puck's in the net. Gump comes charging out at me and starts yelling. "You stupid, no-good so-and-so. Why didn't you just put a goal on the board and keep the game going? Look at all the time you wasted."

Things are a lot different for the officials today. They have the instant replay, which I could put up with only on goals and only if I requested it. If I decided it was a goal and had no doubt about it I wouldn't want any repercussions. If I wasn't quite sure then I would gladly look at a picture of the play.

There are too many people today, the supervisors, second-guessing the officials. I had only one referee-in-chief and that was Carl Voss, who had less courage than any man I've ever worked for. I never spoke to him the last two years of my career. Let me tell you how Jack Mehlenbacher got fired. He was a pretty good referee but never got along with Voss. Jack drove harness horses and one year, just before the season started, Voss went to Greenwood Raceway and asked Jack to pick some winners for him. So Jack marks Voss's program and every horse he marked finished last, just like Jack knew they would. Voss fired him a few days later. True story.

Earlier in this chapter Red mentioned how his career ended on a controversial note, and indeed it did. On April 4, 1959, Red worked the sixth game of the Stanley Cup semi-final series between Montreal and Chicago at the Chicago Stadium. The Canadiens won the game 5–4 to take the series. Claude Provost scored the winning goal at 18:32 of the third period, setting off a wild demonstration by the fans and the Chicago players, who thought Storey should have called a penalty on Montreal just before the goal was scored. In the wee, small hours of the morning after the game, league president Clarence Campbell had a conversation with an Ottawa newspaperman, Bill Westwick, during which Campbell criticized Storey's handling of the affair. Campbell, a long-time friend of Westwick's, thought their conversation was off the record. Westwick didn't. He wrote a story and the next day the headlines screamed that Campbell thought Storey had choked. The league president was quoted as saying his referee "froze" on the play and was "chicken." Storey had come to Boston to work another series. When he read what Campbell had said he resigned because of what he termed a lack of support from the league and never refereed again in the NHL.

I talked with Red about the incident for a previous book, The Habs, *and for this one. Here's his account of what happened on and off the ice that night.*

RED STOREY

It all started when Marcel Bonin went in to check Eddie Litzenberger. Bonin put his stick flat on the ice to trap the puck and Eddie stepped on it and went flying into the air. The Chicago players hesitated because they thought I was going to call a penalty, but there was none. By the time they got their composure the Canadiens had scored a goal.

Then Junior Langlois hit Hull and knocked him flying. It was a good hip check and again the Hawks thought I was going to call a penalty, but I didn't. Then Claude Provost scored and all hell broke loose.

A guy jumped out of the seats and threw a cup of beer in my face. I grabbed him, and Doug Harvey grabbed him from the other side. Doug realized I was going to hit the guy so he yells at me, "Red, you can't hit a fan! You can't hit a fan!" Then, bingo, Doug drives him a couple of times and the guy staggered off the ice. Doug stayed with me, he never left my side.

Another guy had jumped over the screen and he was coming at me from behind. Doug hollered, "Look out!" The guy jumped me so I dipped my shoulder and flipped him in the air. Doug hit him with his stick and cut him real bad. I think he needed about eighteen stitches. Nobody else came on the ice after that.

Danny Lewicki was playing for Chicago and when the game finally ended he gave me his stick. He said, "I think you'll need this more than I will." Now, guess who else was playing for Chicago? My buddy, Ted Lindsay. So now I go down the stairs at the end of the rink and I've got the stick in my hand and Lindsay's there waiting for me. He said, "I'm gonna cut your head off," and I said, "You'd better make it your best shot because if you miss I'll carve you in two." I'll say the two of us came closer to murdering someone than we ever could.

Jim Norris, the owner of the Blackhawks, was also standing at the bottom of the stairs and I have to give him a lot of credit. He grabbed Lindsay right away and threw him into the dressing room. I said, "Mr. Norris, if you hadn't done that you wouldn't have had to pay him any more because I would have finished his career."

But I have to say this about Ted Lindsay. He gave me the greatest moment of my life. We didn't speak to each other from that night until they opened the new Hockey Hall of Fame in Toronto, in 1993. There we were, together, with the rest of the Hall-of-Famers. I see him come in the door and I say to myself that I can't get away from this guy, even at a time like this. But Ted came right over to me and said, "Come on, Red, this has gone on too long. It's all over." With that he jumped into my arms and I picked him up and was holding him like a baby. It was a terrific moment for me.

Looking back, let's face it, you might as well keep the good memories. Being a referee is like being in any other business. If a businessman goes to work for two weeks, that's ten working days. If he has seven good days of work, two iffy days, and one horse-bleep day, then he's average. A referee is no different. He'll go through seven games and do the greatest job in the world. He'll do two games he wished he'd never seen and one he'd wish he'd never shown up at.

The good referees always look better in the better games. With me, I always loved to have a game between Detroit and Montreal. They were the two best teams in the era of the 1950s and I just absolutely loved to be out on the ice when they played. There I was with the greatest hockey talent in the world and it was up to me to control them and yet give them enough rope so they could put on the best show in the world. And I'd say nine times out of ten I did exactly that.

Another referee who joined the NHL in the early 1950s on his way to the Hall of Fame was Frank Udvari, who was born in Czechoslovakia in 1924. Udvari's parents emigrated to Canada when he was seven years old and settled in Kitchener, Ontario. Early in his career Frank Udvari got to know what the Detroit Red Wings' ornery boss, Jack Adams, was all about.

FRANK UDVARI

I was refereeing a junior game in Windsor. The Red Wings sponsored the Windsor team and Adams would be at some of their games. You had to climb stairs to get to the dressing room and one night after the game there was this red-faced fat guy standing at the bottom of the stairs and he really lit into me. I kept going up the stairs and when I got to the room I said, "Who the hell is that red-faced fat bastard?" The other referee told me it was Jack Adams. I was so mad because of what he had said to me that I threw a puck against the wall.

When I got to the National League they started me as a linesman for the first couple of times around the league. Right off the bat I worked a game when Bill Chadwick was the referee. Adams hated Chadwick. After the first period

Adams charged into our room and lit into Bill and I sat there remembering him swearing at me in Windsor when I didn't even know who he was.

A few years later I was the back-up referee to Chadwick at a playoff game. Before the game we were in the room playing cards when somebody told us Adams was on his way to talk to us. Chadwick took off his glasses real quick and threw them into his suitcase. He didn't want Adams to see him wearing glasses.

Another tough executive when I started out was Bill Tobin, who ran the Chicago Blackhawks. Right after I signed my contract I went on a five-game exhibition trip through Northern Ontario with the Hawks. I was a linesman with George Hayes. Scotty Morrison, who was also just starting his career, was the referee. The Hawks were picking up the tab for the officials. In the second-last game Ted Lindsay and Fred Glover went into the stands and there was a hell of a fight. Hayes and I charged into the seats to try and break it up. It was a real mess.

After the game Tobin came into the room and started calling Scotty a curly-haired son of a bitch and that he would never referee a game in the National League and neither would I. He told me and Hayes it was all our fault because we just stood there and watched everything. We were so tired it felt like our arms were dropping off. Then he told us he was cancelling the last game, which he did, and because he had been paying for our hotel rooms on the trip he said we each owed him eighty-five dollars. It was quite an introduction to the National League. I still kid Scotty that he owes me eighty-five dollars.

Carl Voss was the referee-in-chief in those days. A lot of the guys used to say that I was his pet and I know Red Storey didn't like him and I'm sure he had his reasons. But I always got along with Voss and I can't complain.

Before I ever got to the NHL I played baseball in Waterloo with Ted Lindsay, who was about nineteen at the time. Father David Bauer was the playing-manager of the team. I had heard a lot about Lindsay's treatment of referees, but when I got to the NHL I thought surely he wasn't gonna pull that kind of stuff with me. After all, we'd been on the same ball team and all that. Sure enough, the first time I'm on the ice in Detroit I give a penalty about ten minutes into the game and here comes Lindsay. He called me everything under the sun and finally I had to give him a game misconduct. In those days coaches and general managers would come in and out of the referee's room like it was Grand Central Station. So after the first period, in comes Adams putting on his act, saying, "Well, my son, why did you throw Teddy out of the game?" I told him I did it because he had called me an f-ing this and an f-ing that. Adams told me not to worry, that he'd make sure it never happened again. But of course it did.

I always had a philosophy that the less you said to a player like Lindsay the less the chance you could get into trouble. There was a young referee from Montreal named Bill Roberts. He called a tripping penalty against Detroit and Lindsay argued with him. Roberts said, "If that wasn't a trip, I'll be a son of a bitch." Lindsay went and told Adams that Roberts called him a son of a bitch and Adams had him fired. It cost him his job. Can you believe that? Adams was pretty powerful that way. He could get young officials fired before they got established.

Guys in the game today have no idea how tough players were in those days, like Rocket Richard and Lindsay. In the warm-up Lindsay would tell guys on the other team he was going to cut their f-ing head off. I mean, he was mad already and the game hadn't even started. The ferociousness and the way they focused on the game was unbelievable. Those guys had nothing on their minds but playing hockey and it made for some great games.

I never thought Gordie Howe was a dirty player, but if somebody got him a good one he wouldn't forget. One night I gave five penalties in a row to Detroit. I was wearing the number 1 on my sweater at the time. After the fifth call Howe comes to me and says, "You may have number 1 on your back but you're only the second best." Naturally, I asked him who was first, and he said, "Everybody else is tied."

One night in Detroit I was letting a few things go, I guess, and Howe was getting mad. He complained to me that he was tired of carrying guys on his back. Then, right after the next faceoff, he drilled a guy with his elbow right in the kisser and skated to the penalty box before I even blew the whistle.

Who do you pick, Howe or Gretzky? They're different players. Howe was a much better checker and more physical, although Gretzky is certainly more talented. I don't think you can compare them because the defensive hockey was so much tougher in Howe's day.

Rocket Richard was certainly one of the greatest players that ever lived. He brought people to their feet game after game. I was the referee in Boston the night of the incident that led to his suspension in 1955. One thing people forget about that game is that Rocket had a great chance to score just before it all happened. He broke in on the right wing. Sugar Jim Henry was the goalie, and if I'm not mistaken Richard let a backhand go that beat him, but it hit the post. Right after that Hal Laycoe hooked him and his stick went up and cut Rocket above the eye. That's when the big fight started. I saw Richard hit the linesman, Cliff Thompson, right in the eye. I gave him a match penalty and I can't regret calling it, because if I didn't call that penalty I would have been out of a job. Mr. Campbell then suspended Rocket for the rest of the season and all the playoffs. There was the riot and I was sorry about that and that he lost his chance to win the scoring championship. He was such a great player. But if his backhand shot had gone in the net instead of hitting the post I don't think there would have been any problems.

Hockey people have great memories. When I was at the opening of the new Hall of Fame Bill Gadsby was there. A bunch of us were talking and Gadsby says to me, "Remember the night in Montreal when I came to you and said you were having a horseshit game? Remember what you said to me? You said that I should take a look at the scoreboard, because Montreal was ahead 5–0, which meant I wasn't having such a great game either." Imagine, that was about thirty years before and he still remembered. I'd forgotten all about it.

In my day one of the biggest problems we had was a bench-clearing brawl, and I had a few of them when Toronto played Montreal. If you couldn't get up for those games you were in the wrong business. But there was one night, in Toronto, when I had a lot of trouble. I was asleep in the afternoon at the King Edward Hotel and they didn't give me my wake-up call. Luckily I woke up on my own and just made it to the Gardens in time.

The game starts and I'm letting almost everything go, really letting things go. On one faceoff Jean Béliveau says to me, "Frank, what's the matter with you? Is there something wrong?" Halfway through the third period the only penalty I had called was for too many men on the ice. But things were building and late in the third period there was a big brawl. One of the players who was in the middle of it was Bud MacPherson, a big defenceman for Montreal. I ended up giving a lot of misconduct penalties.

I drove home to Kitchener after the game. The next morning I was still sleeping when Mr. Campbell called. My wife woke me up and asked me if I had done something wrong. She was always afraid I had done something wrong when he called.

I picked up the phone and Mr. Campbell said, "Those penalties last night to Mr. MacPherson and the rest, were they misconducts or game misconducts?" I told him they were all just misconducts, and then I said, "Mr. Campbell, I have to tell you, I worked a bad hockey game." He said, "I beg your pardon?" and I told him again that I had worked a bad game. I was expecting the worst but all he said was, "Well, we all have those games," and he hung up. I couldn't believe it.

My last game was the final game of the 1966 Stanley Cup finals and my last call was one a lot of people still remember. The Canadiens were in Detroit leading the series 3–2. The game went into overtime and when the winning goal went in for Montreal I had to make a tough call.

The play went down into the Detroit zone and Henri Richard went between the two Detroit defencemen and they really dumped him. In a regular game I might have called a penalty, I don't know. But this was sudden-death overtime. Dave Balon was following the play and picked up the puck. Richard was sliding towards the net on his stomach. The goalie, Roger Crozier, had been hurt earlier in the series and he might have been afraid of Richard sliding into him. Crozier moved away from the post just as Balon shot the puck. It hit Richard on the elbow, or the shoulder, and went into the net. The only guy who said anything to me was Crozier. He asked me if it was a good goal and I told him it was, that Richard didn't deliberately direct the puck into the net with his body. That's the way I saw it and I seemed to be backed up by the TV replay. At least that's what Campbell and Voss said.

I didn't know for sure that night it was going to be my last game. I had a choice to stay as a full-time referee, or work half a season and do some supervising. I figured it was tough enough to stay in shape if you worked all the time, never mind being a part-time official. I decided to retire and then Scotty Morrison, who had been the referee-in-chief for about a year, offered me a full-time job as supervisor and I took it.

Actually, that game in Detroit in 1966 wasn't exactly my last game. On December 30, 1978, I was at a game on Long Island. The Islanders were playing the Atlanta Flames and the referee, Dave Newell, got hurt with two minutes to go in the first period. They took him off the ice to the clinic so I went downstairs and asked the doctor if Dave could continue. The doctor said no, that they were sending him to hospital for X-Rays because he might have a broken cheekbone. For some reason I said to the Islanders' trainer, "Have you got a pair of size eight-and-a-half skates?" I don't know why I ever said it. Anyway, I kept talking to Dave and suddenly I see the trainer coming back with an armful of equipment, including a pair of eight-and-a-half skates which belonged to Bryan Trottier. So I said, Okay, I'll take over. I put on the skates and a blue sweater to go with the grey slacks I was wearing and I refereed the rest of the game.

I found out three things when I was on the ice that night. One: they all could skate better than when we had just six teams. Two: they could all shoot the puck very hard, every one of them. In the old days you had somebody like the Rocket who could shoot it as good with a backhand as with a forehand, maybe better. And you had just a few guys, like Geoffrion and Hull, who could really fire it. Now, they all can. Three: they were all big, so much bigger. It was something I hadn't really noticed sitting upstairs.

So I worked the rest of the game and it was kind of fun because the players were very co-operative. I hadn't refereed a game in thirteen years but I had been playing a lot of squash so I was in reasonably good shape. As the game went on I found out that the glass all around the rink makes it tougher for the referee to get out of the way if he's caught up in the play. But I survived, and those size eight-and-a-half skates I borrowed from Bryan Trottier are now in the Hockey Hall of Fame.

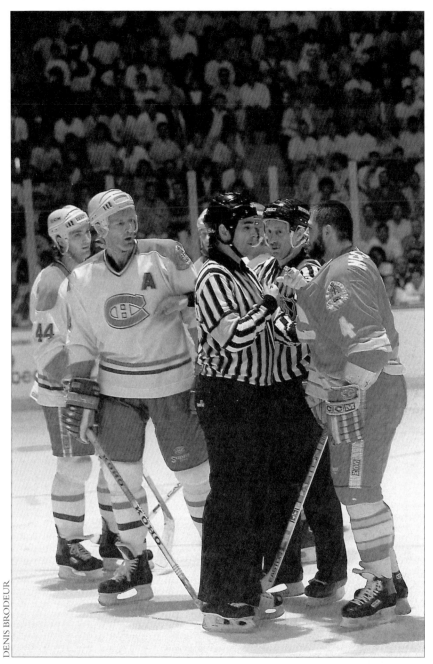

DENIS BRODEUR

Andy van Hellemond explaining things during a Montreal–Calgary game.
Andy's record for most games worked by a referee will likely never be surpassed.

National Hockey League's "Three Blind Mice"

From left to right: King Clancy, Mickey Ion, and Bill Stewart. They were three of the best referees in the game, and yet, then as now, there was an image problem as you can see by the headline. The story accompanying the picture said the headline was used in a "jocular" sense.

Bill Chadwick surveying the result of a knockout punch delivered by Maurice "Rocket" Richard in 1951. Through most of the 1940s and '50s, Chadwick was regarded as the NHL's top referee.

COURTESY RED STOREY

The always volatile Rocket pleading his case to officiating great Red Storey following a fight at Maple Leaf Gardens, December 29, 1954. Another legend, linesman George Hayes, listens in. The Rocket lost this one – Red threw him out of the game.

NATIONAL HOCKEY LEAGUE

Long-time referee-in-chief Scotty Morrison and his senior supervisor Frank Udvari. Their work in the 1960s and '70s established the guidelines used by the officiating department today.

The author and Frank Udvari, both nattily attired, in 1973 following the announcement of Frank's induction into the Hockey Hall of Fame.

DENIS BRODEUR

John D'Amico at work during one of his most memorable games, the Canadiens-Nordiques "Good Friday Night Brawl" at the Montreal Forum in 1984. Bruce Hood, right, was the referee.

NATIONAL HOCKEY LEAGUE

Neil Armstrong, the Hall of Fame linesman who broke George Hayes's record for most games worked in the NHL.

NATIONAL HOCKEY LEAGUE

Above: Veteran linesman Matt Pavelich being presented with a $1,500 cheque the night he worked his 1,500th game in the NHL. Left to right: John D'Amico, Ron Wicks, referee-in-chief Scotty Morrison, Pavelich, and Art Skov.

Right: Referee Ron Wicks looks on as the Canadiens help an injured goaltender off the ice at the Montreal Forum in the early 1980s. Wicks was the youngest official in NHL history when, in 1960, he broke in on his twentieth birthday.

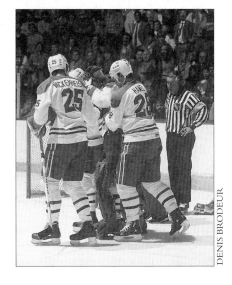

DENIS BRODEUR

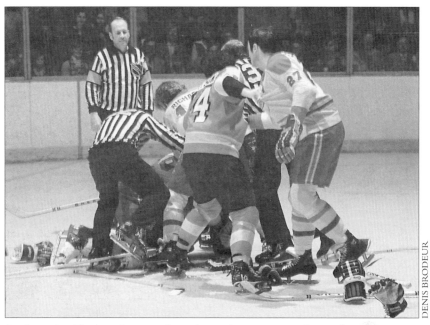

Referee Art Skov sorting out the culprits during a Canadiens–Flyers game at the Montreal Forum in the early 1970s.

Referee Bob Myers on the outside trying to look in. Officials often find themselves doing that when the Philadelphia Flyers are on the ice.

NATIONAL HOCKEY LEAGUE

Lloyd Gilmour was the referee when the Soviet Red Army team left the ice in Philadelphia and threatened to "go home" during their historic series against NHL teams in 1976.

DENIS BRODEUR

Denis Morel in a familiar referee's pose, waiting for the linesman to face off the puck. Morel refereed fourteen years and is now a member of the supervisory staff of the NHL.

NATIONAL HOCKEY LEAGUE

Don Koharski was a teenage linesman in the WHA. He later conquered some tough personal demons to become one of the NHL's top referees.

DIANE SOBOLEWSKI

Koharski and Buffalo tough guy Rob Ray at close quarters. This wasn't their first time in a situation like this and it won't be their last.

3

In Charge

SCOTTY MORRISON BRYAN LEWIS

*My father coached the Montreal Canadiens in the 1940s,
and one of his favourite stories about officiating and discipline involved Red Dutton, who was president of the NHL at
that time.*

*Phil Watson was a fiery forward with the Canadiens in
the 1943–44 season. During a melee in a game in Toronto,
Watson punched linesman Jim Primeau. A couple of days
later Watson and my father appeared before Dutton at a
hearing into the incident in his office in Montreal. Dutton
asked Watson for an explanation.*

*"The linesman grabbed my arms," said Watson, "the
other guy kept hitting me, and I couldn't do anything about
it. I got so mad at the linesman that when he finally let me
go I turned around and belted him one."*

*Dutton, who had been known as a firebrand as both a
player and a coach, wasted no time making his decision,*

"Mr. Watson," said the president. "I would have done the same thing myself. Case dismissed."

Eleven years later, Clarence Campbell was president of the NHL and showed no such mercy on Maurice Richard. After the famed Rocket hit linesman Cliff Thompson, he was suspended by Campbell for the remaining three games of the regular season, plus all of the 1955 playoffs, a ruling that sparked the infamous Richard Riot in Montreal. Obviously, Campbell had changed his thinking from when he was a referee in the NHL.

On March 23, 1937, in a playoff game between the Boston Bruins and the Montreal Maroons, Bruin captain Dit Clapper punched the future president in the nose when Campbell penalized him for high-sticking Dave Trottier. In his game report Campbell exonerated Clapper, claiming the incident took place "in the heat of the moment." He recommended Clapper be fined but the league took no action at all. The Rocket should have been so lucky.

Times have certainly changed since decisions like that were made, or since Frank Calder ordered King Clancy to referee a league game when Clancy had never refereed any game, anywhere. A situation such as in 1942 when Bill Chadwick worked the seventh game of the Stanley Cup finals in his first year as an NHL referee would never happen today.

The league has grown from six to twenty-six teams in the last thirty years. During that time three men, Scotty Morrison, the late John McCauley, and Bryan Lewis, have served as referee-in-chief of the NHL. When Morrison took over in 1965 there were five full-time referees and five full-time linesmen. Today, Bryan Lewis has an on-ice staff of twenty-six referees and thirty-four linesmen. Newer members work in minor pro leagues as well as the NHL. There are also several supervisors, many of them former *officials, who attend hundreds of games each season in the* NHL *and other pro leagues. The most recent additions to the* NHL*'s officiating family are the twenty-six video-replay judges.*

Ian "Scotty" Morrison is a native of Montreal who spent several years refereeing professional hockey, two of them in the NHL. *He was referee-in-chief for twenty-one years. In 1986 Morrison changed jobs within the league to become the executive chairman and president of the Hockey Hall of Fame, a position he still holds.*

SCOTTY MORRISON

I played junior hockey in Montreal but I knew I wasn't going to be an NHLer. What really convinced me was when my team played against the Quebec Citadels in the semi-finals and they gave me the job of shadowing Jean Béliveau. He's 6'3", and I'm 5'7", at best, so you can picture that match-up. Our coach told me to go on the ice when Béliveau went on and to go off when he went off. My job was to keep him off the scoresheet. Well, Jean got a hat-trick and three or four assists that night, so right then and there I knew if I was going to have anything to do with professional hockey it wouldn't be as a player. So I turned to officiating.

I started out in the Quebec Junior League. Young players have heroes and – I don't think people realize this – young referees have heroes too. Mine were men like Red Storey and George Gravel, who I watched doing Senior League games. Others like Sibbey and Ernie Mundey and Kenny Mullins took me under their wing. When I was starting out I got a chance to skate with the Canadiens at their training camp at the Forum. I worked both the morning and afternoon shifts, calling offsides and facing off the puck. After three or four days I was really tired. Your dad was coaching and one afternoon I said I thought I'd take a break because I was so tired. He looked at me with a little smile on his face and said, "A young buck like you, tired already? Get back out there." And of course I did. It was a lot of fun and a great experience.

I moved up to the Quebec Senior League, and in one game between the Montreal Royals and the Quebec Aces I called back three goals against Quebec. It was a tough night and the league president, George Slater, was in our room afterwards trying to console me. Punch Imlach was coaching Quebec. After the game there was a knock on our door. It was one of Imlach's players, Joe Crozier. He had a whistle in his hand and he said, "Mr. Imlach says you were having so much fun with your whistle tonight he'd like to present you with another one. He wants you to take it and stick it you-know-where." Imlach made a big fuss about my work in the press the next day so for the rest of that season I wasn't the most popular man in Quebec City.

I spent a couple of seasons working in the Western Hockey League and in 1954 moved up to the NHL. I did some work as a linesman and my first assignment was an exhibition game at the Forum between the Canadiens and the Senior Royals. The other officials were my two heroes, Red Storey and George Gravel. It was my first game with an NHL team and I was all excited and nervous. I didn't know if George or Red was going to referee. We're skating around before the game and I said to Gravel, "I guess we'd better get started." He said, "Any time you're ready, kid. You don't think that big redhead and I are gonna referee, do you? You're it." And with that he handed me the puck.

For the rest of the night, any time Red would give me the puck to faceoff he'd bend way down to emphasize how small I was and the fans got a kick out of that. With about a minute to go in the game I hear a ripple of laughter going through the Forum. I look around and I'm the only official on the ice. George and Red had climbed into the penalty bench and were sitting there leaning over, with their chins on the boards, taking the rest of the night off. Mr. Campbell was at the game and I don't think he was all that amused. But that's an example of things that happened then that would never happen today.

A few nights later there was an exhibition game between the Canadiens and another NHL team and this time I really was the linesman and Gravel really was the referee. There was a potential icing, the players were chasing the puck, and I waved it off. Rocket Richard and George bumped into each other on the play and the Rocket went down. I can remember George yelling at him "Hey, Rocket, if you can't keep up with me, get out of my way!" My mouth just dropped. I was in awe of Rocket Richard and here was a referee talking to him like that.

Early that season I was in Boston as a linesman. George Hayes was the other linesman and Red was the referee. The newcomer with two old pros. After the game I went with them to a bar. Pretty soon Red and George are into a loud argument. I'm sitting there feeling very nervous and then they said, okay, let's go outside and settle this. So out we go and they hand me their jackets, roll up their sleeves, and right there in the middle of the street they square off. Now I'm really scared and I must have looked like death warmed over. There was no way I was going to jump in between those two big guys. Just when I was sure they were going to start swinging they looked at me and burst out laughing. The whole time they'd been setting up the unsuspecting rookie. Welcome to the NHL, kid.

In Boston in those days the officials stayed at the Manger Hotel, which was right next to the Garden. You'd change in your hotel room, put on a coat, and carry your skates to the rink. The first time I refereed a game in Boston they assigned two local linesmen, so I was by myself going to the Garden. I knock at the back door and a big Irish cop opens it. I go to walk into the building and he puts his hand on my chest and says, "Where do you think you're goin'?" I said I was the referee, and with his Boston accent he says, "Move it, kid, get out of here." I said, "Officer, I really am the referee," and I opened my coat to show him my referee's sweater and the NHL crest. He looked at that, and at my skates, and he finally let me in.

The funny thing is, about ten years later I was at a game in Boston as referee-in-chief and the big Irish cop was still working there. I told him I almost didn't make it to referee my first game in the Garden because of him. We laughed and he said, "Scotty, you looked to me like a little curly-haired kid trying to sneak into the game. I didn't believe a little guy like you could be the referee." [Laughs]

When I refereed for the first time in Detroit the linesmen were two veterans, George Hayes and Bill Morrison. Before the game started I was standing beside Morrison and Ted Lindsay came over and said, "What the hell is this? The first father-and-son combination in the NHL?" Bill took objection to that so I told Ted I was nervous enough without knowing my linesman was upset. Ted just laughed and skated away.

Everyone remembers Toe Blake as a hockey player and coach, but he was also a good baseball umpire. I umpired some games with Toe in the Quebec Provincial League. There were tough days there, let me tell you. One day we were in Farnham. Toe called balls and strikes and I was on the bases. It was a wild game with lots of arguments and the home team lost. Afterwards the fans were waiting for Toe in front of the stadium. The police came to him and told him they could take him out a gate in centre field so the fans wouldn't see him but he wouldn't do it. Toe said, "I'm goin' out the same way I came in, through the front door!" He did, and I went with him. They threw stuff at us, kicked us, spit at us, but we made it. Toe was tough. No way were they going to intimidate him. I learned a lot about officials having to be tough when I umpired with Toe Blake.

When I joined the NHL in 1954 I guess I was the youngest official. I had looked forward to it for a long time but, strangely, I did it for only two years. I had just gotten married and I didn't like being away from home. In those days you were away at Christmas and I didn't enjoy that part of it. After my second year I had an opportunity to go back to the West Coast to work in sales with Goodyear Tire and Rubber, so I took it. Joan and I moved to Vancouver, and I refereed games there in the Western League. A couple of years later I left Goodyear and joined Yardley of London. I ended up back in Toronto as their Canadian sales supervisor and then, lo and behold, I got a chance to get back into hockey at the NHL level.

One day I was in Montreal and met Mr. Campbell on the street. He asked me if I would go up to his office for a chat later on and I did. Carl Voss was retiring and they were looking for a new referee-in-chief. We talked and he told me there were six or seven candidates and that was about it. I don't think he considered me one of the candidates. I didn't think about it again until a couple of months later when I realized I hadn't seen anything in the paper about a new man being hired. I phoned Mr. Campbell and told him I wanted to throw my hat in the ring. He asked me if I was serious and I said I definitely was. He told me to give Carl Voss a call, which I did. Carl came to Toronto from Buffalo, where he lived, and we spent a day talking about the job. The next thing I knew I was in Montreal meeting the six NHL team owners and in June 1965 I was appointed referee-in-chief. It's a small world, Dick. I had the job for twenty-one years.

Mr. Campbell made it very clear that I was responsible for anything to do with the officiating. That meant the hiring, the training, the conduct and efficiency on the ice, the conduct off the ice, all that was my responsibility. He said, "I don't want the owners talking to me about officiating, or about a particular referee or linesman. That's your job." So I had to answer to the owners and the general managers. There were times when things got very hot and heavy, especially in the playoffs. That's when the tension is really there.

People would say to me that I must be having a terrible time with Harold Ballard, that he must be all over me about every call ever made against the Toronto Maple Leafs. They wouldn't believe it when I would tell them Harold Ballard and I never exchanged an angry word. He would say, "You know what I think about that?" and he'd tell me. Then he'd say, "Oh well, Scotty, they've only got two eyes. So what can you do?"

During my first two years on the job we had six teams and were preparing for the first expansion with six more teams coming in. Frank Udvari retired after my first year and I appointed him as my supervisor. When expansion arrived and we were coast to coast I appointed another, Dutch van Deelen, in the West. We had an extensive recruiting campaign and there were some good young officials on the way up through the American and Western Leagues, like Bryan Lewis, Wally Harris, Bruce Hood, and John McCauley.

I changed things a bit from what Carl Voss did. I started a regular officials' training camp, just like the teams. It was near Toronto and we had the Maple Leaf doctors conduct medical tests. People came from the army to set up a fitness program. Frank Udvari was very strict about their weight. We told them there would be three teams for the training sessions and one would be called the Heavy Red Barons. Anyone coming to camp weighing five pounds more than the year before would automatically become a Heavy Red Baron. We set up a two-mile run at 6:00 every morning and there were a lot of complaints about that. But the interesting thing is, within two years we had no more members of the Heavy Red Barons.

The World Hockey Association came along in 1972. Bill Friday, an outstanding referee, received an offer from them he couldn't turn down. Another of our good referees, the late Vern Buffey, left to become their referee-in-chief. A few others went as well. But when the WHA folded and four of their teams joined the NHL we got some pretty good officials out of it. Wayne Bonney was one, Ron Asselstine was another. And life went on.

The toughest part of the job would come when I made the assignments for the playoffs. That's when you have to sit out officials, especially when you get down to the semis and the finals. A referee could have a very good year, maybe we had ranked him fourth overall. Yet only three would be assigned to the finals and you'd have to tell him he wasn't one of them. Maybe he had worked the finals the previous year. It wasn't the monetary end of it they worried about. It was strictly a matter of pride.

I had a hard core of guys I really counted on, especially early in the job. John Ashley, Art Skov, Lloyd Gilmour, Neil Armstrong, Matt Pavelich, John D'Amico. People like them were very important to me. Initially there were just three playoff series. I thought so much of John Ashley that one year I assigned him to referee the seventh game in all three if it came to that. It didn't work out that all three went seven games, but that shows you the confidence you can have in the work of a referee.

Maybe I was considered a tough taskmaster, but I hated excuses about the mechanics of officiating. And I didn't like it when some of our officials got a little careless about their fitness level. I used to tell them, Look, they're gonna question your judgement and they're gonna question calls you make. But I don't ever want them questioning if you're fit to do the job. When a team captain comes to talk to you and he's dripping with perspiration, you'd better be dripping with perspiration too.

While Scotty Morrison's on-ice career in the NHL *was a short one, it was different for Bryan Lewis, who refereed 1,031 regular-season games and another 89 in the playoffs. His last game was in the 1986 playoffs, the well-remembered night in Edmonton when the Calgary Flames eliminated the high-powered Oilers, the game in which Edmonton defenceman Steve Smith accidentally banked the puck off goaltender Grant Fuhr's leg into the Oilers' net for the winning goal. Lewis then went to work as an assistant to referee-in-chief John McCauley. When McCauley passed away in the summer of 1989, Lewis succeeded him in the job now called Director of Officiating.* ⁻

Bryan Lewis followed a familiar path on his way to the NHL. *He was an aspiring junior player and, after failing tryouts with both the Niagara Falls Flyers and the Toronto Marlies, began officiating minor hockey in his home of Georgetown, Ontario. From there he moved up to the* OHA. *A chance meeting with Scotty Morrison gave him his first big boost towards the big leagues.*

Bryan Lewis

I met Scotty at the Weston Arena. We were leaning on a snack bar in the corner and he asked me if I wanted to join the National League. They were looking for officials because expansion was coming up. I had been getting a lot of work doing junior games. At that time they wouldn't use you in games in your own community, which meant that officials in places like Toronto and Hamilton couldn't work in their home arenas. John McCauley and I lived in Georgetown so we got a lot of work.

I got my first big break because of a snowstorm. I was doing a junior-B game in Brampton and there was a big storm and the referee didn't show up. I got to referee that hockey game and got my foot in the door. I wasn't too interested in being a linesman after that. The referee-in-chief of the OHA was Pat Patterson and I remember he came into the room after a game and asked me, "Do you really want to be a referee, kid?" I said I did, and he said, "Then get a haircut and pull your pants up."

Officiating then meant extra money for me over and above my regular job. That's why I told Scotty that night at the Weston Arena, "I'm accustomed to eating steak. I don't have to join the NHL to eat bologna." He said, "You prove to me you're worth the kind of money you need to keep eating steak and I'll see that you get it." That was thirty years ago and I still turn to him for guidance.

I started to work pro hockey in '67–68, the first year of the NHL expansion. On Christmas Day I was in Houston, Texas. I went for a walk thinking, Is this what pro hockey is all about? I can remember the hotel I was in like I stayed there yesterday. My wife hadn't phoned so I wrote her a note saying, What's the matter, don't you care? Right after I mailed it I wrote another one saying, Sorry, dear, disregard what's in the previous envelope, because I felt so bad. I was really low spending Christmas a million miles away from home. I thought I would never survive as a referee.

I had one trip that year where I left home February 2 and got back March 3. The last thing you wanted was to check into a hotel and have them say there was mail for you. That meant more assignments and you would have to stay on the road. Guys like me were getting about five thousand dollars a year. A lot of us worked for Pepsi-Cola in the summertime because lugging those old soft-drink cases around was a great way of making money.

I remember coming off the ice after a tough night in Cleveland in the American League and thinking, Why am I doing this for a hundred bucks a game, or two hundred, whatever it was? I'll never make it to the NHL. Fred Glover was coaching Cleveland, and if he said "Hi" to you before a game there was always a string of profanity before and after the "Hi." At the All-Star weekend this year [1997] in San Jose I refereed the Legends game and he was coaching one of the teams. I went over to him and said, "Freddie, just for old times' sake, please yell at me." And he did. Then he said, "All that stuff I did to you back then was a test to make you a better official."

In my third year as a professional I got three games in the NHL. It was at the end of the season and the games weren't gonna mean anything in the final standings. My first was in Montreal and during the anthem I was shaking so much it's a wonder I didn't fall flat on my fanny. I didn't check to see what the hell side the penalty bench was on. I called my first penalty and then had to look around to find the box. It would have been embarrassing to go to the wrong side.

The next year I shuttled between the American League and the NHL and it was very tough. One night you'd work a game in Boston and the very next night you'd be in

Baltimore. It was like you were always being sent down to the minors. You'd be doing a game one night in the NHL and there would be players and coaches who were your heroes when you watched them on television and the next night you'd be back in the American League. We still do it and it's still tough. I had a young referee in my office a while back and I told him exactly what Scotty Morrison and Frank Udvari told me, that the game in Baltimore or Fredericton is very important to those players. You don't want to stay in the American League and neither do they, so you can't take it lightly.

Like any job, refereeing has ups and downs. A down for me was a game in Pittsburgh when Philadelphia was there and Barry Ashbee punched me in the nose and made it bleed. I remember Brian O'Neill phoning me to tell me he had suspended him for eight games, or whatever it was he got, and he asked what I thought of his ruling. At that point I just didn't care. I wanted to put that behind me because it had never happened before, and it never happened again. I thought, what the hell, that was pro hockey.

Now, that seems tragic because Barry Ashbee died of leukemia and I never had a chance in later years to talk to him, shoot the breeze about that incident and everything else. If Barry Ashbee had played in the Legends game I would have thought no less of him for what he'd done to me.

One of the worst games I ever had was a night when Philadelphia was in Oakland. A few nights earlier in Philadelphia a player named Mike Christie had cut Bobby Clarke badly and the Flyers had gone after him pretty good. They went after him again in Oakland and they tried to annihilate him. Jim Neilson was the only Oakland player who came to Christie's aid. The big fight was in the penalty box. Then all of a sudden Bobby Clarke said, "That's enough. Let him go," and I'll tell you, those Philadelphia Flyers just stepped back like it was a parade and let Mike Christie go off the ice to the medical room. Someone sent me a picture that showed me on top of the boards writing on a piece of paper. I guess I was writing down numbers.

The next day I go up to Vancouver and Philly is there and their back-up goalie, Bobby Taylor, says to me, "Don't worry about us tonight. They've put seatbelts on the benches and we have to wear them at all times." [Laughs]

You'd get your assignments and you'd think, oh my God, Philly at Vancouver, because they always had feuds. But it was nice to know they gave you those kinds of games. I do the assignments now. You take an official like, say, Bill McCreary. There's a case of any game, any time.

I tell young officials that when they feel comfortable to take any game, any time, I'll give it to them. There could be an emergency but, as far as early assignments go, young officials don't get the so-called big or tough games. It's not fair to the teams, the fans, or to the young official. You could kill him right there. Sometimes you guess that a certain game won't be a tough game and you guess wrong. Then again, how are you gonna know if he can do it until you give it to him? But it takes time. It's an apprenticeship.

I did my first game in Montreal, my first playoff game, and my one-thousandth game. I have three pucks from those games hanging in my office and they all have Montreal Canadiens logos. My one-thousandth game was the only time my mother saw me referee a game live up to that point. It was the only NHL game she ever saw me do. Later I was with my brother and my nephew, who both referee, in Georgetown doing a kids' game and we had a family reunion at the arena. My mother was at that one. I would never take my dad to a game because I was sure if somebody said, "Lewis, you're a bum," he would have been up swinging at the guy.

My last game was the playoff game in Edmonton when Steve Smith put the puck in his own net. I tore up my knee that night. I was supposed to work my next game in New York. I went there and tried skating late in the afternoon to try it but I couldn't turn. I had never had a problem like that before but I knew I couldn't work and my year was finished.

But the knee didn't end my career. I remember sitting in Scotty Morrison's office saying I wanted to referee another two or three years. He told me the league wanted me to retire and take a job helping John McCauley. Scotty said there was no guarantee the job would be open in two or three years. So I thought about it in terms of the best interests of my family, and as it was with the same organization, it made sense to take it then instead of spending another two or three years on the ice.

At first I did the job Frank Udvari had been doing. I ran schools and clinics and was always on the lookout for younger people, making sure we had a feeder system. I also spent a lot of time with referees in the minor leagues. John let me be part of everything and there were no secrets. That made the transition much easier when John passed away and I took over his job.

This business is made up of two groups of people, our families and the officiating fraternity, which is a very close-knit group. When I see the wives I tell them that the most important part of our game is them and the families at home. If an official is not happy he's not going to work properly.

The other major part is the game itself. You've got to be prepared mentally and physically. Our physical-fitness guidelines are much, much better than they used to be, and I think it's extended a lot of careers. Years ago before a game you wouldn't get down on the floor and stretch or ride a bike and all that stuff they do now. The guys would have laughed at you. We'd just come in the room and put our stuff on. We had guys sitting there five minutes before the game in their underwear saying, "Yeah, I'll be ready. Everything's fine."

My first year at training camp I was with John Ashley, one of the best referees ever. He took out a rule book, held it in front of me, and fanned the pages. Then he said, "Okay, they can't say you never opened the rule book. Now, go out and use common sense." What the hell's wrong with that?

You still have to know the rule book, and it keeps getting thicker and thicker, and tougher to understand. More logic, more consistency, more judgement. All that stuff. And of course everybody's an expert. You know, back up the video-tape. You and I can look over somebody's shoulder at a tape and after seeing it a couple of times we can say what an awful call the referee just made. The guy had one second to look at it, react, and do what he had to do.

What makes a good referee? Like John Ashley, I say common sense. You have to be consistent, you have to have judgement. Roads are built for you and me to drive on, and if we go too fast the police officer is there. A hockey rink is built for the players and the game is for the players. If someone breaks the rules I have to tell him to go to the bad-boy's box, or take a shower. My reaction as an official is always after the fact. If player X hits player Y over the head with his stick then I have to call it.

I have to have rapport with the players. It might be simple, something like "Cut the nonsense." That's what I call a "one-minute penalty." Our game is filled with those, the ones that aren't called because of common sense. The easiest example I can use is a line change. The rule says five feet from the bench for the players going off and coming on. So the linesman looks and says, "Hey, that's five feet, one inch. You got a penalty," instead of turning to the coach and telling him to watch his line changes. Don't ask for trouble. I know people say, "It's marginal, it's brutal, it's horseshit. It turned the game around." All that stuff. I used to call the late Ted Darling, the Sabres' broadcaster, "No-call" because one of his favourite lines was, "There's no call on the play." [*For years another announcer, Dick Irvin, after what he thought was a bad "no-call," has said, "Play goes right on."*]

When I started it was tough for me to go to the bench and talk to Scotty Bowman or Emile Francis because of who they were. We've got young kids coming into the league and we're asking them to talk to the coaches in a commercial time-out to tell them to watch their line changes, or whatever. I have to realize that's not hard for a veteran like Kerry Fraser or Don Koharski to do but it's sure as hell tough for a Dan O'Halloran or a Blaine Angus. Things haven't changed in that respect. It's just that now the people are different.

The National Hockey League's officiating budget is in excess of fifteen million dollars. We've got a staff of about eighty people. We're probably the largest single department in the NHL. It's a big business and the job is far more technical now. There are far more videotapes and the rules are far more complicated. We don't have to like them, we just have to call them. We send the referees tapes and hold conference calls. There's much more of a hands-on approach to what the league does now.

Anyone in this position has a tough job when it comes to the playoff assignments. Now the officials have to earn their way from round to round so that when you get to the finals you have two of the best teams and three of the best referees. They may not have been your top three in the regular season and that's the good part. You're rewarding them for their work in the playoffs. I don't have any discomfort with that because when the best playoff teams get to the finals so should the best playoff officials.

I phone each and every one of them when their season is over. We used to get a letter sent to us in the mail but by then you knew you didn't have any assignments because the phone hadn't rung. Last year I talked to one guy for fifty-five minutes because he was so upset at not going on to the next round. I understand how he felt but we're not going to change our mind. They don't thank you for sending them home at that time of year and I accept that. But they also have to accept it as professionals.

There are a lot of players out there who dream of being in the NHL and there are a lot of officials who do too. One night, in Anaheim, Blaine Angus took a puck in the face that broke his nose. He went to the hospital and one of the linesmen took over as referee. I happened to be there and I knew the video goal judge, Michel Voyer, was an official in a league in California. I asked him if he had his equipment in his car, and of course these guys always do. I told him to get it. We have emergency sweaters in all buildings. So he worked the rest of the game on the lines. I told him we'd pay him, that we really appreciated what he did, and he said, "I don't want any money. I'd just like to keep the sweater."

Remember the big snowstorm in Vancouver [December 1996]? We didn't know if our crew could make it so we had three local officials standing by. As it turned out our guys got there and I want to tell you, there were three very disappointed young men when they learned they wouldn't be working an NHL game. People are very quick to come forward and tell us there's a good official in Swift Current or in Nanaimo. People are proud when a player comes out of their minor system to the NHL and they are equally proud when an official makes it.

We often hear, "You're a referee? My God, why would you want to do that?" As bad as some people think it is, it's still an extremely good business to be in. Sure, it's like anything else, good days and bad days. I could sit here talking about the bad days but I've been getting paid on the fifteenth and thirtieth of every month for thirty years, always from the same organization. Probably not many people can say they've worked for the same company for thirty years. I can.

We say NHL means No Home Life, Not Home Lately, all that stuff. But I tell you, it's still the best damned place to be. As mad and as frustrated as we get at times, if you made out a list of the positives and the negatives, the positives would far outweigh the negatives.

4

Hall of Fame Linesmen

JOHN D'AMICO
NEIL ARMSTRONG   MATT PAVELICH

There are four linesmen in the Referees/Linesmen section of the Hockey Hall of Fame: the late George Hayes, John D'Amico, Neil Armstrong, and Matt Pavelich. All but Armstrong worked briefly as referees in the NHL and then became linesmen for the balance of their long careers.

There have been many colourful characters in hockey and George Hayes ranks with the best of them. Hayes worked 1,549 NHL regular-season, playoff, and All-Star games between 1946 and 1965. He was constantly in trouble with president Clarence Campbell, who finally fired him February 1, 1965, after Hayes refused to take an eye test. Hayes told Campbell that he took an eye test every day and didn't need another. When Campbell asked him to explain, Hayes said, "I told him I made it a habit to read the labels on the whisky bottles on the other side of the bar, so my eyes must be all right. Campbell told me to get out of his office, that I was a disgrace to the league." A few days later Hayes received a telegram from the president which read, "Your contract has been terminated because of gross insubordination."

George Hayes spent much of his boisterous life embroiled in controversy. He grew up in Ingersoll, Ontario, and became a fine young baseball player. But that part of his athletic career ended in 1940 when the Ontario League suspended him for life for picking up an umpire and tossing him over a fence during a heated argument. He was reinstated three years later but by then Hayes had become an official in the OHA. He joined the NHL in 1946 as a referee and ran into tough times as a rookie.

Late in his first season Hayes was the referee in New York when the Canadiens and the Rangers had a mammoth brawl that some say might have been the wildest ever at the old Madison Square Garden. Before it was over every player was involved, plus some fans and finally the NYPD. A photo of the mess in the paper had the caption, "Hayes in a daze."

Hayes's first playoff game was between Montreal and Boston after which Canadiens GM Frank Selke, normally a mild-mannered type, fumed that it was the worst refereed game he had ever seen. Three nights later, Hayes worked a game in Toronto that featured a wild melee in the penalty box involving Ted Lindsay, Gordie Howe, Gus Mortson, fans, and, again, the police. Early the following season the league asked Hayes to become a linesman, a request he gratefully agreed to on what he called "the happiest day of my life."

Newspaper stories about Hayes often focused on the reputation he had as drinker, a reputation he did nothing to dispel. He liked recalling an incident in a Toronto–Montreal game when he whistled down a play as offside when the Leafs' Bob Pulford was on a breakaway. As Hayes told it, "Pulford came back for the faceoff and said, 'What's wrong,

George? Have three or four beers clouded your eyes?' Jean
Béliveau was taking the faceoff for the Canadiens and he
told Pulford, 'You should apologize to this man. You're
doing him an injustice. What do you mean three or four
beers? He drank the whole case.'"

But George Hayes was far from being all play and
no work. He loved his job and did it very well. In an interview near the end of his life he said, "I liked everything
about hockey but the fights were the best. I liked breaking them up, but you had to know who you were dealing
with. You never grabbed Rocket Richard by the throat.
That's what got that linesman in trouble in Boston when
Richard hit him. You had to know your players and how to
handle them.

"I couldn't work today. Take fighting, for instance. It's a
joke. They grab with one hand and swing with the other.
A two-fisted fighter, like Fernie Flaman, would have
killed them."

Hayes was a big man, standing 6'3" and weighing 220
pounds, and was always part of the show. When he would
pick the puck up after an icing he would head back up the
ice at top speed, swerve a couple of times from one side to
the other, arrive at the faceoff circle with an elaborate, snow-
throwing stop, and then ceremoniously hand the puck to
the referee. His express-train trip was always accompanied
by whoops and hollers from the fans, who loved it.

Red Storey, who once described Hayes as "twenty-four
hours of delight," was one of his best buddies and is still
one of his biggest boosters. Red told me, "We had our fun
but I'll tell you this: there have never been two officials
who were in better shape at game time, mentally or physically, than Red Storey and George Hayes.

"I know a current official who told kids at a hockey
school that in Red Storey's day all they did was sit in a

hotel room and drink beer. What a bunch of crap. If that's the image they have of guys in our day they're wrong. Dead wrong. George Hayes walked miles every day. He was in better shape than the guys of today ever will be."

Hayes was always a nonconformist. He never wore a tie. The league once fined him fifty dollars because he hadn't shaved before a game. He was suspended for two weeks for travelling overnight in a day coach on a train, instead of first class, in order to save money. He had a lifelong distrust of doctors and remained in character to the end, refusing to see a doctor or enter hospital for severe circulation problems in his legs which led to his death in 1987, at the age of sixty-seven.

When Hayes died he had not yet been elected to the Hall of Fame, although other officials had proposed him for induction. Hayes blamed his long-time nemesis, Clarence Campbell. He once said, "The ghost of Clarence Campbell is still prowling around. I don't know any other reason. They're going to have to put me in one of these years or else say why." They finally did put George Hayes in the Hall of Fame in 1988, a few months after he died. Most people felt it was done that way because the league was fearful of what Hayes might say at his induction ceremony.

In researching this book I was told by three Hall of Fame officials, Red Storey, Frank Udvari, and Matt Pavelich, that, in their opinion, George Hayes was the best linesman in the history of hockey.

Late in the 1992–93 NHL season the Hockey Hall of Fame announced that John D'Amico had been named to its Referees/Linesmen section. The next day I was in the press room at the Capital Center, home of the Washington Capitals, in my role as the radio broadcaster of Canadiens games on station CJAD in Montreal. I was halfway through *my free meal when in walked John D'Amico, who was there in his role as a supervisor of officials.*

John and I go back a long time and he has always been one of my favourite people. I congratulated him on his well-deserved selection and we sat down to tape an interview for my show that night. As John talked about what it meant to him to be in the Hall of Fame tears welled up in his eyes. As the interviewer listened to and watched John's emotional description of his feelings, he too became teary-eyed. I'm sure others in the room were wondering why those two grown men hunched over a tape recorder in the corner of the room were crying.

A native of Toronto, John D'Amico worked more than 1,700 NHL games from 1964 to 1988. He was a linesman in the Stanley Cup finals twenty times and handled the lines at seven All-Star games plus four Canada Cup tournaments, the Challenge Cup in 1979, and Rendez-Vous '87. D'Amico was a quick study when it came to officiating hockey games. His career in a striped sweater had barely begun when he found himself working in the NHL.

JOHN D'AMICO

I started working junior hockey almost right away. I did the Memorial Cup in Toronto in 1964, which was about a year and a half after I started in amateur hockey. One of the executives of the OHA, Bill Hanley, recommended me to the NHL. They were looking for another linesman because Ron Wicks was moving up to be a referee. I got a letter from Carl Voss asking me to do some NHL exhibition games. My first was in Kitchener between Toronto and the New York Rangers on a Thursday and Mr. Voss was there. He came into our dressing room afterwards and told me he was gonna hire me as a linesman in the NHL. I looked at him and said,

"I've only worked a year and a half in the OHA and you're gonna hire me?" He said yes, and told me he wanted to watch me again on Saturday night at Maple Leaf Gardens when Toronto would be playing Detroit.

To be honest with you, I don't even remember showering and I don't remember the wheels on my car touching the road going home. I charged into the house and told my wife. I was working in construction at the time. I had watched and worked junior games in the Gardens but I'd never been in the building for an NHL game. I couldn't believe that I was going to see my first NHL game at Maple Leaf Gardens two nights later. Never mind see it, I was gonna work it.

In those days they had glass behind the nets but nothing along the boards and, sure enough, during the warm-up I see Carl Voss in a seat along the boards at the visitors' blueline. Now the game starts and after five or ten minutes I knew why I wasn't a player in the NHL. I couldn't believe how great these players were, how fast they were skating. Gordie Howe was doing things with the puck I had never seen before.

The funny thing was, I hadn't felt like that in the game in Kitchener. I guess it was the Gardens itself, the big crowd, the cheering, the whole atmosphere. And you know what? I think I was intimidated by the building, just like I was the first time I did a game at the Montreal Forum. My focus when the game started was more as a fan than as a linesman. A couple of plays went in offside and the Leaf bench was yelling like hell. All of a sudden a light went on in my mind telling me, Hey, John, wake up! You're an official now. I came off the ice at the end of the game with my head between my legs. I'm thinking to myself that I was hired on Thursday and sure as hell I'll be fired tonight, on Saturday.

Carl Voss came into our room and looked at me and I said, "Before you say anything to me, I'm not apologizing, but I learned something tonight in my first game in this building.

I became a spectator, which an official should never be. I made two or three errors in the first period. Thank God there were no goals scored, but they were blunders and I admit it. I'll always do that. If I'm wrong, I'm wrong, and I'll admit my mistakes." He looked at me and said, "You're being very honest with me. You'll have a good career." And he left the room.

Two weeks later I got my first set of NHL assignments in the mail and also a cheque for $250. I thought, Holy shit, look at all this money. Two hundred and fifty dollars. I showed it to my wife and then deposited it in the bank. Later I found out it was a $250 advance for expenses on my first road trip. I thought it was part of my salary. [Laughs]

Just before the season started they had all the officials at a meeting at the same time the owners were meeting. Matt Pavelich and Neil Armstrong were there, and Frank Udvari, Vern Buffey, John Ashley, and Art Skov. I don't know why, but George Hayes never went to meetings like that. We went into a boardroom and there they were, the six gentlemen who owned the teams in the NHL. There was Jim Norris, Senator Molson, Mr. Smythe, Weston Adams, Bill Jennings, and Bruce Norris. We were standing there and Carl Voss says, "Gentlemen, here are your officials for this year. Any questions?" Nobody asked any questions. Then somebody said, "Thank you very kindly," and we all walked out. You talk about intimidation. It was like being in front of a firing squad.

I started in Boston on opening night, October 12, 1964. I went from there to New York the next day and then went to Montreal for my first game at the Forum. That afternoon Mr. Campbell's secretary, Hilda Turriff, called me and said he wanted to see me. I thought, oh-oh, what have I done? I had worked only two games and the president wanted to see me.

So I went up to his office in the Sun Life Building and he said, "I have something here for you that you're going to like. It's your contract." I had to get a co-signer so I said, "Would you do me the honour and co-sign it for me?" and he said he would. Mr. Ford, the controller, and Hilda Turriff were there and I signed my first NHL contract. I never even looked at the amount of money written down.

I went home the next day and told my wife I had signed my first NHL contract. She said, "How much are you making?" and I said, "You know something? I really don't know." I had to admit to her that I had worked three games in the NHL and had no idea what they were paying me. So I phoned the office in Montreal and they told me it was three thousand dollars. I was ecstatic. That was in 1964 and I thought it was the biggest thing since sliced bread.

I always remember my father telling me to make sure your eyes and ears are open all the time, and don't say anything unless they say something to you first. I always remembered that and that's how I started in the NHL. I worked hard and everything seemed to be going good. About three-quarters of the way through the season one of the officials said to me, "John, you're doing a good job. Keep it up. But I don't think Mr. Voss will give you any playoffs because it's your first year." In those days there were only two rounds. Well, not only did I do the first round, I worked the very last game of the finals, in Montreal, when the Canadiens beat Chicago for the Stanley Cup in 1965.

In that first year I was doing a game in Montreal between the Canadiens and Toronto. Vern Buffey was the referee. Dave Balon of the Canadiens went around Kent Douglas like a hoop around a barrel, skated in on Johnny Bower, and scored. I got the puck and went to centre ice. Buffey was at the penalty box telling the timekeeper who scored the goal. I guess Balon said something sarcastic to Douglas when he skated by him because all of a sudden I see Douglas turn around, swing his stick, and hit him with a two-hander. It caught Balon on the side of his head and cracked him on the shoulder. I immediately called a match penalty, which a linesman could do then. Buffey hadn't seen it and he asked me, "What are you calling?" I said I was calling a match penalty because the guy gave him a two-hander. Buffey said, "Wait a minute," and I told him to call it anything he wanted, but that's what the guy did.

There was a hearing and Douglas got suspended for three games and fined, which hurt players in those days. He was making something like $7,800. Two weeks later I'm at Maple Leaf Gardens and when the Leafs skate out for the game, guess who's coming right at me? Kent Douglas. I'm thinking, what's he gonna do to me? I figured he might shoot the puck right at my head, but he said, "No hard feelings, John. You did your job." I'd been thinking about the next time I'd see him, so that broke the tension. It was a ton of bricks off my shoulders.

Another time early in my career I had back-to-back games in Montreal, on Thursday and Saturday. In the first game there was a very close play that was actually offside. I didn't call it and the Detroit player went in and scored on Gump Worsley. I couldn't sleep for two nights thinking about it. Saturday morning I went to the Forum to sort of apologize to Worsley because he was in a fight for the Vezina Trophy.

As soon as I got into the Forum I bumped into Toe Blake. I was sure he would be mad at me because of the call I missed, so before he said anything I told him why I was there. He took me aside and said, "If you're honest with the players, if you never lie to them, and if you admit you missed an offside, you'll have them with you for your whole career. And you'll miss some offsides, but you're going to have a good career. I like what you're doing because you're being honest about the whole thing." It was very good advice from a gentleman I really respected and who coached all those Stanley Cup–winning teams. And good hockey sense too.

Toe's captain in those years was Jean Béliveau, another man I had nothing but the highest respect for. Big Jean didn't say much but when he did, you listened and you thought about it. One night he asked me, "John, are you having a bad night or are all those plays really offside?" [Laughs]

After two years they asked me to become a referee. Expansion was coming a year later and they needed more referees. Scotty Morrison asked me to give it a try with the promise that if things didn't work out I could go back to being a linesman. So in 1966–67 I worked as a referee in the American, Central, and Western leagues.

I didn't have too much trouble on the ice but I couldn't leave the game at the rink. I started as a referee in the NHL the next season and worked twenty-one games, but I still had problems with my nerves. I'd break out in a rash thinking about the game I had just done and the next game I was going to do. After a game in Toronto I told Scotty how I felt, that I didn't want to kill myself. I know he was disappointed but he was true to his word and I went back to being a linesman.

People often ask me about the toughest games I had to work. I had a few. One of the biggest fights I was involved in was a Boston–New York game during the playoffs in the 1970s. It was in New York and it was really a heated game, really bad. Just as I was going to drop the puck in the Rangers' end, Derek Sanderson left the circle and skated up to the goalie, Ed Giacomin, and told him he had better stay in his crease because the first time he came out of it he was going to cut his head off. I finally drop the puck, Sanderson skates by the net, Giacomin gives him a two-hander and

Sanderson gives him one right back. Before I know it the
benches have emptied and away they went. What a night
that was. I think that period alone took about an hour and
half to play. Johnny McKenzie was all over the place. That
was one of the biggest altercations I was ever in.

Another one was the famous Good Friday Massacre in
1984 at the Forum in a playoff game between the Canadiens
and the Quebec Nordiques. Games with those teams were
always among the most tense I worked no matter what
time of the season it was. It was worse in the playoffs.
Bruce Hood was the referee and Bob Hodges and I were on
the lines. The first big brawl happened at the end of the
second period. Chris Nilan, Dale Hunter, guys like that
were into it. I was trying to break up Louis Sleigher and
Jean Hamel. Mario Tremblay jumped in as a peacemaker
and Sleigher threw a punch over his shoulder and knocked
Hamel out cold.

We finally got them off the ice and then there were a lot of
people trying to sort things out. There were the three of us
plus the standby officials, Andy van Hellemond and Wayne
Bonney, Scotty Morrison, John McCauley, and Brian O'Neill.
It was quite a scene. Nobody told the teams to stay in their
rooms until we sorted things out so before we could tell the
teams what players were being thrown out of the game they
went back on the ice for the third period. Claude Mouton
started announcing the penalties and everybody started
fighting again. That was an awful night.

I had some injuries. I was cut for fourteen stitches trying
to break up Pierre Bouchard and Stan Jonathon the night
they went at it in Boston. The Hall of Fame book mentions
that I kept working in a game after I had broken my arm.
That was in Boston too. I had hopped up on the boards to get
out of the traffic and Mike O'Connell shot the puck and it
hit me on the arm. It really hurt but I kept going. Between

periods I started to lace up my skates to go back out and the bone in my arm snapped like a twig. They put a pressure bandage on it and I finished the game. I went back to Toronto and had it set. I missed a few games after that.

If an injury can be funny, sort of, I had one. I was working with Andy and Ray Scapinello on Long Island in the 1983 Stanley Cup finals between the·Islanders and Edmonton. We went out for our normal pre-game skate about five minutes before the national anthems. The three of us are skating around and I decide that instead of going the same way they were I'd turn and skate the opposite way. As I do here comes Andy cutting around the net, right at me. He was moving pretty good and so was I and before we can react we collide. His helmet hit my nose and broke it, smashed it all to hell. There was blood all over the gol-darn place.

They take me off the ice and as they do here come the Oilers out of their dressing room and down the corridor. They're looking at me like, what the hell is going on? Just three guys skating around on the ice and one of them comes off bleeding. They get a doctor and he sticks gauze up my nose so far I can hardly breathe. But in a few minutes they managed to stop the bleeding, and I did the game.

The most emotional game for me was the final of the 1976 Canada Cup in Montreal, the one where Darryl Sittler scored the winner in overtime. It was Canada against Czechoslovakia. There were two goals called back in that game and the tension was unreal. Bobby Clarke got upset about one of my calls and he said to me, "What side of the ocean do you live on? There's a new season starting soon. I'll get even with you." It was the most emotionally draining game I was ever in.

I was also on the ice when Canada beat Russia in the 1987 Canada Cup, in Hamilton. I was about ten feet from the Russian net when Mario Lemieux scored the winning goal.

A linesman can't cheer, of course, but for a split second I was between a rock and a hard place. But only for a second. I might have been a Canadian but I was also a pro. I picked the puck out of the net and went back to centre ice to give it to the referee for the faceoff.

When I was in my last year John McCauley told me the league wanted to make me an officiating coach before the season was over, to work with the younger officials in our league and in the minors. I told him that was okay, that I'd do anything the league wanted me to do. I am a firm believer that I should always help the people who helped me. I worked my last game in Toronto. Winnipeg was there. [March 5, 1988.] When it was over I walked down the corridor with my wife. *Hockey Night in Canada* had a camera on us. That was tough.

You look at the players. Does any player want to retire? I don't think so. I had the opportunity of working another two or three years on the ice. But I never wanted to embarrass myself. I felt that, if I go, I'll go on a high note and still be with the league in another capacity. I'll give something back to them for the twenty-five years I was on the ice. So I made the decision to be a supervisor and not stay as an official. The league was very generous in giving me that opportunity, and I'm still doing it.

It's tough to walk away from something like what we do. You're programmed. You know exactly what you're going to do, especially on the day of a game. And the camaraderie was always there. I think George Hayes, in the short time I worked with him, taught me more about hockey and how to officiate than anyone else. We never stopped talking about it on train rides and at our pre-game meals or just sitting around hotel lobbies reading papers and smoking cigars. There was always talk, talk, talk.

I think it's tougher to officiate today. I really do. One reason is that there are so many teams. We used to see the same teams so often. You knew their players and their systems. You knew what to look for on a power play. Now, an official might work a game tonight in Montreal and not see the Canadiens again for another two months.

An official has to respect the players. They make your game for you and they can make it very miserable for you if they really want to. I remember Fred Shero coaching Philadelphia saying to his players, "You guys play. Let the officials work their game. If you're thinking about the officials you're not thinking about your game." And that's true. The players made John D'Amico's career.

George Hayes's record for most games worked as a linesman was surpassed by Neil Armstrong, and it isn't likely anyone who saw Armstrong's debut in 1957 thought he would work in the NHL for the next twenty years. They probably wondered if the lanky, pencil-thin newcomer would last through his first game. Armstrong was always the frailest-looking man on the ice and yet constantly amazed fans, and likely the players too, for his uncanny ability to break up fights.

When Neil Armstrong retired he had worked 1,733 regular-season games and another 208 in the Stanley Cup playoffs. Throughout most of his officiating career Armstrong spent the off-season working as a golf professional. Since 1981 he has been a scout for the Montreal Canadiens, which makes him part of a family rivalry within the NHL. His son Doug, who introduced his father at his Hall of Fame induction in 1991, is the assistant to the general manager with the Dallas Stars.

NEIL ARMSTRONG

I came from Galt, which is now Cambridge, and at a very early time in my hockey career knew I was either gonna be a bench-warmer or not play at all. I was going on nineteen when the gentleman running the minor-hockey program told me they were looking for young referees for peewee and bantam games and I told him I was interested. He said they would need me to do four of five games on Saturday starting at 7:00 in the morning. I said, "That's fine. What's the pay?" He said, "Fifty cents a game." That made me think for a while but finally I said I would do it. It turned out they used me for kids' games and industrial-league games at night, all kinds of leagues in that area. I got a fast start that way.

I was a referee then. The following year I worked the Ontario Minor Hockey playdowns and a couple of years later a good Ontario League referee from Galt, Larry Lewin, had me work as one of his linesmen for junior-A and senior-A games. I'd work with him on the lines and then referee on my own for the B and C leagues. At the same time, through a friend of mine, the late Bill Wiley, I took over his job as an assistant pro at the Westmount Golf Club, in Kitchener. Bill's father-in-law owned a clothing store so I worked there in the winter. It was a good combination.

I started to work in the OHA and was one of the linesmen for a Memorial Cup final in Toronto. During the 1957–58 season I was hired by the NHL as a local linesman. I was still living in Galt. I did games in Toronto, Detroit, and Chicago. The following year I joined the league full time.

My first game was in Toronto. It was in November and I remember it was Grey Cup day. I walked into the officials' room at Maple Leaf Gardens and Carl Voss handed me a sweater. There was no number, no nothing on it. George Hayes was the other linesman and he was very aloof. All he said to me was something like, "You're not in the amateur leagues now, rookie." He seemed to resent having new kids come along. But he was a good guy. When the Lord made George he threw away the mould.

Anyway, Boston was playing Toronto that night and everything was going good until there was about a minute and a half left when all hell broke loose. There were fights all over the place. I grabbed Fernie Flaman. I got him against the boards but I knew he knew I was a rookie. He could have thrown me to the other end of the rink if he wanted to. I'm hanging on to him and suddenly he starts yelling, "Hey, kid, you're in trouble. You've broken my arm! You've broken my arm!" I thought it was over for me right there. Then Flaman breaks out laughing.

I was sure I had done a lousy job, and after I was thinking, well, at least I can say I did one game in the NHL. Then about ten days later Carl Voss phoned me again and told me he wanted me to do a game in Detroit. I ended up working eleven games that season and almost two thousand after that. But I thought my first one in Toronto was gonna be my last.

When I started my first season full time Carl Voss told me I would work with George Hayes for a few games. Mr. Voss said, "I want you to do two things when you work with Hayes. Listen to him on the ice but don't listen to him off the ice." That was my introduction. It was like there were two sets of rules, one for George and one for the rest of us. Not many people remember this but George Hayes was the first full-time employee Clarence Campbell hired after he became president. I know they had their problems but I still think that, deep down, Campbell had a soft spot in his heart for George.

When I started, George and I were the only full-time linesmen. Everyone else was part time. Art Skov and Matt Pavelich were full time with the league but they would referee in the Eastern Pro League for a couple of weeks and then come back to the NHL and work the lines for a couple of weeks. But George and I carried the load. In a 210-game schedule, which was 70 games a team, I did 98 league games in my first year.

It was funny that after starting my career working with George Hayes I was the one who broke his record. I did it in Detroit and they had a little ceremony for me. Mr. Campbell sent me a cheque for $1,545.00. He gave me a dollar a game for setting the record. You can see how times have changed.

One of the real characters in those days was Rudy Pilous when he was coach of the Chicago Blackhawks. He had a nickname for most of the officials. He called me "Tangle-foot," Frank Udvari was "The Monkey" because he was always climbing up on the screens and the glass to get out of the way. Vern Buffey was "Pretty Boy." George Hayes was "Beer Eyes." He called Matt Pavelich "Sabu" and Matt would get mad. When he'd yell at me I'd laugh, so one day Pilous said, "I'm not gonna say anything to you. You don't even get upset. You're laughing at me."

People used to wonder about "the skinny guy," as they called me, breaking up the fights. Andy Bathgate called me a "one iron." I'm a little over 6'2" so, being a fairly tall person, I sort of submarined myself up between the guys. I wasn't big and burly so I had to do it that way. Remember that in those days there weren't too many players who were as tall as I was. The two Mahovliches. Jean Béliveau. Not many more. There was a big difference in the average size of the players when you compare those days and today.

Like most officials I had a few situations with Ted Lindsay. He had a unique way of doing things. He would stand beside Howe and curse you up and down and you'd say, "What did you say?" He'd say, "I'm not talking to you, I'm talking to him," and he'd point at Howe. He tried to work all the angles.

When it came to toughness I'd say the strongest, by far, was Tim Horton. Howe was Howe but Horton was in a class by himself for brute strength. John Ferguson was quite a battler. One of my most memorable games was the night Fergie and Eddie Shack decided they'd fight and they went at it for the longest time. I got between them and broke it up and all of a sudden I go down on my rear end. This happened about three times and Fergie would stop punching long enough to bend down and say, "It wasn't me."

I was never manhandled on purpose. I was really lucky. Maybe it was because I was so skinny but the players seemed to get along with me. I don't know how you get it other than longevity, but respect is something you can't buy. If you get it then you can go a long way. What you try to do is not be arrogant, not try to be the show. Then the players will protect you. It happened to me.

One New Year's Eve I was assigned to work in New York. I was madder than hell because it was the only game that night and I was one of the senior officials. Chicago was playing there and I was not too happy. I have to admit I wasn't at my sharpest and the players could tell right away. I can remember Vic Hadfield on the Rangers' bench and Stan Mikita on the Chicago bench telling me to just stand on the blueline, stay out of the way, and we'll tell you when to blow the whistle. It didn't quite work that way, of course, but they could see that I wasn't in the game. If they didn't like me they could have made it really tough.

I learned that early, the first time I had to referee because of injury. It was in Toronto and Vern Buffey got hurt and couldn't continue. Walt Atanas and I were the linesmen. There was a big stink about who would referee. He had more experience but he was part time and I had just become full time. So they told me I'd referee. I hadn't refereed a game for five or six years. Everything went fine. The only complaint I had all night was from Frank Mahovlich, and it surprised me to see him come after me. But it was only that he wanted an assist on a goal. So I was feeling pretty good when the game ended. Bert Olmstead was playing for Toronto and when we were skating off the ice he came over and said, "Hey, kid, don't let that go to your head. If we wanted, we still could have been out there and you wouldn't have been able to count the penalties." He let me know, in spades, that the players can decide how a game is going to be played. They got me through the night.

Sometimes things that happened in the past can help you out. I was a stickboy for the junior team in Galt when it was sponsored by the Detroit Red Wings. Terry Sawchuk and Marty Pavelich were playing then and so was Fred Glover. Years later he coached the Oakland Seals and he was a referee-hater. He was always ranting and raving at the officials but he left me alone. The other guys couldn't understand that but it went back to when I was his stickboy in Galt.

Everybody used to know everybody else and that made it easier on the officials, and on the players. But as the league got bigger that changed. When Gump Worsley was playing in Minnesota I did a game there and when I came out on the ice he started chasing after me. I told him to bugger off but he kept after me and finally said, "Who's 47?" He was referring to the number on the back of one of our officials. I told him I didn't know and he said, "I got a misconduct last night from that goddam 47. He blew one and I told him to open his eyes and he gave me a misconduct. What would you have done?" I told him I probably would have told him to go fuck himself. Gump said, "That's right. That's the problem these days. These new guys don't understand." Everybody thought Gump was mad at me because he was chasing me but all he wanted to know was the name of 47. You'd be hard-pressed to find an official today who knows every player in the league.

John Ashley was quite a character as a referee. John and I worked a game in Toronto on Saturday night and then took the overnight train to Chicago. The Maple Leafs were on the same train. We all got off at Dearborn Station and it was cold as hell. Punch Imlach and King Clancy hailed a cab but before it got to them we jumped in. It was stopped at a red light so they ran back and got in with us. We were all laughing and kidding around and they got off first, at the LaSalle Hotel. We were going to the Bismarck. When they got out Imlach said, "You guys got in first, so you pay the cab," and he and Clancy took off.

Now the game starts that night and right away Bobby Baun runs at someone and knocks him flat. John blows the whistle, and Baun is gone for two. A minute or so later, another penalty to Toronto. A couple of minutes after that, another one. "Chrome-dome," as we used to call Imlach, was yelling and screaming at John. Don Simmons was the Toronto goalie, and right after all the penalties he gets hit in the shoulder and goes down and there's a delay in the game. Johnny Bower was the back-up and I look over at Imlach and see him give Bower a five-dollar bill. What he told Bower was, "Go out and tell that son of a bitch Ashley to lay off. Tell him I'll pay for the cab after all." Ashley sees Bower coming and says to him, "If you give me that money you're gone, and he's gone too." By then Imlach was laughing, and so were we.

I was assigned to do a lot of seventh games in the Stanley Cup finals, but as it worked out I only did one. That was in Toronto in 1964 when the Leafs beat Detroit 4–0. Believe it or not, I found playoff games and playoff overtime easier than regular-season games because everybody was so cautious. When I first broke in it was considered a sin by a team like Montreal to go offside. You take the Rocket. You could see fire in those eyes of his if somebody went offside on him. He would be as mad at his playing partner as he was at the opposition. I would think that, at that time, Montreal had the fewest offsides and of course they had the best team.

When I retired, well, they had a self-imposed thing about having to get out when you were forty-five. At least that's what I was told. This was before the stuff about age discrimination. I didn't fight it. If they didn't want me, they didn't want me. That year I was rated high enough to do all the playoffs. They had twenty-one linesmen and I was one of the four that worked the finals. How could I go from the top four on June 1 to number twenty-one a month later, without doing a game? So it was basically an age thing. I would have liked to have gone to two thousand games but it wasn't in the cards.

Getting into the Hall of Fame was a day I'll never forget. The most pleasing and proudest part of it was having my son Doug introduce me. When Bob Clarke was GM in Minnesota he hired Doug and then he hired Bob Gainey. Doug has been working with Gainey ever since.

I've been scouting for the Canadiens for fifteen years. The life is a lot like officiating, with plenty of travel, but it's not a lonely life. I've been accustomed to travelling alone and I've been all over the world. I've been to all the European countries and I've been to rinks the *Hockey News* doesn't even know about. Big rinks, little rinks, and I've met so many nice people everywhere I've gone. What else could I do and meet so many nice people?

The section in the Hockey Hall of Fame reserved for officials had a "referees only" sign on the door from 1961, when

Chaucer Elliott, Cooper Smeaton, and Mickey Ion became the first to be inducted, until 1987, when Matt Pavelich made it as a linesman.

Matt Pavelich came from a hockey-oriented family. His older brother, Marty, played ten seasons for the Detroit Red Wings. He was the right winger on Detroit's checking line along with Glen Skov and Tony Leswick when the Red Wings won four Stanley Cups in the early 1950s.

Matt Pavelich was an official in the NHL for twenty-three years. He worked his first game in Boston October 11, 1956, and his final game in Montreal, May 21, 1979, when the Canadiens defeated the New York Rangers to win the Stanley Cup. He then served for several years as a supervisor of NHL officials. He is now retired and living in Windsor, Ontario, where he is involved in supervising officials in junior hockey and the Colonial Hockey League.

MATT PAVELICH

The first time I refereed I was fourteen years old. I got off the bus one night and went over to the rink near our house to see what was going on. A game was starting but they didn't have a referee. I said I would do it. I didn't have any skates but I went out and refereed with my boots on. I liked it so I got in touch with the Soo Hockey Association and asked if there was a possibility I could officiate for them. That's how I got my start.

I worked my way up through the leagues in our area. One night I was having a tough game in Marquette, Michigan. There was no glass around the boards in those days and a fan leaned over and hit me on the side of the head. The sheriff of the town used to go to the games and sit beside the penalty box. I went to him and said I wanted the fan thrown out of the rink. The sheriff said, "The way you're refereeing, I should throw *you* out." I knew right then the only friends I had were the two linesmen.

Another time, I was refereeing a game in Blind River when a team from the Soo was there. A Blind River player hit the puck with his stick over his shoulder. It went to a Soo player, and he scored, which was a legal goal. There was a big row and when I came off the ice a guy taps me on the shoulder and says, "Mr. Pavelich, are you Catholic?" I said I was and he said, "Well, I'm Father Skillen and I'm the manager of the team here in Blind River. The way you officiate, I should excommunicate you from the Church." [Laughs]

I never was hit by a player but I went after Jack McCartan one time in the Eastern Pro League. He had been the goalie for the States when they won the Olympics in 1960. There was a scramble and he thought he held the puck long enough for a whistle, but I didn't blow it. Bob Sabourin was playing for Sudbury and he got the puck and scored. McCartan chased me and gave me a little push so I gave him a push right back. I was worried about it so I phoned the president of the league, Ed Houston. I told him I had given McCartan a little push and he asked me what McCartan had done. I told him he had given me a little push. Mr. Houston said, "Well, you're both even. Don't worry about it."

The NHL didn't have any scouting for referees then. I got there by word of mouth, maybe some of it from my brother. He was playing for Detroit and I might have put a bug in his ear. My first year in the league was his last. I worked two years on the lines and then Carl Voss asked me if I wanted to try refereeing, and I did. They sent me to the Eastern Pro League and the American League, but when I came back I only refereed seventeen or eighteen games in the NHL. It wasn't for me. I took the games home with me, worried too much. I was more suited for the lines.

I was a standby referee for the playoffs the year Red Storey had his hassle in Chicago. I was standby for a game in Toronto and was supposed to go to Boston to standby for the game Red was going to work the next night. Carl Voss called to tell me I was going to Chicago instead. He knew there was a chance Red wasn't going to work and that meant I would have refereed the game. They sent Eddie Powers to Boston and as it turned out he worked because Red quit. I said, oh-oh, they don't have much confidence in me.

When I started, George Hayes took me under his wing a bit. He was a great guy to travel with. We'd get to a city and he'd say, "Okay, young fella, we're going on a tour," and we'd walk for miles. The tour would be between sightseeing and beer parlours. [Laughs] Sometimes during a game he'd say, "I don't like this game. We've only had three fights." He was over six feet and most players then were 5'9" or 5'10". George could always get in between them. I think he was the greatest I ever worked with.

Rudy Pilous was coaching Chicago and he was a real character. In a close game at the Montreal Forum he'd get a towel and go to Mikita or Hull and wipe their brow. He had nicknames for the officials. I was "Ho Chi Minh" or "Sabu." Ron Wicks told Pilous he collected stamps so Wicksie was "Stamp Collector." Then he heard a good story about Ron. We travelled by train in those days and sometimes we'd sit up all night in the coach cars to make a couple of extra bucks on our expenses. When Ron was a rookie Frank Udvari asked him, "Aren't you gonna get into your pyjamas?" Ron said, "Do I have to?" and Udvari told him yes. So Ron changed in the washroom and went to sleep sitting in the coach car with his pyjamas on. After Pilous heard that story he always called Ron "Pyjama Wicks."

I always enjoyed the fans. There was a guy in Boston who would yell, "Hey, Pavelich, we've named a town after you down here. Marblehead!" He used that line on everybody. Then he'd say, "Where's your seeing-eye dog?" and I'd point down and skate around like I had a dog on a leash. When they'd throw stuff on the ice and we'd be picking it up fans in Boston and New York would yell, "We know what you'll do when you retire. You're gonna be a garbage collector!" There was no glass around the boards then and you got to know the people sitting there and you'd kibitz with them, back and forth. I might have been in Montreal fifteen or eighteen times a season when I first started and you knew everybody. At the end of my career I might have worked there twice a year. That was a big change. You didn't get to know the fans and they didn't get to know you.

The greatest game I was ever in, for emotion and everything, was not a playoff game. I worked 240-some playoff games and now they all sort of intermingle. My greatest game was the one in Philadelphia between the Flyers and the Red Army, in 1976. The Flyers were the Stanley Cup champions and the Red Army team was Russia's best. The tension was unbelievable.

There were a couple of deals in that game. First, early in the game Alexandrov got into a pushing match with Reg Leach. I got between them and grabbed Alexandrov. He gave me a little shove and skated away and as he did he said something to me, in Russian. I said, "That'll be two minutes for unsportsmanlike conduct," and he looked at me like, How does this guy understand my language? But I did. I'm Croatian and I can speak Russian.

The Flyers were outplaying the Russians badly and then the big controversy happened when Ed Van Impe hit Valery Kharlamov a terrific bodycheck. Kharlamov was lying on the ice and I heard the other linesman, who was a Russian, telling him to stay down so there would be a penalty. Kharlamov was still lying there and one of their players, Vasiliev, looked over at me and he gave me a big wink as if to say, this guy's puttin' it on.

Lloyd Gilmour was the referee and that's when the Russian coach, Tikhonov, told the interpreter to tell him his team wouldn't play that kind of hockey any more. He said they had the Olympics coming up and he didn't want his players getting hurt playing animal hockey. We were all standing in front of their bench and I told Gilmour, "They're leaving." He said, "No, they're not." I said they were because I heard Tikhonov tell the interpreter. And right then, they left and went to their room. Clarence Campbell, Scotty Morrison, and Alan Eagleson were all there and there was a big argument. The Russians kept saying they weren't coming back, but after a few minutes they did. It would have cost them too much not to. It was quite an afternoon. That game stands out as the tops in my career.

I retired when I was forty-five years old. They had offered me a job as a supervisor. They said I could keep working on the ice but there was no guarantee the supervisor's job would be there down the road. I had done everything I could have done. My feeling was that I always wanted to work in the Stanley Cup finals. If I wasn't good enough to do that I didn't want to be an official any more. From the time I began working in the NHL as a linesman I worked the Stanley Cup finals every year. I only missed the finals the two years I was a referee.

My last game was in Montreal, in 1979, when the Canadiens beat the Rangers and won the Stanley Cup. I knew it was my last game and I felt very sad. I felt I was still pretty well at the top of my game, although I also felt I might be slipping a bit. Maybe the next year I wouldn't have worked the finals and wouldn't have felt as good. I was retiring when I wanted to, not when they told me to.

I enjoyed supervising, and especially when I worked with younger officials in the minors. In my day it was lonely down there, you didn't have anybody to talk to. The linesmen were all local. A lot of them would walk in five minutes before game time wearing their official's uniform and just put on their skates. When it was over I didn't even have my skates off and they were gone. I was young and I might have had a tough game with a coach like Fred Glover giving me a hard time. If there had been a couple of linesmen or a supervisor to talk things over with it would have helped. That's what I tried to do when I became a supervisor. I remember when Mike Keenan was coaching in the American League, in Rochester, and he was always hollering and screaming. I took him aside and asked him why he was there, and he said he was trying to help some of his young players get into the NHL. I told him that was why I was there too, so let's work together.

After I became a supervisor I'd be interviewed by the media and they'd ask me about violence in the NHL. I'd say, "Violence? We haven't had a bench-clearing brawl in years and baseball had sixty-seven bench clearings last season." There are still fights, but no bench clearings, and if there are secondary fights the guys are thrown out of the game. A lot of the fighting has been eliminated. It's not like those old-time games with Montreal and Toronto when Shack and those guys were running around banging heads and there'd be two or three fights at the same time. They'd get misconducts and be back in the game again. Today, everybody would be gone.

A lot of people would tell me that it looked as though I enjoyed what I was doing, and I did. We had officials who were uptight before games, but I never felt that way. I failed public speaking in high school because I was afraid to get up before twenty or thirty people. But when I was officiating I felt comfortable in front of fifteen thousand people. I felt at home, like I was in my own little world.

5

Expansion Years

RON WICKS ART SKOV
BOB MYERS LLOYD GILMOUR

A story that has made the rounds in hockey the past few years concerns Hall of Fame coach Al Arbour and a couple of referees. A few years ago a rookie referee, Richard Trottier, was working a game involving Arbour's New York Islanders. Early in the piece Trottier made a call that upset Arbour. For the next period or so, every time Trottier skated by the Islanders' bench Arbour would yell at him, "You're the worst referee I've ever seen! You're the worst referee I've ever seen!"

In previous years there were times when Arbour and long-time referee Ron Wicks didn't exactly get along, even though they were from the same area of Northern Ontario. So while Arbour was berating Trottier, linesman Ray Scapinello said to the coach, "If he's the worst you've ever seen, what about Wicks?" For the balance of the game, every time Trottier skated by his bench Arbour would yell, "You're the second-worst referee I've ever seen!"

Ron Wicks has heard, and laughed at, the story many times, yet doesn't recall all that much bitterness between him and Al Arbour while he was an official in the NHL for a record twenty-six years. Along with the other referees featured in this chapter, Wicks worked through the NHL's most significant transition period, beginning in 1967 with the expansion from six to twelve teams. In the next few years the league's map and travel schedule exploded from a cosy six-team set-up of train-connected cities to a continent-wide organization extending from Montreal and New York in the east to Vancouver and Los Angeles in the west, with temporary stops in places like Oakland, Kansas City, and Cleveland along the way. The NHL had entered an era when, as Neil Armstrong pointed out, it was becoming impossible for all the officials to know all the players as they once did.

When Ron Wicks retired in 1986 he was the longest-serving referee in NHL history. His 1,034th game surpassed Bruce Hood's record. He finished with 1,067, a figure later surpassed by Andy van Hellemond.

Wicks's career got off to a record-setting start in October 1960 as a linesman at New York's Madison Square Garden on his twentieth birthday. That made him the youngest official ever to work an NHL game. Amazingly, his big-league debut came a mere three years after he refereed for the first time in his home town of Sudbury, Ontario.

RON WICKS

I started when I was seventeen. Bob Davidson was scouting the north country at that time for the Toronto Maple Leafs. The NHL didn't have much of a scouting or supervisory staff and Carl Voss had team scouts on the lookout for young referees. Bob spotted me and sent my name in to the league so at least they knew about me. The Eastern Pro League held a meeting in Sudbury and Clarence Campbell was there. I saw him in the lobby of the hotel, introduced myself, and told him I was a young referee. He asked me to write him a note, which I did, and he replied. I still have his reply. He sent my note to Mr. Voss, who called me, and I guess I talked my way to their training camp in Toronto the next year. When the camp ended they signed me and I started right in the NHL as a linesman. No one was more surprised than I was. I went straight from the midget league to the big league.

I was single in those days and reasonable when it came to money. I was coming from the City of Sudbury Assessment Department, where I was making $1,800. I signed with the NHL for $2,500, which worked out to forty bucks a game and they gave you seventy-five bucks for each playoff game. We used to make more money on our expenses. Maybe I shouldn't say that but the statute of limitations must be over by now. [Laughs]

Before I signed they had some of us work exhibition games with NHL teams. They'd send three tryout linesmen and we'd each work a period with George Hayes. It was a hell of an experience. I remember one game in Peterborough when Chicago was playing and I talked Elmer "Moose" Vasko out of beating up on a guy. My boss was impressed and told me I had done a good job with Mr. Vasko. I said, "Thank you, sir. I talked nice to him and he just kind of stopped." There was no way I was going to get physical with the biggest guy in the league. I wasn't Leon Stickle.

My first game in New York was on my twentieth birthday. Frank Udvari was the referee and Hayes the other linesman. How did I feel? Well, my knees were rattling. How's that? I kind of pinched myself. You know, the old feeling, what am I doing here? Detroit was the visiting team and as we're warming up, my heroes are all skating around with me: Andy Bathgate, Gordie Howe, and so on. But I got along very well. I was so small, I weighed 150 pounds, and I think they were afraid of hurting me.

Early in my career I was on a train from Detroit to Chicago and the Montreal Canadiens were on the train. I was twenty-two years old. I walked through the Canadiens' car and the guys grabbed me and cut my tie off. Then they invited me to have a beer. It was Christmas Eve. As I was leaving I passed the compartment at the end of the car and the coach, Toe Blake, was sitting there by himself. He invited me in and, as I recall, I had a beer with him too. I was very flattered. We were from the same area. I'm from Sudbury and he was from Coniston. He told me to enjoy the evening but warned me not to get too chummy with the players. Be civil with them, but don't snuggle up to them. That was maybe the best advice I was ever given by a hockey person. I kind of stayed away from them after that.

I was a linesman in Chicago in the 1961 playoffs the night Toe hit the referee, Dalton McArthur. Dalton had given Dickie Moore a penalty in the third overtime period and Murray Balfour scored on the power play. It was my first year and my third playoff game. I was standing by the penalty box and when I first saw Toe on the ice he was about six feet from Dalton with his arm cocked. George Hayes was the other linesman. We all went out after the game and we were still out at 7:00 in the morning when we heard Mr. Campbell wanted us at a hearing in his hotel suite at 8:00. So we went right from the bar to his hotel suite for the meeting. He fined Toe two thousand and it was the end for Dalton McArthur.

Another time Howie Young, who was playing for Detroit, tried to get at Frank Udvari. George Hayes and I tripped him and knocked him down and then one of his own players, Bill Gadsby, knocked him down too. Mr. Campbell said it was too bad everybody knocked Mr. Young down because if he

had got to the referee Mr. Campbell would have had more
evidence to work with. I don't know if he meant Udvari
deserved a punch in the nose, or what. I said that to Frank
but he didn't find it very humorous.

At 150 pounds I became very agile when the fights
were on. I talked nice to them, used a lot of friendly per-
suasion. When you're a linesman nobody is on your ass. I
might still be working today at the age of fifty-six if I had
stayed as a linesman. The mortality rate for referees is
a little higher. I occasionally say when I became a linesman they gave me a bag of marbles and when I lost my
marbles they made me a referee. [Laughs]

I was a linesman for three years and then they sent me to
referee for three years in the American, Central, and Western
Leagues. In 1967 I was back in the NHL, along with 120 new
hockey players, the expansion babies.

There were some interesting times in the minor leagues.
One year I worked the opening game for a new franchise in
Memphis. The linesmen were local linesmen – they were
part of the group that got the team for that city. The first
time the Memphis team scored, one of the linesmen
applauded the goal. Pat Stapleton was playing for Dallas, the
visiting team, and he was ready to decapitate the guy. I told
Stapleton to hang on, that I'd talk to him. So I had to say,
"Excuse me, Mr. Linesman. You must be neutral when
you're on the ice. At least appear to be neutral."

There were some down days then. Like everybody else I
didn't like being away at Christmas time. The year our
daughter was born I left Sudbury December 24 and got back
January 17. With local linesmen in those leagues you'd be
all by yourself for three weeks. I think I saw every state
capital and every library and museum there was in the
cities I was in. You had to become your own best friend or
you'd go nuts. Sometimes you hear players today moan

about the long road trips. My wife won't buy that stuff. She says she can write them a note and tell them what it used to be like. The old days were great but often you celebrated your Christmas in July.

When I came back to the NHL I realized my three years in the league as a linesman had helped my refereeing career. Actually, I did a few games as a referee the year before expansion, in 1966. When I did my first game, in Chicago, Stan Mikita came up and whacked me on the ass and said, "Good luck, Wicksie. Where the hell have you been the last three years? We're sick of these other guys." I was a fresh face but I had some acceptability. They knew who you were. In 1967–68, the first year of expansion, I refereed about twenty-five games in the NHL and fifty in the American League. The next year it was reversed: I did about fifty NHL games. After that I was in the league full time.

In '67–68 I did my first game at the Met Center in Minnesota. The North Stars played Oakland and one of the coaches threw a bunch of sticks on the ice at me. Great start. [Laughs] Maybe my toughest call ever came at the end of that season. I called a goal back against Los Angeles in their last game of the season, in Oakland. The game ended 2–2 and it cost them a tie for first place. The Kings' owner, Jack Kent Cooke, called Mr. Campbell in the middle of the night and said he was bilked out of first place by a green-horn official. Mr. Campbell called me and said he had just finished listening to a raving maniac for the last twenty minutes. I guess Mr. Cooke wanted me shot, for want of a better term.

Mr. Campbell called people in Oakland and Los Angeles who had been at the game or had watched on TV and they told him I had made the proper call. I was dead right. A couple of weeks later Mr. Campbell called me in Quebec City, where I was doing an American League playoff game, and the first thing he said was, "You were right." I said, "Excuse me?" and he said, "You were right. Brian O'Neill and I have just reviewed a TV tape of the game in Oakland and you made the right call." Then the league issued a press release and said I had made the proper call. By that time I had gone from 160 to 150 pounds worrying about it, but I survived. It was a different era. We didn't make a helluva lot of money, but we had a lot of fun.

About that Al Arbour story: well, actually I got along very well with Al. Once he said that maybe I wasn't the best referee in the league. I think he got fined for that. I remember one night in an Islanders game I got knocked out on the ice. Butch Goring, who is much shorter than I am, turned the wrong way and we hit dead on. I was TKO'd when I hit the ice. I got up and I remember waltzing across the ice to get off. Gerry Gauthier, the linesman, told me it was pretty funny watching me weave through the traffic. I got to the Islanders' bench and I was out on my feet. Al escorted me to the trainer's room and I had a bump on my head the size of an egg. I had the weekend off after that one.

There were a few coaches that maybe I didn't get along with. Most of them liked to hoot and holler at you once in a while. I occasionally would say to a new coach, "Do us all a favour and get a little time in the league under your belt before you start calling me an asshole." Wren Blair, in Minnesota, would go absolutely bananas on the bench. He'd bang his fists on the boards and parade up and down. At the end of a period you'd skate off and he'd be standing there with his hand in the ice bucket. His goalie, Cesare Maniago, would say, "Throw the bugger out," but I'd say, "No, he's fun. He's not hurting anybody." The players knew what was going on. As long as you had the players in your corner, you'd survive. I was okay with Don Cherry but I don't think his boss Harry Sinden and I got along too well. I shouldn't say too much about Harry because my lawyer once told me to beware of libel laws.

Anyone who refereed in that era is always asked about the Philadelphia Flyers, the Broad Street Bullies. A while back I was at a skate-a-thon in Toronto and Borje Salming was there. I told him I used to save his life in Philly and he laughed. One night in Toronto a Flyer named Dave Hoyda knocked Borje out with one punch. I threw Hoyda out of the game and the Philly management went ballistic. That was the year they put in new rules about major penalties with the aggressor getting five minutes and a game. I think I was the first guy to invoke the rule because of one punch but the teams were going right back to play in Philly. One year my record at the Spectrum was something like seven losses, no wins, and one tie for the Flyers. I was not popular in Philadelphia.

I had the game in Minnesota [January 4, 1975] when Dave Forbes of the Bruins injured Henry Boucha and it ended up in court. They had been in the penalty box for fighting majors and when they came out they had to cross the ice to get to their benches. There was an icing on the play and I was not made aware they were out of the box. I heard a roar. When I turned around Boucha was lying on the ice and Forbes was punching his face into the ice. Unbeknownst to me Boucha had already been butt-ended in the face. He suffered an eye injury and that led to the end of his career. He didn't play much after the incident. He was a local hero, a native Indian from Minnesota, and had been a Minnesota State high-school hockey star.

I threw players out of the game because of all the fisticuffs. Cesare Maniago had left his net and jumped on Forbes's back. It was close to civil insurrection. Everybody in the rink had seen it except the three game officials. We were watching the play going down the ice, the icing, and coming back up the ice. We changed our procedure after that so the minor officials would have to inform the referee that the guys were coming out of the penalty box.

I took statements from all the minor officials in the penalty box. By the time I got there after the incident they were all there and also a police officer. They said the S.O.B. butt-ended him in the face, blah, blah, blah. I told them to put it all in writing and bring it to my dressing room at the end of the game. The game may have been televised but not that specific part. [*Forbes was suspended for ten games, the third-most severe penalty up to then.*]

Quite frankly, it became a political issue. [*Forbes was indicted on a charge of aggravated assault.*] I ended up in front of a grand jury giving a statement and then I had to appear in County Court. It was all very unnerving. I wasn't skilled in the art of dealing with lawyers. There were a lot of witnesses, like the police officer. He was a Minneapolis cop. The case ended with a hung jury.

One night in Chicago I was the back-up at a playoff game. Don Koharski was the referee. After the game Bob Pulford, the general manager in Chicago, kicked the referee's door open. I was standing behind it getting ready to light a cigar and it hit me right in the nose. Pulford said Koho would never work another game in the Stadium so Koho threatened to throw him out of the room. On his way out Pulford growled at me and I just smiled. I said right then that Koho would go a long way because he had balls. I remembered when he hitchhiked to Bruce Hood's school in Haliburton. I could see right there he'd make it. I said, "That kid will have my job in ten years." And he did.

Acceptance by the players is important. One night I blew a call, a guy scored, and Brad Park gave me shit. I said to him, "Have you ever had a guy go around you and score the winning goal?" He knew I was admitting that I had screwed up on the play without sending him a telegram about it. Later he patted me on the ass and said, "Gotcha. No problem." I never had any more trouble with him.

I tried to make sure I was not a homer. Scotty Bowman once said, "I will take Wicksie on the road any time." He figured he was gonna get a fair shake. I think if you study my stats, 90 per cent of my first penalties went against the home team and it was because they deserved them.

It was a great business but when I left it I was ready to go. I won't go into all the reasons. Maybe I'll write my own book someday. But it was time to get on with the rest of my life. I had been part time in real estate so I went into it full time. That cushioned the blow. I sent in my resignation from my real-estate desk.

Some guys can't get away. I see guys today who are still vaccinated with the NHL pin. If you took it off them they might expire. I have people say to me, "Are you the Ron Wicks who refereed?" and I tell them, yeah, I was a referee in my first life. I don't say I was humble because everybody was proud. I was sure as hell proud to be there for half my life. But it was time to get on with other things.

As it was with the Pavelich brothers, the Skov brothers were, briefly, playing and officiating at the same time in the NHL. Glen Skov's ten-year playing career was winding down with the Chicago Blackhawks when his younger brother, Art, was beginning his nineteen-year officiating career.

A native of Windsor, Ontario, Art Skov began refereeing in his early twenties by working three games on Saturday nights in the local Bell Telephone League. In 1955, while he was a referee in the International League, Skov was hired by the NHL as a part-time linesman. He also kept working, full time, for Chrysler Canada in Windsor. As he says, "I wasn't home very much." After a year of a tiring triple-duty workload, Art Skov signed a full-time contract with the NHL.

ART SKOV

My first game in the NHL was in Chicago and I worked with Red Storey and George Hayes. You couldn't work with two more senior guys, or two nicer guys. Montreal was playing there that night, and before the game George said if there was a fight involving Rocket Richard he would handle him and I would take the other guy. I was in awe of everything that night, seeing guys like Richard and Doug Harvey on the ice, and I don't know if I even blew the whistle. Red and George whistled a play down for me a couple of times. At the end of that season, Carl Voss told me I would start refereeing the next year in the minors. I wasn't ready for that and in the summer I called Red and asked for advice and I kept doing that for years. Everything I knew about refereeing was taught to me by Red Storey. It didn't matter when I called him, he was always there for me.

Early in my career as a linesman I had a game in Toronto. Eddie Powers was the referee and George Hayes the other linesman. The Toronto brass sat behind the penalty bench and we would leave the ice down an aisleway right beside where they were. The first period was a rough one. Hayes and Powers must have smelled something because those buggers left the ice real quick. By the time I was getting off Conn Smythe was waiting for me and he was yelling something terrible about a penalty I gave one guy, and another penalty I gave another guy, and I'm thinking, hey, I'm a linesman not the referee. A lot of people are walking by and hearing all this and I'm feeling pretty small. Smythe keeps yelling and screaming at me so I finally put my hand on his arm and pushed him aside. He yelled, "You can't push me, sonny. I'll have your job." I get into our room and Carl Voss is there and I had to explain what had happened between me, a raw rookie, and one of the most powerful men in hockey. But you know something? I never heard any more about it. I think Smythe was testing me to see if I had courage. I didn't push him, I just put my hand on him so I could get by. I think the sucker was teasing me.

I was a linesman in New York the night Gordie Howe and Lou Fontinato had their famous fight. Frank Udvari was the referee and Bill Morrison was the other linesman. Bill was around for a lot of years, almost as long as George Hayes, and when fights started he had a habit of you-go-first-and-I'll-follow. I was young and ambitious so the fights and the brawls didn't bother me. I liked the rough games.

In the first period Eddie Shack kept trying to get Red Kelly going and they were jostling quite a bit. After one whistle a lot of players gathered around and Fontinato came romping in from the blueline. He yelled at Howe, "You stay out of it, big guy, or I'll take care of you." I thought, Oh my God, you don't talk to Gordie Howe that way. Anyway, we got that sorted out and I dropped the puck. The play went to the other end, and back again, and the same damn thing happened. Shack and Kelly start shoving and I see Louie coming in from the other side and I see Gordie standing there and he's shaking his glove loose. I stopped dead in my tracks about ten feet from the play. I stayed back because I knew when the time came Morrison wouldn't be the first to go in, it would be me. Louie skated in and Howe cranked him and smashed his nose. I don't think Louie ever saw that punch. Then Gordie grabbed him by the shoulder and held him down and hit him about three times with his right hand. Howe dislocated his baby finger. Then they swung around and Howe hit him with a left uppercut. Everybody had formed a half-circle and we just stood there. Andy Bathgate was beside me, and after what seemed like a long time for a hockey fight he said, "Art, I think we'd better go in and break this thing up," and we did. By then it wasn't so much a matter of breaking them up as holding them up, Howe was tired from swinging and Louie was tired from getting hit. I grabbed Louie and he had his head down. When it came up it seemed he didn't have any nose at all. There were two little holes at the side of his face and the bridge of his nose was flat. There was blood like you wouldn't believe. My sweater was covered with it.

Frank gave them both five minutes for fighting. I still don't know why he gave Louie five minutes because I don't think he ever hit Howe. We had to push Louie through the gate at the bench because he could hardly walk. Phil Watson was coaching the Rangers and he grabbed Louie's arm and held it in the air like, he's the winner.

I was working a game in Montreal the next night and when I got there I received a call telling me Clarence Campbell wanted to see me in his office. I'm thinking I'm gonna get hell about the fight in New York because I didn't go in and stop it. It was my first time in the president's office and I'd never seen such a gol-darn big desk as he had. He asked me to tell him all about the fight and I told him exactly what happened. He started to laugh a little bit and I thought that was a good sign. Finally I finished my story and he said, "You know, maybe we should do that more often and let these guys fight. Thank you, that's all I want to know." I thought I was gonna get a real earful, but that was it.

That same year, 1959, I was a linesman in Montreal when the Canadiens beat Toronto to win the Stanley Cup. The season was over so we had a little party. I was going home the next day and had to get up early to take a 7:00 plane to

Toronto and then a connection to Windsor. There were only about ten people on the plane so I went to the back and snoozed off right away. When I woke up, the plane was full and I'm wondering where all the people came from. The stewardess came by and asked if I wanted lunch. Lunch? Then the pilot comes on to tell us what the weather will be like when we land in Calgary. Nobody woke me up when we landed in Toronto so I was still on the plane when it took off for Calgary. When I got off there I walked around the airport for about an hour before getting up the courage to tell the agent what happened. He said, "So you're the one. We knew we had one extra passenger." [Laughs]

They got me on a plane back to Toronto but by then it was too late to catch a flight to Windsor. So I rented a car. They told me there was a chap who wanted a ride to Windsor and I said I'd be happy to take him with me. Turns out he was a priest. By that time I figured I needed one. Then, to cap the day, the car started acting up and I had to get another one at the airport in London. I finally got home at 1:00 Monday morning. I should have been there at 10:30 Sunday morning.

When I started refereeing I did games in the American League and the Eastern Pro League. At the same time, I did some games as a linesman in the NHL. They wanted to keep my face up there so the players would know who I was. In my third year I refereed about ten games in the NHL, fifteen the next, and twenty-five the year after that. Then I went full time. When I was a linesman I always wanted to be a referee. I thought refereeing was the greatest thing in the world. The game was yours. You were in charge but at the same time you had to remember people paid to see the players, not the referee. So you stay in the background and do your best to keep the players on the ice.

When I refereed in the American League every rink had local linesmen. The first time I worked in Rochester there was a linesman who was something terrible. You could see he was a homer. The other guy was young and not too sharp but honest, a good kid. I remember we went into the room at the end of the first period and the older guy says, "Well, we're winning 1–0." I said, "How's that?" and right away he said, "Rochester's winning 1–0." I told him he'd better keep it that way. I had him in other games I did in Rochester but I never spoke to him again. I hated that, just hated it.

In the NHL sometimes local goal judges were a problem. In my day we didn't have replays to rely on. I won't mention any names but Boston had a goal judge who wasn't too honest. And, believe it or not, there was one guy in Montreal who wasn't too honest either. In those days, if there was a disputed goal, you'd check with your two linesmen. If you didn't have enough ammunition to make a definitive call then you'd talk to the goal judge. With some, like those guys in Boston and Montreal, you usually knew what he was gonna call so you would take his view with a grain of salt. If there was a good goal judge, and you knew he was honest, a lot of times you'd gamble that he was right. I say the most important call in hockey is, "Is it a good goal, or is it no goal?" I think the replay they have now is great. I would have welcomed it 100 per cent.

I was the referee in New York when the Rangers' coach, Emile "The Cat" Francis, had a big fight in the crowd over a call I made. The Rangers were ahead by one late in the game when Detroit scored. The puck went in and out so fast I didn't blow the whistle and the play went on for a few seconds before I noticed the red light was on. I stopped the game and the goal judge, a nice little man named Arthur Reichert, told me the puck was in. I asked him if there was any doubt in his mind and he said, "Art, it was in." So I ruled it a goal and of course the Rangers started arguing. While the argument was going on Francis ran around to where the goal judge was. As it turned out he was met there by one of the goal judge's pals plus a couple of his friends and they started fighting with Emile. Suddenly I see some New York players climbing over the glass. I didn't know who was fighting in the crowd. I grabbed one of Vic Hadfield's skates as he was climbing over and he yelled at me, "I gotta go, Art. It's the Cat." That's when I realized Francis was in the middle of it. That was an awful mess. Emile and Arthur's friends ended up in court over that one.

That was an unusual case involving fans, but they're there, they like to heckle, and you hear them. They're gonna stand up and they're gonna yell. All a guy who is yelling at you wants is recognition. If you turn around and say something to him, he's got you and he'll never stop the rest of the game. Don't let him know he's got your goat. If you ignore him long enough, he'll sit down. He won't yell any more.

I think my memory of a best game would have to be in 1974 when the Flyers beat Boston 1–0 to win the Stanley Cup. It was on a Sunday afternoon and, let me tell you, it was up and down the ice all day. The goalies were Bernie Parent and Gilles Gilbert and they were just fantastic. I called a penalty in the third period on Bobby Orr when he grabbed Bobby Clarke and Orr really went after me. Clarke had got in behind him on the play. Scotty Morrison was supervising the series and after the game he asked me if a penalty shot had entered my mind. I said yeah, but it was too far away from the net to call a penalty shot. But I said there was no doubt in my mind on the call, that he had turned Clarke completely around. That was one hell of a hockey game. I was wiped out.

When I was refereeing I rarely called anybody by his number. It was always Gordie, Bobby, Teddy, John, whatever. You knew everybody, knew their skating styles and habits. Like Yvan Cournoyer. Who wouldn't know him flying up and down? Then came expansion and that changed. New players and a lot of helmets too. I remember doing a game in New York when the Oakland Seals were there and I put my arm up in the air for an Oakland penalty. The play keeps going and I've still got my arm up and then I thought, Geez, I don't know who it was. Finally I got a chance to blow the whistle and I said, "Oakland, two minutes!" I went to the penalty box and told the timer, "Some Oakland guy's got a penalty. When one of them comes near here tell him to get in the box and sit down for two minutes." [Laughs] That was when I realized I had to start looking at numbers, not faces, because I didn't know everybody any more.

In the last five years of my career my knees gave me trouble. I would be walking down the street and suddenly I'd start limping. It would stay that way for a couple of hours and then go away. As the years went by I couldn't keep up with the play any more. I told Scotty I didn't want to be a hanger-on and I packed it in. I had worked nineteen years and about 1,200 games.

About two years after I retired something hit me at home one day and I couldn't walk, do up my shoes, nothing, and I thought, Holy mackerel, what's wrong? They got a doctor and he arranged for X-Rays and I found out, for the first time, that my problem was my hips. I needed replacements and I had it done. After that I skated pretty good and did some Red Wings oldtimers' games. But I'm having trouble again because one of the replacements is starting to wear out.

The travel got to me in the end, although there was a time I enjoyed it. I used to love being on a train after a game when we'd leave Montreal for New York or Boston and the Canadiens would be on it, and I would get a chance to sit in the club car and talk hockey with Danny Gallivan. He was so interesting, and such a nice man. But when it was all plane travel and you would spend so much time in airports when the weather was bad, I began to wonder if it was worth it.

When I retired I didn't miss the travel but I missed the games, especially at playoff time. I used to love the playoffs. That's when you could look the players in the eye and see that they knew it was a big game. For me, there was always a lot of satisfaction when the game was over. People could say, "Nice game," but they still couldn't know how it was to feel good about the game you had just done, how great you felt.

The two referees whose memories will complete this chapter, Bob Myers and Lloyd Gilmour, were involved in some of the best-remembered incidents in the NHL in the 1970s and 1980s.

First, Bob Myers, who has lived all his life on his family's farm in Copetown, Ontario. Myers was the referee in Montreal when the Boston Bruins, coached by Don Cherry, were caught with too many men on the ice late in game seven of the 1979 semi-finals against the Canadiens. Guy Lafleur tied the game on the ensuing power play and Yvon Lambert's overtime goal won the game, and the series, for the Canadiens. If you are not familiar with that story you haven't been paying attention to "Coach's Corner" on Hockey Night in Canada. *Also on Myers's dossier is the game in Chicago in the 1982 playoffs when Vancouver Canucks coach Roger Neilson waved a white towel of surrender at him, setting off a white-towel mania in Vancouver the rest of that playoff year.*

Since leaving the NHL Myers has worked for the Colonial Hockey League, first as its commissioner and in recent years as director of officiating.

BOB MYERS

When I was in my early twenties I was playing senior-A hockey and refereeing junior games in the OHA. Around Christmas the OHA office told me I would have to make up my mind what I wanted to do. I liked officiating from the moment I started doing kids' games so I made the decision to stick with it. Hughie McLean, a former NHL referee who was back in the OHA, took me under his wing. I went to the NHL training camp, in Toronto, at a time when the expansion was starting. They hired about seven or eight of us. Dave Newell, Bryan Lewis, Will Norris, John McCauley, and I were all hired at that time.

I went right in as a linesman. I didn't want to do that because I had been a referee in the OHA but they didn't have any room at the time. I worked the lines for two years and did a bit of refereeing in the Central, American, and Western Leagues. I spent a lot of time on trains and buses. Scotty Morrison knew I wanted to referee because I had been bugging him about it for two years. I ended up taking John D'Amico's place when he went back to being a linesman around Christmas time.

My first game as a referee was in Toronto, and Philadelphia was the visiting team. The Broad Street Bullies. Nice way to start. As time went on I had a lot of Philly games but that was all right because you looked forward to them. It was nice working with them, and Boston and Montreal. Right from the drop of the puck it was physical. I thrived on that type of hockey.

When you have a team with·a lot of tough guys, you can't let them out of your sight. I tell that to the young referees I work with in the Colonial League. Players like Dave Schultz or Tiger Williams. They still have to commit the foul but they're the guys who will get you in trouble.

With the Flyers, Schultz and Don Saleski, every fight they got in, every penalty they got, it was our fault. No matter if it was in Philly or on the road, no matter what penalty they got, they had to yap and complain. Schultz was probably one of the worst. Funny thing is, when he was playing I never talked to him except when we were swearing at each other. Now he's coaching in the Colonial League and he's a real nice guy.

Tiger Williams was different. He would certainly get upset with the officials, but not every time. He'd take his lumps and go to the penalty box. I used to tell Tiger that he was a marked man, but that he should just think of the penalties we didn't call on him because we were calling four or five a game against him as it was. On a scale of one to ten we'd let him get away with the fours and fives while the other guys couldn't get away with the fours and fives.

John Ferguson was the same. The odd time he'd lose his cool but normally he'd have his fight and then go straight to the penalty box. The best fight I ever saw was between Fergie and Orland Kurtenbach. I was a linesman that night and I just stood there and watched. When they finished they were on their hands and knees. But know what? At the end they picked each other's gloves up and went right to the box. We didn't have to do anything.

I was in the league for over twenty years and my favourite was always Jean Béliveau. He had class towards the officials and class towards the other players. Bobby Orr was certainly a great player and a terrific competitor but he had no class with the officials on the ice. The first couple of years Wayne Gretzky was in the league he was a real whiner. Many nights I told him Béliveau and Bobby Hull never acted that way. Later he improved a lot, at least with me.

I had respect for many of the players I had confrontations with. One night in Boston Wayne Cashman said he was gonna cut my head off with his stick. I said, "Okay, I'll get a stick and we'll go at it out in the parking lot." The next time he saw me he laughed and said, "The other night, geez, that was great." If a referee said that to a player now he'd be on the carpet. I was a bit of a hollerer and it was accepted, although not in the later years of my career. It got me in trouble. Someone like Andy van Hellemond, who was calmer and more diplomatic, had more success than I did. I used to swear a lot and Scotty told me I had to stop because it was getting reported so often. He was also concerned that the younger officials were picking it up from me. Toronto was a bad place for me because the rink would get so quiet. Scotty would get upset because his wife would be at the game and she could hear my language. [Laughs]

Coaches? I often think of Fred Shero when he was coaching in Philly. With all the penalties they took he never said a word. I always had time for guys like Al Arbour and Scotty Bowman. When they questioned me or hollered at me, 99 per cent of the time they were likely right. Then there was Michel Bergeron. He hated everybody and we always had battles. Guys like him and Bryan Murray yelled all the time. I just don't know where they came from, why they did it. I had no respect for them.

I noticed a big difference when the players started wearing helmets. I remember being in Los Angeles and the Canadiens were there. Mario Tremblay and Doug Risebrough had just joined the team and both wore helmets. One of them got into a fight and I gave the wrong guy the major. Red Fisher never let me forget that. That's when I started carrying a writing pad and marking down names when there were fights or bench-clearing brawls.

My worst injury was when I had my nose smashed in Minnesota. One of the Sutters got hit and his stick flew up and smashed my nose in twenty-odd places. It wasn't one of those stories where I courageously finished the game. I thought I was dying. It took three operations to reconstruct it. That was around the end of January, or early February, and I missed the rest of the season and the playoffs. I wore a helmet my last year and a half mainly because my kids said I was stupid not to. I didn't enjoy wearing it but today I think an official is crazy if he doesn't wear one.

I never took games home with me. I was fortunate I had the farm. When I went home on a schedule break I always had two weeks' work to catch up, what with the cattle and everything else. I'd have a game in Buffalo, or Toronto, and at 3:00 in the afternoon I'd look at my watch and say, "Holy smokes, I've got a hockey game tonight." I'd never even think about it when I was home on the farm.

John D'Amico was the one who called the too-many-men infraction against Boston in that playoff game, in Montreal. I get reminded of that penalty all the time. It seems like Cherry mentions it once a week. I got the hassle, but D'Amico made the call. I heard later that the tape showed there was a period of seventeen seconds when they had too many men. Some people say there were eight of them on. I remember D'Amico trying to grab one of their players, I think it was Don Marcotte, because nobody wants to call a penalty in a situation like that. Cherry? He had no reaction at all, really.

Lafleur scored the goal that tied the game. When he shot it I was a little bit behind him and I said to myself, "The goddam thing's going in." The goalie fanned on it. He should have had it in his back pocket. But I had a feeling as soon as Lafleur shot the puck that it was going in, and it did.

As far as the white-towel game goes, well, it was turning into a rough series. I had the game in Chicago and Frank Udvari told me I was to tighten things up, the hooking and holding, all the shit Vancouver was doing. So I did. By the third period I guess they'd had it with me. I called another penalty and they got scored on and that's when Roger Neilson started waving the towel. Bob Hodges and Ron Finn were the linesmen and I asked them what Neilson was doing and they said, "He's surrendering to you." Nobody had ever seen that before. Hodges asked me what I was going to do with him. I said, "I don't know, but he's not staying in the game." I threw Neilson out and I threw Tiger Williams and Gerry Minor out too. That towel thing really caught on in Vancouver. I should have been selling them. I could have made a lot of money.

There is a story hockey types like to tell about Lloyd Gilmour to prove he was a bit of a character. Gilmour was refereeing a game in Vancouver between the Canucks and the Philadelphia Flyers when the Broad Street Bullies were in full bloom. The Canucks were a tough team too. There was a fight every few minutes, and the game was moving along at a snail's pace. Late in the third period Flyers coach Fred Shero sent a few of his heavyweights over the boards again, presumably for one last battle. Gilmour skated over to Shero and said, "Come on, Freddie, don't put these guys on. Look at the time. If there's another fight we'll miss last call."

The Flyers were a big part of the final season of Lloyd Gilmour's career, which had begun when the NHL was a six-team league. He had the emotional exhibition game at the Spectrum in Philadelphia in January 1976 when the Soviet Red Army team left the ice in protest after Ed Van Impe flattened Valery Kharlamov and Gilmour didn't call a penalty. In the same building, four months later, he refereed his last game.

Lloyd Gilmour

I'm from Vancouver and got my start in pro hockey in the old Western League. One year the Rangers and the Bruins came west to play exhibition games. The Patrick brothers were running the teams. Muzz had New York and Lynn was with Boston. I went on the tour with them. They started in Calgary and ended up in Los Angeles. Muzz recommended me to Mr. Campbell and Carl Voss.

Like most of the guys, I worked most of my games in the minors and they'd bring me up for three or four NHL games. After a while the players would say, "Hi, Lloyd. How are you doin'?" I thought I was doing pretty good but Voss didn't think so. It turned out I wasn't one of his favourites and he gave me a pretty good shafting. He wanted me to go to places like Memphis, Tennessee, at Christmas and New Year's. I had a wife and family in Vancouver so I told him to go to hell. I came home and finished the season in the Western League. Mr. Campbell and Al Leader, who ran the Western League, were close, and between them they arranged to get me back to the NHL.

My first game was in Toronto. Boston was there and I was trying so hard to be sharp and not miss the first penalty. We'd played about six or seven minutes and I put my hand in the air for what I thought was gonna be a penalty but it didn't happen. So there I was, kinda stuck, and when the play stopped Eddie Shack came over and asked what was going on. I told him I had anticipated a penalty and he said, in that foghorn voice of his, "Ah, that's all right." The players in those days took it kind of easy on you in your first game or two but from then on they treated you like you were a veteran. It wasn't long before they'd start giving you static when you had it coming.

When I was in the Western League there were plenty of tough guys, and Larry Zeidel was one of the toughest. We used to call him "The Rock." I had a game in Portland when he took a run at somebody and the guy put his stick up and actually scalped him. Zeidel went after him and we had an awful job trying to keep them apart. He was bleeding like crazy and the other players were just standing there with their mouths open at the sight of all the blood. I finally said to him, "Come on, Rock, you've got all kinds of time before the end of the season to get hold of this guy. Right now you better get off the ice because you're bleeding to death." In this day and age they would have called 911 but he was still ready to go.

I liked working tough games but I didn't like them having sticks up. When the Philadelphia Flyers were in their heyday they were a tough hockey club. Most of their guys didn't use the stick, but Ed Van Impe was a stick man. I watched him like a hawk. I used to tell him, "If you're gonna cut guys open with that stick when I'm here, you're not gonna play."

Then you had a team like Montreal. They were all business. They had been drilled by great coaches like Toe Blake. I didn't know him that well and didn't have the seniority to walk around calling him "Toe," but I travelled with him a couple of times. We had to fly with his team one night because of bad weather. There was me, Matt Pavelich, and Claude Bechard, and he told us to sit with him in first class. He didn't want us sitting with the players.

The Canadiens had a few tough guys, like John Ferguson, but they were kind of curbed so, basically, they made it easy for you because you really only had to watch the other team. Then Bowman came along and he was never my favourite. I pitched him one night and he took it personally and said he'd like to punch me out, or something. I told him he didn't have the guts. I said, "I'll meet you, if you want."

Usually I got along with coaches, although that was tough to do sometimes with Punch Imlach. They put in that coincidental-major-penalty rule and you couldn't get that across to some of the players. George Armstrong was Toronto's captain and I was trying to explain it to him. Imlach was standing at the gate. We had a rule that coaches couldn't step on the ice. I said, "Punch, if you come on the ice, you're gone." I look over again and there's Imlach putting on his skates. Because the rule said a coach couldn't "step" on the ice, he was gonna put skates on. [Laughs]

So many players didn't know the rules. You take Alex Delvecchio. He was Detroit's captain, the nicest guy in the world, but he didn't know the rules and couldn't care less. George Armstrong knew the rules, and Jean Béliveau did too. Béliveau never raised his voice, never used bad language, and he never wanted you to swear at his players. He told me one night, "My players, they don't swear at you, so don't you swear at them."

I had two games with no penalties. We called them "no-hitters." The first was in Buffalo on a Sunday night, Scotty Morrison and his wife, Joan, were at the game, and afterwards Scotty said, "You could have sat in the seats with me and let Joan referee." The other was in Vancouver in my last year. The Rangers were there and Phil Esposito had just been traded to them. With about a minute to go Espo split the defence and a Vancouver guy hooked him down from behind, real bad. As it turned out they scored on the play, which took off the penalty, but Espo had noticed that I hadn't put my arm up. At the faceoff he said, "Geez, you weren't gonna send that guy for a penalty. He could have ripped my head off." I said, "I've got a no-hitter going," and Phil said, "Oh, I'm sorry."

I had that sort of rapport with a lot of players and I kind of liked it. I hardly gave any misconducts, especially to guys who would act up with two minutes to go and the score was 8–1. They just wanted to get out of there and get to the bar before anyone else. I wouldn't give them a misconduct for that reason. I went nose to nose with a few guys and there were some who knew I didn't like them because I told them so. I would never penalize a team because of that, but they knew who I didn't like. I didn't go for the bad language, and the backstabbing jazz when they'd go to the coach, and the showbiz stuff. Like Cherry. He'd put his foot up on the edge of the bench and give it to the linesmen. I ripped into him a few nights, I'll tell you, and I pitched him a couple of times.

I had the game when Bobby Orr got walloped by Pat Quinn, likely the hardest check he ever took. In my opinion Orr was the greatest who ever played and he got walloped. There was nothing wrong with it and nobody said a word. If that was this day and age and it had been a guy like Gretzky, they'd have a war. I never had a problem with Orr cussin' me but he gave it to my linesman a couple of times. One night I think it was Bob Hodges, but after the game he called him over and apologized. He's a class guy.

Ask me who the toughest players were and I'd flip a coin between Gordie Howe and Fergie. Today they fight funny. They hang on with one hand and hit with the other. If you fought Howe or Fergie you wouldn't be grabbing them because you'd be on your ass. Fergie could flip his gloves off and hit you so fast your head would spin. And Gordie would just take one look, blink once, and wham, you're gone. A lot of guys challenged them, like Shack. Fergie had him on the run a few times. Shack wasn't tough as a fighter but he was tough as a hockey player.

I worked a lot of years and did a lot of games, but the one they still ask me about is the game in Philly with the Russians. The hassle all started when Van Impe came flying from the blueline to centre ice and whacked Kharlamov. He went down, and stayed down. My two linesmen were Matt Pavelich and a Russian. The Russian linesman was bending over Kharlamov telling him to stay down so I would give Van Impe a major penalty. What he forgot was that Pavelich is a Croatian and speaks Russian. Matt came over and told me what was going on so I told the Russian coach to get the son of a bitch up on his feet because there was nothing wrong with him. So they took a hike and went to their room and that's when Bob Cole said on TV, "They're goin' home!"

Mr. Campbell was there, and Scotty Morrison, and of course Alan Eagleson. I told Mr. Campbell the story Matt told me and he got very hostile towards the Russians. He said, "They're not pulling that bullshit on us," and he went into their dressing room. I wasn't there with him, but apparently what he said was, "You've got five minutes to come back and play. There is one more game for you on this trip and if you don't come back that game will be cancelled and you'll never play against the National Hockey League again as long as I am its president." The Russians were making a lot of money on the trip, so they came back. There was one of their players, I can't remember his name, but he was a good guy. When they came out he had a little smile on his face and he winked at me. It was like he was saying, well, we tried, but it didn't work.

When it came to retiring, I'd been a referee long enough, I was getting up in age, and there was the travel. My home was in Vancouver and every game I had, except there, was back east or in California. I took my wife with me one time for an eighteen-day swing. During that trip we couldn't fly out of Montreal because of a snowstorm. Bob Hodges was with us and we had to rent a car to drive to Burlington, Vermont, and then charter a plane to get from there to Boston. That wasn't much fun and my wife wondered how I was able to do it all those years.

The last game I did was in Philly, in 1976, the night the Canadiens won the Stanley Cup. The Flyers had won the previous two years but they couldn't handle Montreal. It was over in four straight. I remember sitting with you, Dick, and the people from *Hockey Night in Canada* the night before the last game on the roof of the hotel. It was hot as hell and I was telling you it was going to be my last game, and it was. After that I ran a restaurant in Nanaimo for nineteen years. Called it Nanaimo Harbour Lights. NHL. It was filled with hockey memorabilia. I ended up selling it and now I'm a man of leisure.

I had a wife and three kids at home and as you get older the travel is so difficult. I'd been on the ice with the greatest players in the world. I'd been on the ice when the Stanley Cup was won. How much more could I want?

6

Wild Times in the WHA

BOB FRAMPTON BILL FRIDAY

The World Hockey Association lived from 1972 to 1979, upsetting a few NHL apple carts along the way. Anyone who spent time in the WHA, including two of my Hockey Night in Canada *cohorts, Harry Neale and John Garrett, has tall tales of the chaos, and the fun. In one of my previous books,* Behind the Bench, *they told some of their favourite WHA stories.*

At one time Harry coached the Minnesota Fighting Saints. He described how the owner raced into the Minneapolis– St. Paul airport a few minutes before the team was to take off on a long road trip carrying a brown paper bag which contained the players' meal money. There was six thousand dollars in cash in the bag, and after the plane took off Harry and his assistant, Glen Sonmor, started counting it out on their tray tables. A woman passenger told the pilot she thought two bank robbers were on the flight.

Luckily for Harry and Glen the pilot was a hockey fan and recognized them.

John Garrett played goal for the Birmingham Bulls when the line-up included the likes of Gilles "Bad News" Bilodeau, Dave "Killer" Hanson, and one of hockey's all-time tough guys, Steve Durbano. John told the following story of a game the Bulls played in Cincinnati on the eve of American Thanksgiving: "To give you an idea of our game plan, I didn't start because our other goalie, Wayne Wood, was six-foot-two and weighed over two hundred pounds. He rarely played but our coach, Glen Sonmor, said Wood was starting because he was sure there was going to be a big brawl. Just before the game a minister came on the ice and offered a prayer for Thanksgiving and thanked the Lord for the fine group of sportsmen who would be playing that night. He called for a display of true friendship and sportsmanship. About twenty seconds after the minister gives the prayer they drop the puck, and another ten seconds later Robbie Ftorek clobbers Durbano and the gloves are off. Everybody on the ice, including the goaltenders, got into the fight and they were all thrown out of the game."

Among those who tried to bring some semblance of order to the WHA's on-ice chaos were two long-time NHL employees, Bob Frampton and Bill Friday. Frampton was director of officials, Friday the league's highest-profile referee.

Bob Frampton is a Montrealer who captained the Montreal Junior Royals when they won the Memorial Cup in 1949. From a hockey standpoint Frampton was born several years too soon. He would easily have made a team in today's expanded NHL, but in the old six-team days he was always on the fringe, playing just briefly for the Canadiens. He began officiating after he retired as a player in 1954.

BOB FRAMPTON

I was working for Dominion Bridge and playing for the Montreal Senior Royals and not doing a good job at either. I had to make a decision so I stopped playing halfway through the season, in January, and right away started refereeing in the Quebec Junior League. I did the Memorial Cup Eastern finals that year and Carl Voss offered me a contract with the NHL.

There was no training camp for officials in those days; you just started with your first game. Mine was an exhibition in Providence and I hadn't been on skates since the previous season. Boston played the Rangers. They had met in the playoffs the year before and there were still some old scores to be settled. Right away Fernie Flaman was yelling, "I'll get you bastards!" Stuff like that. He and Jack Evans went at it ten seconds after I dropped the puck. The benches emptied and I'm saying, What the hell am I doing here? It was unbelievable. I gave out thirty-three penalties. That was my first pro game, my initiation into the NHL.

Most of my refereeing was in the American League and I worked the lines in the NHL. I didn't give up my job at Dominion Bridge, so I would be a linesman in Montreal during the week and travel on weekends. For example, I'd be in Toronto Saturday, New York Sunday, and back in my office Monday morning. I worked fifty to sixty games a year. I was in the NHL from 1955 to 1970. It was tough.

The WHA came along in 1972. Vern Buffey, who had been retired for a year after refereeing eleven years in the NHL, was hired as referee-in-chief. He signed several officials away from the NHL like Bill Friday, Bob Sloan, Ron Ego, and Brent Cassleman. Friday was the big catch. He was a top referee in the NHL. Buffey offered him a three-year contract at fifty thousand dollars a year. The NHL didn't come close to matching it so Bill jumped. I was hired as supervisor of officials, mainly to assign and supervise the linesmen. They were all young and in many cases local linesmen, and they weren't very good. We set up a camp in those early years and eventually got some guys trained pretty well.

I've never seen an organization so loosely run in all my life. Teams came, teams went. We'd lose three, add one, lose two more. After the first season Buffey fell ill and they named me director of officials. The biggest problem I had was assigning the guys. I'd book them four weeks down the road and then have to change everything two weeks later because two teams had dropped out. Bill Friday's three-year contract ended in 1976. After that I kept him, and everybody else, on a one-year contract because we never knew if the league would last through the season. [Laughs]

I did all my WHA business out of my house in Montreal. I never quit working at Dominion Bridge. Sometimes I'd leave my office at 4:00 Friday afternoon, fly to Los Angeles, and get there in time for the game that night. I'd go to Vancouver Saturday morning and watch a game there that night, go on to Calgary, Edmonton, or Winnipeg for a game Sunday night, take the red-eye home and be back at my desk in Montreal at 8:00 Monday morning. During the week I'd fly to places like Quebec City and Hartford in the late afternoon and be back at Dominion Bridge first thing the next morning.

We used to have meetings between the coaches and referees before each game. One night Winnipeg played in Quebec City. Marc Boileau was coaching Quebec and Bobby Kromm was with Winnipeg. They got into an argument during the meeting and the next thing we knew they were having a fistfight, right in the referee's room. Another time, after Bill Friday had a rough night in Quebec, the Nordiques' general manager, Maurice Filion, sent me a telex that read, "Don't ever send that fucking Friday back to Quebec." Bill was on his way to another city so I got hold of him, told him what Filion had sent to me, and asked him if he wanted to go back to Quebec for a game the next night. He said, "I'd love to go back." So I changed some assignments and put Bill right back there. He had a good game, and Filion and I have been friends ever since.

Those of us involved with the officiating had carte blanche when it came to changing rules because the owners didn't know anything about the game. When Wayne Gretzky started with Indianapolis I watched three of his first five games and I have to confess I never thought he'd make it. I thought he was gonna get killed in pro hockey. In fact, at one time Glen Sather said exactly that to me – "They're killing the kid" – after Gretzky had moved to Edmonton. Sather was complaining about the way the older players were giving Wayne a going-over on faceoffs. Before a game he took me to the dressing room and told Gretzky to take off his underwear and show me his body. He was marked from his neck to his knees like you wouldn't believe. We put in the faceoff-interference rule because of that.

That game was in Hartford. Bill Friday was the referee and I told him about Gretzky and said we had to clamp down on faceoff interference. The game starts and right away some guy runs Gretzky in the faceoff circle. Up goes Friday's arm, he gives the penalty, and thirty seconds later Edmonton scores. By the end of the first period Friday had called three more penalties against the Whalers for the same thing, all on Gretzky, and Edmonton was leading 4–0. Then I hear on the P.A., "Would Bob Frampton please report to the New England Whalers' directors' room." Howard Baldwin owned the Whalers and he was also chairman of the board of the WHA. I didn't go near the director's room, but when I went downstairs after the game Baldwin was waiting for me.

Edmonton had won the game 9–2 and he's standing at the referee's door. I said, "Mr. Baldwin, are you going to talk to me as owner of the Whalers, or as my boss?" He started right in about how they were trying to put people into the building and we had spoiled the game. I said I didn't think we had spoiled it but we had to do something about the interference. It was a touchy night.

Let's face it, we had some terrible teams. In the NHL in those years 90 per cent of the players were good journeymen, 6 or 7 per cent were stars or superstars, and 3 or 4 per cent were gorillas. In the WHA we had 90 per cent gorillas, 7 or 8 per cent journeymen, and 2 or 3 per cent stars. Paul Stewart, the same one who is now a referee, was one of the tough guys and, I think, the best fighter I ever saw on skates. He would get into some awful battles, but once the referee told him to end it he'd beat the ref to the penalty box. A lot of intimidating tactics were tried and often they brought people into the buildings.

I was in Quebec City one night and had just gone to bed at the Château Frontenac when my phone rang. It was Ron Harris, one of our referees, calling from Winnipeg. He asked me if I was sitting down and I told him I was lying down, asleep. He said I had better sit up because they had just had a real nightmare of a game out there between the Jets and Birmingham and he wanted to tell me about it. I thought, Oh, oh, Birmingham.

Anders Hedberg had scored a goal for Winnipeg and when he had his arms in the air, celebrating, Steve Durbano speared him. Bobby Hull then cross-checked Durbano and everybody got into it. Durbano grabbed Hull's hair transplant and pulled it out by the roots. Hull was bleeding all over the place, the benches emptied, and they finally had to call the police. Birmingham was on a road trip but we kept them in Winnipeg and I flew out for a hearing. We held it in a huge boardroom at Great-West Life and I interviewed the players who were the main participants, Durbano being one of them. I made my recommendations and Durbano was out for the balance of the season and the playoffs. We never saw him in the league again. It was a familiar situation for us, the gorillas against the stars, and our main responsibility was trying to keep it under control.

The league was poorly organized with bad management and bad owners. In the first three years they lost fifty or sixty million dollars and likely broke more millionaires in a shorter time than any business in history. But I have to say that the officials were always paid. There were a few times when the cheques were a couple of days late and I told my guys to cash them as quickly as possible. But they always got their money. In the late '70s I felt that, man for man, our top four officials were better than the top four in the NHL. I think I had a staff that was more consistent and officiated games better. When the WHA ended and the four teams joined the NHL, Scotty Morrison took on six of my guys, and they were all great.

At one time the WHA asked me to apply for the job as full-time director of officials and I was to make my presentation at an owners' meeting in Las Vegas. Benny Hatskin, who owned Winnipeg and was the chairman, opened the meeting by going over the financial situation of the league and then he said, "Each member team is hereby assessed a half-million-dollar payment, due and payable tomorrow morning." Everybody started laughing, then they got up and walked out to the gaming tables. That was the end of the meeting. They had wanted me to quit Dominion Bridge and go to work for them full time and they left me sitting there. It was ridiculous. I'll never forget that as long as I live.

When the Winnipeg Jets signed superstar Bobby Hull away from the Chicago Blackhawks in 1972 it was said the World Hockey Association had achieved instant credibility. The signing of referee Bill Friday did the same thing from an officiating standpoint. It meant the WHA would begin play with one of the best referees in the business dropping the puck. The NHL was upset with Friday because he jumped leagues and, although the WHA lasted just seven years, it stayed upset with him for more than twenty years.

BILL FRIDAY

I did it for money, pure and simple. The WHA offered me $50,000 a year for three years. I had been with the NHL twelve years and I was making $22,000. I went to Scotty Morrison and he offered me a three-year contract, which was something the league had never done before. He said he would give me 26, 30, and 34. I thought, Hey, I've got five kids at home. Fifty thousand dollars was pretty good money. I couldn't afford not to take it so I moved. Despite all the money problems the WHA had I never missed a paycheque in seven years. Once they asked me to hold my cheque for three or four days, but that was the only time. They treated me royally.

I don't know how Mr. Campbell felt about me leaving but Scotty Morrison was really upset. When it was all over for the WHA in '79 I had refereed nineteen years and I wanted one more year real bad. If the NHL had wanted me back for one or two years I would have been more than happy. But I never got the opportunity. I think, and I could be wrong, I was kind of ostracized. Then in 1994 they asked me to referee the Legends game during All-Star weekend, in New York, which I did. That was the first time anyone had contacted me. Now I'm working for the league as the video-replay judge at games here in Tampa where we spend the winter, and I really enjoy being around the scene again.

Things happen in your life you never forget and one for me is the first game I refereed in the NHL. It was in the Montreal Forum with Detroit. With about three minutes to go the score was 9–3 for the Canadiens and, all of a sudden, I got so excited I could hardly skate. My knees just turned to jelly. I finally realized that I had just done my first game in the NHL and it really hit me. Those last three minutes seemed like three hours. I had never had that feeling on the ice before, and I never had it again.

When I first joined the league in 1960 I worked twenty-four games on the lines so I would get to know the players. Probably twenty of those were with George Hayes and I enjoyed the man immensely. He was a character but he took his job seriously from the time we dropped the puck until the game was over. If I were going into a game in the NHL, WHA, any league, and I know the game is going to be tough, give me George Hayes. The other linesman could be anyone else, but give me George.

I was on the ice with some of the greatest players in history. You can start with Gordie Howe. He was tough and you had to watch him, especially if he got behind you. You knew he was going to retaliate if something happened and he figured you weren't looking. He never gave me trouble, never chased me or hollered at me. But he'd get upset when you caught him if he thought you weren't watching.

I've got a cute Howe story for you. When we were in the WHA together we were in an exhibition game in Hamilton. That's my home town and my kids were sitting right behind the bench. During the game Gordie would come off the ice and sit with them, take off his gloves, sign autographs and all that. The kids were thrilled. When the game was over he was saying goodbye and he asked them, "Does your dad like his new glasses?" The kids said, "Dad doesn't wear glasses." Gordie said, "Well, tell him he needs them," and he took off. [Laughs]

Ted Lindsay was tough and, I thought, mean. He would curse you. I was doing a TV series with oldtimers called "The Original Six." They played no-contact hockey but Lindsay cross-checked Pierre Pilote and drove him to the ice. I gave him a penalty and he started giving me a lot of sass so I gave him a ten. He turned around and said, "I'm gonna run this stick right through you." I said, "No you won't. I'm looking at you." Red Storey was the commissioner and we threw him out. He went home and never played again in that series. Imagine, an oldtimers game. Years later I was with him in Jamaica doing a TV show with Bobby Orr and he was the nicest guy in the world. Off the ice Ted was a completely different person.

I was doing a game between Toronto and the Rangers and the Leafs were ahead 3–1. With about thirty seconds left Tim Horton blasts one from the point and the puck hit me right on the knee. I couldn't skate and until the game ended I was hanging on to the boards. Gump Worsley was the Rangers' goalie and when the horn sounded he skated by me and said, "Thanks for stopping one for me, Bill." I was really hurting but I got no sympathy from him. That was Gump.

I was involved in an incident with Emile Francis that caused a new rule to be put in the book. He was coaching the Rangers and they were playing Chicago. Francis had pulled his goalie, there was a big scramble, and one of the Rangers slid the puck into the crease. A Chicago defence-man was lying there and it went under him. I blew the whistle and Francis thought there should be a penalty shot. I explained things to his captain, who told Francis, and the next thing you know he starts coming on the ice after me. Vic Hadfield and Rod Gilbert each grabbed him under an arm, picked him up, and carried him back to the bench. Francis is a little guy and his little feet were still going when they got him off the ice. I wrote up a report. There was no rule then to cover something like that but the next year they put it in. Any coach steps on the ice, bench minor.

When I went to the WHA I knew games would be rough and dirty because there were guys that didn't belong but they had to have bodies. Some of the bodies were real goons. They would put tape and stuff on their fingers and hands and we tried to stop that. If you got in a fight and you had stuff on your fingers and hands you got a match penalty if you injured the other guy. That rule came out of the WHA.

I had a game in Minnesota one night when Winnipeg was there and Harry Neale was coaching Minnesota. Winnipeg had a good team and they started their big line of Bobby Hull, Ulf Nilsson, and Anders Hedberg. Incidentally, that was the best line I ever saw in hockey. They weren't fighters, of course, and neither were Lars Sjoberg and Barry Long, who started on defence. Harry started his heavies, the two Hanson brothers, Curt Brackenbury, John Arbour, and Billy Butters. I dropped the puck and it just lay there because the five Minnesota guys jumped the five Winnipeg guys and we've got five fights. When it was all over I gave the Minnesota guys each five minutes for fighting and the Winnipeg guys each two minutes for roughing. By the time the penalties were all served the score was 5–0 for Winnipeg. I skated by the bench and said to Harry, "Don't ever do that to me again." Harry said, "No. There's no way."

The only player I ever thought was going to physically attack me was Steve Durbano when he was playing for Birmingham. I gave him a penalty and he shot the puck at me. Right away I gave him ten and he started to charge. He was coming at me with his stick and I thought, Do I grab the stick or what? But before he got to me four or five players, including Paul Henderson and Frank Mahovlich, came over the boards and jumped him. They got him down and dragged him off the ice. That was the only time I was really scared refereeing a hockey game.

Quebec was funny. When the WHA started they had a team of little guys. A team like the Los Angeles Sharks would run at them all night and I'd keep pitching the L.A. players. They loved me in Quebec. Then they changed their team around and got goons like Brackenbury and Gordie Gallant. Now Winnipeg comes to town and Quebec is running at them all night and I'm pitching the Nordiques. Now I'm the worst referee in the world. But that's the way the game goes.

I got to work games when Wayne Gretzky first played professional hockey. When he started he would take the odd dive. I remember one night in Edmonton, down he went, a big dive. He was on the ice looking back at me and I just stood there. No penalty. That got the crowd going. Al Hamilton was the Oilers' captain and I called him over and said, "You go tell Mr. Gretzky that this swimming pool is frozen and if he ever does that again I'm gonna whistle his butt for ten." At the time I'm about forty-two, forty-three years old and I guess Gretzky is nineteen. The next time he came out for a faceoff he gets set, his head is down, and he doesn't look up. I'm hanging on to the puck and I hear him say, "It won't happen again, Mr. Friday."

I had one rule and I never broke it in nineteen years. I never swore at a player, not once, because I didn't think it was fair. If he swore at me I could give him ten. If I swore at him he couldn't do anything. My theory was, if I swore at the players how could I earn their respect?

People used to say I was a showman and I think it was mainly because of the way I skated. I was pretty intense. Nobody could talk to me before a game, even the linesmen.

They wouldn't say anything to me unless I spoke to them. I used to worry about every game but once I dropped the puck everything was fine. I enjoyed my job and, I guess, the notoriety. I enjoyed people telling me I did a good job. It made me feel good, made all the bad things about refereeing good.

I have to admit that when I was in the WHA there were a few times I found myself wishing I had stayed in the NHL. I think I could have lasted longer. Then again, I probably made more money in my career than I would have by staying. Other people were affected by what I did. They had offered Bob Myers a raise of five hundred bucks, but when I jumped he got five thousand. So there were a lot of referees who made a lot more money after I jumped leagues and that gave me a good feeling.

7

Lights Out in Boston, Doughnuts in Jersey

DENIS MOREL DON KOHARSKI

Almost every official I talked to for this book had experienced a well-publicized, and usually not very pleasant, incident. There are a few cases when the not-so-welcome moment in the media sun marked the end of an officiating career. On March 13, 1955, Cliff Thompson, a local linesman in Boston, was struck by Maurice Richard. Clarence Campbell suspended Richard for the balance of the regular season and the playoffs, a decision which sparked the infamous Richard Riot in the streets of Montreal. Thompson never worked another game. In 1961 Montreal coach Toe Blake punched referee Dalton McArthur after a playoff game in Chicago. McArthur never refereed again in the National League.

Quebec native Denis Morel refereed for seventeen years in the NHL. *He too had his share of incidents, including a blackout in the Boston Garden in the Stanley Cup finals,*

*and a brawl in Los Angeles that might have forced him into
retirement earlier than he had planned.*

DENIS MOREL

I refereed hockey games when I was a kid before I learned to
skate. It was a familiar story, I guess. I was at a rink and they
needed a referee. I said okay, I'll do it, and I went out in my
boots and ran back and forth blowing the whistle. I loved it,
so right away I bought a pair of skates. I started officiating in
the Quebec Junior League when I was twenty years old. By
then I was teaching physical education in La Tuque.

You learned in a hurry in a league like that, especially
when it came to taking abuse from coaches and managers.
They had some dandies in those days, guys like Phil Watson,
Maurice Filion, Jacques Marcotte. They'd come banging on
your door after games. One night in Shawinigan Marcotte
came down from the stands during the game and really
gave it to me. It was a small arena and everybody heard
every word.

I did my first NHL game in 1978. Montreal played Atlanta.
Pierre Bouchard was with the Canadiens then and in one
game in Montreal early in my career he was all over me.
Pierre owned a restaurant, so right in the middle of his
tirade I said to him, "Hey, Pierre, can you get me a reserva-
tion for eight at your place for after the game?" He stopped,
then said, "Okay," and skated away. He got me the reserva-
tion, and we went.

Soon after I started, the Quebec Nordiques came into the
NHL. I was always asked how I felt as a French Canadian
doing the games between Quebec and Montreal because
they had such a big rivalry. A lot of people tried to put pressure on me. I'd work two or three games a year between

those teams and I didn't feel any extra pressure at all. I was a pro and I approached those games just like all my other games. Don't forget, there were a few other pretty good rivalries then too, like Calgary and Edmonton, and the Islanders and the Rangers. Just because the Canadiens and the Nordiques were two teams from *la belle province* didn't make any difference to me.

I worked over 1,200 games and if you ask me when I was the most nervous before a game, my answer might surprise you. It was an All-Star Game, the one in St. Louis in 1988. I know people feel there's no pressure in those games but there was for me. Big time. The best players in the world are all there, in the same game, and I didn't want to make a farce of it. It turned out to be a good game. Mario Lemieux set a record for most points in an All-Star Game and he scored the winning goal, in overtime. The next day I had a sore back, the only time that ever happened to me. I guess it was my nerves.

Early in my career I worked games in a playoff series between Montreal and Philadelphia and it gave me a great feeling. In 1989 I was the referee in Montreal when Calgary won the Stanley Cup. Referees get a great thrill out of something like that, just like the players. A night like that is one of the big goals in an official's life.

The strangest playoff game I worked was in the finals the year before that when the lights went out at the Boston Garden. It was a Boston–Edmonton final. The Oilers scored to tie the game 3–3 near the end of the second period, then, bang, the lights went out. I thought maybe Harry Sinden had done it. [Laughs] I sent the teams to their dressing rooms and then the security people said everyone had to be out of the building in thirty minutes. I didn't have the authority to cancel the game. Only John Ziegler, the president of the league, could do that. They told him the power failure was going to last quite a while so the game was called off. That was the fourth game and Edmonton was leading the series 3–0. They went back to Edmonton and won the Cup two nights later.

The game that hurt me the most was in Los Angeles, February 28, 1990. Edmonton was there, it was the last game of the season between them, and they had had a big rivalry going since the Gretzky trade. There are a couple of penalty records from that game that are still in the book. [*Most penalties, both teams, one game: 85. Morel assessed 26 minors, 7 majors, 6 ten-minute misconducts, 4 game misconducts, and one match penalty. The other record is for most penalties, one team, one game: Edmonton, 44.*]

Kelly Buchberger sucker-punched Tomas Sandstrom and broke his jaw. I missed it and there wasn't any video of it. I went to Toronto for a hearing and I felt I was on a real hot seat. I lost a lot of confidence because of that game. It took me two years to get over it and during that time I didn't perform the way I used to. Maybe that's why they did what they did and I had to retire after '93–94. I wasn't ready to quit. I wanted to go two more years but they had other ideas. They said they didn't want me on the ice any more and offered me a supervisor's job. I took it. I've never talked about what that game in L.A. did to me until now, never told anyone. Maybe I should have. My wife never knew. I was so stubborn, like an alcoholic who won't admit he's an alcoholic. It hurt me.

I've always thought the two basic things for a referee to remember are be prepared, and be yourself. Don't try to copy anyone else. After what happened to me because of the game in L.A. I tell young referees that if they feel bad and upset about something, talk about it. Get it out. That's what supervisors are for.

Refereeing is a passion with me. I started doing it when I was thirteen years old – that's forty-five years ago. I couldn't give up the life completely and I feel comfortable now. I'm not out of place. It's nice when players, managers, and coaches come to talk to me. Before, that only happened in the heat of battle. Now, I think they respect me, and it's a good feeling.

There are two dates that represent significant incidents in the life of referee Don Koharski. The first, May 6, 1988, was when the coach of the New Jersey Devils, Jim Schoenfeld, screamed at him, "Have another doughnut, you fat pig!", a now-famous taunt that was heard on national television, coast to coast, in Canada and the United States. The second, September 13, 1990, was the day he quit drinking.

Koharski arrived in the NHL in the late 1970s as a bit of a free spirit, a reputation he did little to live down, considering his obvious zest for the high life, on and off the ice. By 1989 he was one of the league's top-rated referees, but during that year's Stanley Cup playoffs he was caught breaking curfew in Philadelphia. He was fined a thousand dollars and banished to the minors for a few weeks at the start of the next season. His side of the story is simply, "I was out late and had a brown bottle in my hand." Sixteen months later, with support from his wife, Susan, Koho quit drinking. He later told hockey writer Mike Ulmer, "I didn't want to be called an alcoholic. I didn't go to A.A. I did it myself. That's the proudest thing I look back on."

If I were in the movie business looking for someone to play the role of a tough drill sergeant, or an equally tough prison guard, the brushcut-wearing, confidently cocky guy everyone in hockey calls "Koho" would be my man. Don Koharski has never been shy about his ability, a trait that was evident early when, while still a teenager, he sold himself to some professional hockey executives to get his foot in the officiating door.

Don Koharski

I was born and raised in Dartmouth, Nova Scotia. I'm a good old Bluenoser, through and through. My dad was in the navy, and when I first got involved in organized hockey we were living on a navy base. They had great sports facilities for kids. I didn't learn to skate until I was thirteen. I used to public-skate at the Shannon Park Arena and chase my favourite girl around. Her name was Susan. I finally caught her and ended up marrying her.

One night public skating was over and some guys were gonna play a pick-up game of shinny. They asked me and my friend Mike Clark if we would referee. I phoned my folks to make sure I could stay out late because the ice was rented from 11:30 p.m. until 1:00 in the morning. They said it was okay so I blew the whistle for offsides and did some faceoffs. When it was over we were taking off our skates and one of the guys came over to thank us. He told us there was some beer money left over that the players wanted us to have, and gave us each ten dollars. That was the first time I officiated a hockey game. Right from the start I liked the idea of being able to control something, have fun and be in control.

The next weekend Mike and I went to the minor-hockey people, told them we seriously wanted to get involved in officiating, and they gave us some work. Mike was probably a better official than I was, but when the time came to go to referee schools and camps, he couldn't afford it. We would work Saturdays from noon to 9:00 or 10:00 at night and Sundays from 9:00 in the morning until 6:00 or 7:00 in the evening. No pay, just ice time. At lunch they'd give us a hot dog and a Coke, and we'd get two hot dogs, chips, and a Coke at suppertime. We thought it was real cool. It was a blast.

I won a trophy one year for being the kid who did the most work for the community. Besides hockey I refereed soccer and football. I would go to the football field with my whistle and my hockey referee's sweater in case an official didn't show up. Along with the trophy I got fifty dollars. Wow, fifty dollars! Right away I wanted to buy a car. My dad, God love him, straightened me out on that one. He told me the money was meant to improve my officiating skills, so I used it to fly to Vern Buffey's referee school, in Ontario.

I was doing bantam, midget, and junior-B games in Nova Scotia. They said I was too young to referee so I was always a linesman, but in the back of my mind I always wanted to referee. I'd watch the ref and tell myself that was what I wanted to do. All part of me being a control freak, I guess. When I was at Buffey's school, Red Storey was there and he took me under his wing. The next year he arranged with Bob Frampton for me to go to the WHA rookie camp for linesmen. Wayne Bonney and Ron Asselstine, who are linesmen for me now, were instructors and I was calling them Mr. Bonney and Mr. Asselstine. [Laughs] I went back the next year when I was a seventeen-year-old snotty-nosed punk and then a year later they hired me as an eighteen-year-old linesman.

I worked the 1975–76 season and it was a great experience. Then they lost four teams and didn't need as many officials. Last hired, first fired, so I was back in Dartmouth. My aunt worked for Baxter's Dairy and she got me a job as a milkman, the only full-time job I've ever had outside of hockey. I was living at home and driving a milk truck making deliveries to grocery stores.

The Canadiens' American Hockey League team, the Nova Scotia Voyageurs, operated out of Halifax. I called Gord Anziano of the American Hockey League, told him I had just finished working ninety-four games as a linesman in the WHA and would like to get on his league's staff. He said he would call me back and when he did he told me Jack Butterfield, the president, said his budget was all spent but maybe they'd consider me for the next season. So I said, "Okay, you don't talk for the next ten minutes, you just listen to me. I know the guys working the games in Halifax and they can't carry my bag to the rink. There's no way they're doing the job I would do for you." I pulled out all the stops. I wasn't gonna take no for an answer. I told him I'd pay my own way to their training camp and they'd be making a grave mistake if they didn't take me up on it. We finally hung up and an hour later he called back and said Mr. Butterfield agreed to have me at the camp and they'd pay my expenses. It turned out they hired me and I worked the lines at every V's home game that season.

That same year the hockey people in Nova Scotia decided that since I was working at a pretty high level they'd let me referee some amateur games. But the only friggin' one they gave me was a university game, St. Mary's at Dalhousie, on Valentine's Day. The game is usually called the "Valentine's Day Massacre." The guys who worked that league were scared shitless to do it because it almost always ended up in a riot. So they give it to me, and I'm nineteen years old.

Pierre Page was coaching Dalhousie and I always tell this story about him. It was the first game I ever refereed past midget, there was a big crowd of noisy college kids, and suddenly I'm not so sure about this refereeing stuff. Maybe I want to be a linesman after all. Page used to flip out and, sure enough, I do something that upsets him and he goes after me. I was trying to explain it to him and finally I got mad and said, "Pierre, if you don't shut up I'm gonna throw you out." He starts in, "You can't throw me out! You can't throw me out! You do and you'll never referee another game!" He keeps it up, calling me this and that, so finally I said, "See you later," and I threw him out. Tossed his ass right through the gate. He left like a little puppy dog with his tail between his legs. It was the only Canadian university game I ever refereed and I threw Pierre Page out, right at Dalhousie. He chased me for an hour after the game. Every door I went to go through he was waiting for me. He followed me to my car, right to my car, still yelling at me that I'd never referee another game. When I see him now I keep reminding him, "Hey, Pierre, never referee another game?"

Dan McLeod was a supervisor for the NHL and saw a lot of my games in Halifax. He gave me good reports and that led to me being hired by the NHL as a linesman. I did it for two and a half seasons. In my third year they asked me if I'd like to try refereeing. I don't know if that was because I was a bad linesman, but I like to think it was because of my age, with a lot of years ahead of me if it worked out. That's what John McCauley told me and I had to believe John.

I started refereeing junior A, my first experience outside of that cameo appearance where I tossed Pierre out of the game. It meant a lot of travel. For example, I might work Tuesday in Vancouver as a linesman. Wednesday in New Westminster as a referee, Thursday back in Vancouver as a linesman, then go down to places like Seattle and Portland and referee three or four games. In the East I'd shuttle between doing the lines in Pittsburgh or Buffalo and refereeing in Rochester or Johnstown. My last game as a linesman was New Year's Eve, in Buffalo, when they played an exhibition game against the Russians. For the balance of that season, my third with the NHL, I concentrated full time on refereeing in the minors and in junior A out West.

Back then we'd wear our NHL sweaters everywhere. Remember Perry Turnbull? He was a real tough guy and I was the referee the first time he played junior A. He saw my sweater and he was like, wow, we've got an NHL referee tonight. I signed a program for him. He lives three blocks away from me now, in St. Louis, and we play summer hockey together. He says, "I got your autograph in junior. I must have had rocks in my head." [Laughs]

The next year I got a full slate of American League games and did three rounds in the playoffs. The year after that I did the American League finals. In those two years I also did a few games in the NHL. My first game as a referee in the big leagues was New York Rangers in Washington. Four penalties. I worked with Bob Hodges and Leon Stickle. I was young, spry, and cocky. I grew a moustache to make me look older. So I work my first game with "Mr." Hodges and "Mr." Stickle and there's only four penalties. I got off the ice and they had champagne waiting for me.

That was a Wednesday. Then Hodgie and I went to Pittsburgh for a game Friday. Toronto was playing there and those teams had a big rivalry at that time. He takes me out to dinner on the Thursday and says, "Koho, you had a bit of a cakewalk last night. This game's gonna be a little different. You'll be calling a lot of penalties." I'm saying, "Yeah, sure. Four penalties. There's nothing to refereeing in this league. Let's have another glass of wine."

We get to the rink the next night and the first thing I find out is that Frank Udvari is there supervising and, suddenly, I'm a nervous wreck. He's the tough taskmaster. He hires people, he fires people, and he's gonna be watching me all night. The game starts, bodies are flying all over the place, they're whacking each other with sticks, and I'm not calling anything. I figure, a four-hitter last night, I'll try for a three-hitter tonight. There were about eight scrums with everybody pushing and shoving and I call nothing. At the end of the period Hodges grabs me and says, "Koho, you've got to start calling some penalties. You've got to get control. I'm whipped already. I don't know if I can go two more periods breaking up all this stuff."

In the second period, exact opposite. I call everything. If a guy steps on somebody's stick, tripping. I'm inconsistent, big time. Now, in the third period, I let almost everything go again. The score is tied 3–3 and with about two minutes to go I give Pittsburgh a penalty. After I make the call one of the Pittsburgh players comes charging right at me, bends his knees, and does a swan dive. Slides right by me head first into the boards, because he thought the Toronto player took a dive. So I give him two for unsportsmanlike. I've had the whistle in my pocket almost the whole period and now I've got Pittsburgh down two men with two minutes to go in a tie game. Greg Millen was their goalie and he must have made a dozen saves in those last two minutes and the game ends 3–3. The Pittsburgh crowd is ready to lynch me and I'm thinking, I go from four penalties in Washington to this. Take me back to Portland and Rochester where I'm comfortable. I'm not ready for this crap.

I go back to the room and I'm sitting there, not even starting to take off my skates, waiting for Udvari to come in. I was sure he was gonna send me to Siberia for at least the next two years. He comes in, walks into the bathroom, has a leak like he always did after a game, and comes back out. There's dead silence and we're all waiting for him to explode. He looks at me and says, "Kid, you've got balls," and walks out of the room.

I had made an agreement with Scotty Morrison that if refereeing didn't work out for me he would take me back as a linesman in the NHL. At the same time Susan and I made a decision that I could work another five or six years in the minors, until I was thirty, when we figured referees like Bruce Hood, Ron Wicks, Wally Harris, and Bob Myers would be getting to the end of their careers. But I was back in the

NHL, to stay, a lot quicker than we figured. Lo and behold, I worked my first Stanley Cup final when I was thirty.

That game in Pittsburgh, my second in the NHL, was a wake-up call that I was getting a little too cocky. I knew after that game I wasn't ready for a full shot. I needed more training and experience in the minor leagues. This business is so humbling. There is a fine line between confidence and cockiness.

You've got to go out there and look confident. If we go out like we're scared because it's a big game, the players get uneasy. We're like salesmen. I tell young referees the important thing is to portray confidence, to sell yourself to the players and the coaches. Even if you're shaking in your boots, let them know you're there to do your job, make things safe for everybody, and we're gonna have some fun. On the other hand, don't put yourself above the game because you're not above the game. Talk to players and coaches civilly, the way you'd want to be talked to. The players play the game and the coaches coach the game. We're just there to control it. Sure, we get pumped up for some games and the first thing you know your arm is up for a call because you've overreacted. But be honest. Tell the player that you made an error, that if you had it to do over again you wouldn't have called it. We're there to protect the players. They don't know the rules because they're not paid to know the rules. We are. We're paid to call penalties.

On May 6, 1988, Don Koharski refereed the third game of the Eastern Conference finals between the New Jersey Devils and the Boston Bruins at the Meadowlands, in New Jersey. Boston won 6–1 to take a 2–1 lead in the series. At the end of the game, the Devils' coach, Jim Schoenfeld, confronted Koharski in a hallway and, with television cameras and microphones recording the incident, shouted,

*among other things, "Have another doughnut, you fat pig!"
Schoenfeld was suspended for the next game. The Devils
then served the league with a restraining order granted by a
New Jersey judge allowing Schoenfeld to stay behind the
bench. When that decision came down just prior to the
fourth game, the officials assigned to handle it, referee Dave
Newell and linesmen Ray Scapinello and Gord Broseker,
refused to work. Amateur officials from the area were
brought in and, after a delay of one hour, the game was
played. The incident was a major embarrassment to the
NHL. The Bruins eventually took the series, winning the
seventh game 6–2, a game refereed by Koho.*

DON KOHARSKI

He was mad over two penalties I'd called, one late in the
second period that carried over, and another early in the
third that put them down two men. The score then was 4–1
for Boston and the Devils started running around a little bit.
To this day I don't know why it wasn't Harry Sinden who
was waiting for me. I gave Boston the last five penalties in
the game because they started retaliating for what they
thought Jersey got away with earlier. Jersey was on a power
play almost the whole third period.

When we were coming off the ice I told my linesmen that
Sinden's gonna be all over me for this one. Somebody said,
"Look over your shoulder. Schoenie's waiting for you." I said
we'd stay put for a minute and let him go down the hallway
to his dressing room but he wouldn't leave. So we started
down the hallway and that's when it happened. NBC was
there, ABC. There were reporters and cameras everywhere.
That line "Have another doughnut, you fat pig!" has stuck
with me ever since.

People ask me what was the highlight of my life in hockey, my most memorable game. I've done Canada Cup finals, like the game in '87 when Lemieux scored his famous goal against the Russians, a lot of big games. But my most memorable game was the year of the Schoenfeld incident, the seventh game, New Jersey at Boston. Back then, if you did the third game of a series, you did the seventh game if there was one. I remember coming out of the hearing in Boston when they told us about the restraining order and walking down the street with John McCauley and Ray Scapinello. I told John that if there was a seventh game, and I didn't do it, I was scared what it would do to my confidence. I told him I knew I could go in there and do it, I thrive on pressure. I love it. He said, "Could you do it?" And I said, "If it happens, please don't take me off the game." As it turned out there was a seventh game. John called me and said, "Koho, go to the Boston Garden and do your thing." New Jersey didn't quarrel with it. Schoenfeld said that if they'd asked him to pick a referee for a seventh game I would have been his guy.

The Garden was crazy that night. I skated out and everywhere I looked there were Dunkin' Donut boxes. People had them all lined up behind the glass, they were waving them at me from the seats, they had doughnuts hanging from their ears as earrings. It was wild. The game went off without a hitch. A great seventh game. I think we ended up with only four penalties. Four penalties and Dunkin' Donut boxes everywhere.

There's a good follow-up to the story. Schoenie lost his job in New Jersey, was a commentator on ESPN hockey games for a while, then got hired to coach Washington. Right after he goes there I get a game in Washington and it's on ESPN. It was the first time I refereed one of his games since the incident, although we'd seen each other. I played in some celebrity golf

tournaments that summer and in about five of them I ended
up on the same teebox as Schoenie. I'd always got along with
him. It was too bad that isolated situation had to happen. So
this night in Washington just as I'm set to faceoff I hear him
calling me over to the bench. I think, should I go, or shouldn't
I? One of the linesmen says to me, "Go on over. It'll be good
for hockey." So I go to the bench and he leans down and starts
whispering. I can't hear him so he leans closer and says,
"Stay here for a minute because ESPN wants us like this
for the opening of their show." I said, "You son of a bitch.
You conned me." But there we were, Koharski the doughnut
man and Schoenfeld. Crazy.

The best part of refereeing? The games. No matter what
kind of a day I've had, bad travel, whatever, when I get to the
rink it's exactly where I want to be. Just get me a coffee and
let's start the game. I can't wait because you never know
what might happen. One night I had a game in the old
St. Louis Arena when Detroit was there. Petr Klima was
with Detroit and the day before he had been arrested for the
tenth or twelfth time. This time it was for speeding but not
under the influence. The St. Louis papers had played it up
big that day. Petr's a good guy on the ice, likes to joke and
tell stories, but he can be a loose cannon. I'm standing on
the goal line, there's a line change, and Klima comes off
the bench and starts skating right at me at top speed. I'm
thinking, has this guy flipped out? Is he taking a run at me?
He keeps coming, full tilt, puts on the brakes about three
feet in front of me and sprays me with snow. He looks me in
the eye and says, "Hey, Koho, what's the speed limit out
here tonight?" I started to laugh. The linesmen comes over
and I tell him and he starts to laugh. We had a tough time
dropping the puck we were laughing so hard.

Our son, Jamie, is refereeing minor hockey in St. Louis.
He gave up playing for officiating and says he wants to be a

referee so you may have a Koharski to talk about for a long time yet. But his father isn't about to pack it in. I train every day now. Yesterday I was thirty-one pounds lighter than I was when the doughnut incident happened. I can tell you that today I thank Schoenie. I've lost all that weight. I quit drinking on my own. It put longevity on my career. Life went on and now I think I'm a better person and a better referee.

8

Like Grandfather, Like Grandson

PAUL STEWART

Hockey has always been a "family game." Brothers acts have been frequent, from the Patricks and Cleghorns of the early days through to the Bentleys, Richards, and Espositos of more modern eras. During a good part of the 1980s and 1990s it seemed that no matter what rink you were at there was a Sutter in one, or both, of the lineups. Cal Gardner, Butch Bouchard, and Bryan Hextall are old-timers whose sons became NHL players. And of course the Howe boys, father and sons, ended up playing on the same team.

The same can't be said of the officiating ranks. If Jamie Koharski becomes a referee in the NHL, it could be the first time a son followed in the footsteps of a refereeing father. Today, for the first time, there are two brothers blowing whistles in the NHL, referee Paul Devorski and his brother, Greg, who is a linesman. Their father, Bill, was a long-time referee in Ontario minor hockey, but Paul claims the *father's background had no bearing on the sons becoming officials. "I played junior hockey," he told me, "then started refereeing commercial-league games for beer money." I guess the officiating genes took over and he started doing it for a living.*

The only official in the NHL today who can claim a family link to a former NHL referee is Paul Stewart, a native of Boston whose grandfather, Bill Stewart, refereed in the 1930s and 1940s. Today, Paul Stewart is one of hockey's most talkative, colourful, and controversial officials, and I looked forward to getting together with him for this book. We did, and right away Paul started talking about his grandfather, who, in his day, was also talkative, colourful, and controversial.

PAUL STEWART

My grandfather was quite a guy. He refereed in the National Hockey League for fourteen years and at the same time he was an umpire in the National Baseball League where he worked for twenty-two years. I never saw him skate but I saw him throw a baseball. He used to give clinics and even late in his life he could throw a big curve ball and a spitball. He was 5'6", a solid barrel-chested guy. He was the light heavyweight boxing champion of the navy in the First World War and he once beat Jim Thorpe in a track meet. They were opposing anchors in a relay race and after they passed them the batons my grandfather beat him.

He coached baseball at Boston University. He turned Mickey Cochrane into a catcher and he went on to be a Hall-of-Famer. And he coached the U.S. national hockey team in 1957 and they had a record of 53–4. Most of the players on that team played on the American gold-medal team at the 1960 Olympics. We've got all the clippings.

I used to go with him when he gave speeches at sports breakfasts at the Catholic Church and at the Gridiron Club Dinner, which was a big event at the Statler Hotel, in Boston. My dad was usually there too. When it came to his officiating career, the story he used the most was about the night in Montreal when two fans jumped over the boards and came after him. There was no glass around the boards in those days. When the first guy got to him my grandfather hit him with a short right and he hit the other guy with a left hook, which was his whistle hand. The whistle cut the fan and there was quite a bit of blood. Then another fan leaned over the boards to get him and my grandfather hit him with an uppercut and knocked him out. My dad was at the game and, prior to his death, I took him to Montreal because he wanted to see the Forum again. We walked into the darkened arena and he pointed to a seat by the boards and said, "Right here is where your grandfather hit the guy and knocked him right out of his seat. Knocked him cold." He said the fans were waiting for my grandfather when the game ended so I asked him how they got out. He said, "I held his coat and he had his skates in each hand with the sharp edges exposed. We walked right through the people and out of the building and nobody went near him." My grandfather was one of the referees at the Forum the night they played the longest game ever. The Maroons and Detroit. They had a two-referee system then and they played into the sixth overtime period. The game ended about 2:30 in the morning.

In 1937 he was hired to coach the Chicago Blackhawks and they won the Stanley Cup the following spring. They played Toronto in the finals and before one of the games he had a fistfight with Conn Smythe in a corridor at Maple Leaf Gardens. Chicago was owned by Major Frederic McLaughlin, who was always changing coaches. He fired my grandfather New Year's Day the next season. How many men won the Stanley Cup the only time they coached for a full season? He went back to refereeing the next year. The president of the league, Frank Calder, offered him a hundred dollars per game. My grandfather said he'd be happy if they gave him a contract for five thousand dollars. Calder said he wouldn't do that because then they'd have to pay him if he got hurt. They paid him the hundred dollars per game and he worked fifty-four games, so my grandfather beat him for four hundred dollars. The only time he missed in fourteen years in the NHL was when he got cut in the arm and he was out about two weeks. In twenty-two years umpiring major-league baseball he only missed twenty days, with appendicitis. He was a resilient competitor.

An author's aside here: Bill Stewart was present on two occasions that are memorable for me. The first NHL game I attended was the second game of the 1938 Stanley Cup final when Chicago played Toronto, at Maple Leaf Gardens. I was six years old and my father was coaching the Maple Leafs. Paul's grandfather got the best of Dick's dad in that series. The first major-league baseball game I saw was at Wrigley Field, in Chicago, in 1947, the year Jackie Robinson broke baseball's colour barrier. Robinson was playing first base for the Brooklyn Dodgers, against the Cubs, and Bill Stewart was the home-plate umpire in the game.

When Paul Stewart finished talking about his grandfather I started to ask him, again, about his career as a referee. Not so fast, Dick. There were a few stories about Paul's playing career he wanted to tell me. A couple of items he didn't mention that I later checked: games played, 285, penalty minutes, 1,242.

PAUL STEWART

I played college hockey at the University of Pennsylvania. The other guys wanted me to drink beer and party all the time but I was more interested in working out and hanging around the rink because the Philadelphia Flyers practised there. Nobody would talk to me in the dressing room. I wasn't one of the guys, and by my senior year every day was an emotional wrench. I was an outcast. One day in practice I was standing in front of the net and this guy cross-checks me in the back of the neck. It cracked my third cervical vertebra. After three weeks, against doctor's orders, I showed up to play again. Before practice I went up to the guy who had hit me and said, "I'd just like to ask you why you hit me from behind. What did I ever do to you?" He said, "Screw you. I'm not here to be your friend." So, during the practice, I hit him a real shot in the chest with the point of my shoulder. I knocked him backwards and both his elbows hit the dasher. He dislocated his clavicle and separated his shoulder. A couple of his buddies came after me but I took care of them and then I yelled, "Anybody else want to try me?" Later, when I was alone, I cried. I just couldn't get along with those guys. That's when I decided to turn pro and a few days later I signed with the Birmingham Dusters in the North American League.

I played for a lot of teams in places like Rochester, Utica, and Cape Cod. The final count was eleven teams in six years, in six leagues. I played for Cincinnati in the WHA and for Quebec in the NHL. My dad had refereed college hockey in New England and I used to go to some of his games. Jack Kelley was a college coach and then he went to Hartford when they got a WHA team. He knew me because of my dad and before a game he told me to watch out for one of his players, Jack Carlson. I hadn't had a fight yet in the WHA but that night I fought Carlson toe to toe. It was punch for punch. We even switched hands. There was no hair grabbing or wrestling, just solid haymakers. We both had to be helped to the penalty box we were so tired. When we came out of the box, we fought again. Bill Friday was the referee and he said to us, "What have you guys been drinking, green beer?"

Quebec took me in a draft after the WHA folded and they went to the NHL. Jacques Demers was the coach. My first day at camp I got on an elevator in the hotel and there was Curt Brackenbury, Wally Weir, and Bob Fitchner, guys I'd fought in the WHA. They all moved to one side and gave me a look and you could tell there was no love lost. Then we got on the ice and scrimmaged and Weir and I started to fight about who would wear number 2. We fought about five times that day. When all was said and done I acquiesced and took 22.

I didn't make the team at camp but Jacques Demers brought me up for a game in Boston, Thanksgiving night, November 22, 1979. Robbie Ftorek had cut Bobby Schmautz in a game in Quebec and Jacques wanted me to keep an eye on Schmautz. Wayne Cashman and I had a little stick fight in the warm-up. In the game I ended up fighting Terry O'Reilly, Stan Jonathon, and Al Secord. After my third major I was automatically ejected and when I skated off the fans really cheered the hometown kid. It was all very exciting. I couldn't sleep the night before and I couldn't eat the day of the game. When I got to the hotel I knocked on Jacques Demers's door and kissed him, I was so grateful. That was my goal in life, to play an NHL game in the Boston Garden.

That same season Schmautz got traded to Colorado when Don Cherry was coaching there. We're playing in Denver and Schmautz went by our bench and I clipped him with an elbow. When I got on the ice he tried to spear me and we squared off with our sticks. Bryan Lewis was the referee and he finally threw us out of the game. Schmautz went off the ice at one end and I went off at the other. I was so mad at him I kept going down the hallway. He came around the corner and there I was, waiting for him. You should have seen his face. We sort of hacked at each other a little bit and then the police separated us and that ended that.

Now, finally, to Paul Stewart's career as a referee. He was colourful as a player, and he's been equally colourful as a referee. When we learn Stewart is working a game, media types go through the "nudge, nudge – wink, wink – say no more" Monty Python routine, like, what will he come up with tonight? Stewie has nights when he is showbiz in a striped sweater. Mario Lemieux accused him of that in the first week of Stewart's NHL career and was promptly thrown out of the game. Ten years later the beat was still going on when Stewart tossed Montreal forward Chris Murray after Murray said to him, "You sure know where the cameras are."

A few years ago I met Paul as I arrived at the arena in Tampa for a 7:30 game. He asked me, "Want a quick one, like around 10:00?" Not many games end as early as that and I replied it wouldn't be a bad idea. "You got it," said Stewie. After the game, same doorway, same guys meet, and the smiling referee said to the broadcaster, "What did I tell you? Was that fast enough?" The game had ended at 9:58.

Now to the question, How did someone who was a goon as a player wind up as a referee handing out penalties to goons? Paul Stewart is the only former NHL player now officiating in the league. (Another former NHLer, Kevin Maguire, is apprenticing in the American League as this is being written.)

After retiring as a player in 1981, Stewart tried a variety of jobs. He was a substitute teacher, a radio talk-show host, a high-school hockey coach, and a part-time employee of the police department in South Yarmouth, Massachusetts. His marriage of seven years had ended, and he was drifting. He decided he wanted to get back into hockey, so in July 1983 he picked up the phone and called Scotty Morrison, the NHL's referee-in-chief. Considering Stewart's admiration for his grandfather and father, both of whom were referees, it's surprising he waited so long to make the call.

SCOTTY MORRISON

When Paul Stewart called me he kind of caught me by surprise. I hardly knew him as a person but I knew of his reputation as a player and I had read a lot about his grandfather being a good referee and a good umpire. The first thing I said to him was, "Are you serious?" He said he was, so I said, "If I make arrangements to send you to a referees' school, will you go? We'll pay your costs." He assured me he would go, so I sent him to Bruce Hood's school in Milton. I was doing some instructing and I was able to watch him. Good skater. Very keen.

When that was over I said to him, "All right, I'm gonna bring you to our training camp." Paul is a very outgoing guy, and we had a lot of fun. We put him on our training program and the next year we hired him for the American League. In one of his first games two players drop their sticks and gloves and they're gonna go at it, but at first all they do is shadowbox. No punches are being thrown and I guess Stewie had enough, so he says, "Are you guys gonna fight? Because if you're not I'm gonna put this whistle in my pocket and beat the shit out of both of you." The players stopped and started to laugh.

The next morning I get a call from Jack Butterfield, the president of the league, and he tells me the story. I said,

"Come on, Jack. He wouldn't say something like that." He assured me that was exactly what he had said, so I called Paul. "Well, Mr. Morrison," he said, "they were just fooling around and wasting time. I guess maybe I did say that." I told him referees can't talk to players that way, and then I called Frank Udvari. I said, "Frank, when you're doing your next assignments, mark in Paul Stewart. I want you to go down and watch him, give him one of your Mark of Zorro discussions, and set him straight." We still laugh about that one. Paul was different but he's turned out to be a good referee. He advanced very quickly because of his determination and his temperament. He's certainly a player's referee, with a sense of humour, and it's nice to see development like that.

PAUL STEWART

When I played in Binghamton I was the property of the New York Rangers and I played for them in an exhibition game against Philadelphia. John McCauley was the referee. I had fights with Stevie Short and Bob Kelly on the same shift. I knocked Short down, picked him up by the hair, and hit him a couple more times. John threw me out for gross misconduct. A year or so later, after John suffered the eye injury that ended his officiating career, he was supervising a game in Binghamton. I got thrown out of that one too. I went around to see him to apologize for the trouble I'd given him in the Rangers game at a time when he was there mainly to get in shape. He said, "When you get through playing you ought to become a referee." I told him I'd think about it. Then I saw Scotty Morrison in Philly when I was playing for the Firebirds and I told him that when I finish I might become a referee. And he was the one I ended up calling.

I had tried to do some high-school and college officiating but they didn't want me because I didn't have any experience. One of the administrators, Brian Petrovek, told me because of my playing style I wasn't the type who would best exemplify the qualities of an official. We had played against each other in college so I told him, "The next time you watch me work you can pay to get in." Then I called Dale Hamilton, Harry Sinden's secretary, and she gave me Scotty Morrison's number.

I think the reason I went back to the game as an official was because I thought it was a noble profession and because the two people I admired most in my life, my dad and my grandfather, did it. And to do things at the top was always my life's recipe.

Three years after I started working in the minors I did my first game in the NHL and of course there were some interesting situations along the way. One night in the International League I was working a home game of the Salt Lake City Eagles. Between periods they had a contest where fans had to shoot the puck through a hole in a board to win a car. I came out to start the period and I could tell there was something going on. They told me a guy had shot the puck through the hole but it had stopped right on the goal line. Everybody was standing around saying they didn't think the puck was over the line so it wouldn't count for the car. I skated over to the net, kicked the puck in, and said, "Now it is." The general manager of the team was livid, but the owner, Art Tees, was happy as hell. The next morning my phone rings at 7:00 and it's Scotty Morrison telling me I had to apologize to the owner. I said, "Apologize? He thanked me about ten times last night. He said I'd just given them about a million dollars' worth of publicity."

I did an American League game between New Haven and Maine. New Haven was first in their division and Maine was last and Maine was winning the game. There was a fight and a Maine player brought his knee up, but then pulled it down. It may have appeared that he kneed the fellow but he never made contact. In retrospect I might have given him two minutes but there was no contact, no harm done. Robbie Ftorek was coaching New Haven and was angry. He called his team over and wouldn't let them line up for the faceoff. I warned him but he said, "No, I'm not putting my team out." The score was 3–1 or 4–1, and the game was almost over. The captain came over and I told him to tell his coach if he didn't put his team out I was gonna drop the puck and he said, "Ftorek doesn't think you have the balls to do it." I said, 'Is that right?' The Maine centreman was there and I said, 'Are you ready?' He said he was and I dropped the puck. He took it and shot it into the empty net. Did I get in trouble for that one!

My first NHL appearance as a referee was on March 27, 1986, and, as luck would have it, at the Boston Garden. It was also by accident. The Bruins were playing Montreal and first place was at stake. I was working in the AHL and IHL then and was at the game as a spectator. The referee, Dave Newell, collided with Mats Naslund and broke some ribs. John McCauley was there and asked me to finish the game. I get dressed and go out and, just after the puck was dropped, Ray Bourque shot it at Patrick Roy. I lost sight of it and blew the whistle a split second after Geoff Courtnall knocked it in. Here comes Bobby Smith, here comes Ray Bourque, and here comes my signal, no goal. I ruled I had blown my whistle before the puck entered the net. The game ended in a 3–3 tie and the Canadiens ended up one point ahead of Boston and had home ice when they met in the playoffs. Montreal won the Stanley Cup that year. I learned from that one to get to the net, hold the whistle as long as you can and, if you err, be honest. I told Bourque, "Ray, I made an incorrect call. I was quick on the whistle. I'm sorry." He said. "I'm sorry too but you'd better tell our coach because he's having a spasm." I told the coach, his spasm stopped, and I had my first NHL tough call for my files.

[*Note: Patrick Roy was in his rookie year and, the night before in Hartford, had started his trademark looking at his goalposts after the national anthem. As Roy told me for my book,* In the Crease: *"I made some good saves and we tied. We went to Boston the next night and I tried the same thing. We tied again. I got a good call from the ref, Paul Stewart, on a shot from Ray Bourque that I think went in. They didn't count it. After that I kept doing it."*]

The first week I was full time I gave game-misconduct penalties to Mario Lemieux, Wayne Gretzky, and Steve Yzerman. Three different games. Brian O'Neill called me and asked, "Are you having a problem getting along with superstars?" So I told him the stories. Lemieux told me he was the show, people paid to see him play and I wasn't a player. I said I had played and he said, "I hear you were a horseshit player and you're a worse friggin' referee." I told him if all the people there had paid to watch him they were going to have a hard time getting in the shower because that's where he was going.

Then I went to Hartford and after the game Gretzky handed me his stick. I asked him what that was all about and he said, "You might as well have it. You took it out of my hands all night." I told him he could have a game misconduct for that one.

The Yzerman game was in New York. A Detroit guy boarded Ron Greschner from behind and I gave a penalty. Yzerman protested the call and I ended up giving him two, ten, and a game. In my report I wrote that he questioned my ancestry, my sexual preference, and my right to eject him, so I awarded him "the whole ball of wax." I got a call from the league and they asked, "What's 'the whole ball of wax'?" The funny thing is, all three of them are wonderful guys. I think at that point it was just a question of them testing my mettle.

After my first year I refereed in the 1987 Canada Cup final. Canada against Russia. I had the second game, in Hamilton. Mike Noeth and Don Koharski had been picked for the finals. Noeth was an American and had some unfortunate circumstances in the first game. Koharski was a Canadian and not the obvious choice for the Russians for the second game. They hadn't even used me in our own playoffs after my first season. I was at training camp when John McCauley told me I would be doing game two of the series the next night. Dave Newell and Andy van Hellemond brought me to their room, we ordered up some lunch and sat around and talked. It was my first big game, pretty early in a guy's career for something like that, and it could make me or break me. Dave and Andy gave me good advice. They told me to keep my phone off the hook the next day, not listen to anybody, and in the game do what I did best, which was skate hard and be in position.

My brother Jimmy, who was stationed in Toronto with U.S. Customs, came with me. John D'Amico was one of the linesmen and the other was a Swedish guy. I took a shower before the game and D'Amico was surprised. I told him it relaxed me. I just wanted to be relaxed. Fran Rosa, a hockey writer from Boston, saw me in the hallway before the game and asked me if I was uncomfortable. I said to him, "To quote General George Patton: I'm the right man, in the right place, with the right tools to do the job."

It was a hell of a game, a hell of an experience. Mario scored the winner. That tied the series and he got the winner again late in the third period in the final game. Koho refereed that one. In my game I had an interesting challenge from Mike Gartner, who had been a teammate of mine in Cincinnati. Mark Messier, who was also with me in Cincinnati, was in the box with a minor. Gartner was killing the penalty and he bodychecked the Soviet goalie when he came out of his crease, thinking he was fair game. I gave him a penalty for charging. Mike challenged my interpretation and yelled, "I bet you're wrong!" I said, "For a hundred dollars, you're on!" At the end of the period I sent the rule book into the Team Canada room with rule 47 underlined, proving I had been right. Mike sent a hundred-dollar cheque to the Christian Children's Fund, which I thought was just great.

I'm more relaxed with the players today, more accepting of the fact that I can't dominate them. In the past I may have been little too intense. I called a penalty on Tie Domi this year, in Toronto, for tripping. The player never lost his balance and within two strides took a shot on the net. If I had to do it over again I would have sawed my arm off at the elbow. Later in the game I said to Domi, "I didn't like that penalty I called on you." He said, "Pretty brutal, wasn't it," and I said, "It was worse than brutal."

I don't know, what with all the money today, that players feel they can afford to be characters, let their hair down. But a few still do once in a while. A few years ago I did the opening game of the season in St. Louis. Before the game the Blues' stickboy brought me a package, all gift-wrapped, and there was a card on it that read, "Stew, enjoy the gift. Best wishes from Brett Hull." I opened it and it was an NHL schedule, in Braille.

I had four days off in Winnipeg and went to get a haircut and the barber told me I should tint my hair. My old teammate in Cincinnati, Bryan Watson, had told me my hair was getting grey and it didn't look good on TV. So I got the tint job. Calgary played there the next night and I've got different-colour hair. The game's on, I'm sweating, and Sandy McCarthy skates by and says, "Hey, Stew, what's all that brown gunk running down your neck?" That's where the tint job ended up.

Still with my hair, one time in New York I got it cut for four bucks by a Russian guy in a shop on Times Square. I fell asleep in the chair and he took so much off I looked like Forrest Gump. In the game that night Peter Zezel says to me, "New haircut, eh? Who did it?" I said it was a guy in Times Square and Zezel said, "See if you can get his name. Nobody should be allowed to do that to one of our friends."

When Tom McVie was coaching Washington there was a problem with the ice and I had to stop the game. He finally called me over to find out what was wrong and I told him they were fixing a hole in the ice. He said, "Do everybody a favour. Go jump in it."

I gave a player a penalty and he said, "Come on, Stewie, when you played you did that lots of times." I said, "Yes I did, and every time I did Bill Friday gave me a penalty. Sorry, have a seat."

I write a weekly column on officiating for a magazine and every month I have them print the five best questions people have sent in. One was, "Paul, when are you planning to retire? The games I saw you ref at New Jersey were the worst I had ever seen." It was signed, "John Buckman, via the Internet." I answered, "Gee, John, what type of answer do you expect from such an intelligent question? Should I turn the other cheek as the Lord told us to? Should I ignore it and hope you go away. Or should I hope that somewhere in the Internet there is a net they can get you with."

I also told him I have no plans to retire, and I don't. I still love to skate and the body contact with the players. Officials do bump into them once in a while. I still love coming out of the dark tunnel into the lights when the game starts, the music, the enthusiasm of the people. I love it when I make a good call and I'm in great position and the player knows he has a penalty. Same thing when they score and you signal the puck's in the net and they look at you and sort of nod and skate away. It gives you a wicked satisfaction.

I don't mind the travel. I'm single. I have a fern on my window ledge and that's it, that's all I have at home. When I work I have an obligation to the fans, the teams, and my linesmen to do my best. No excuses. The best advice Frank Udvari ever gave me was "Excuses are for losers." Having played, I know the players deserve my best because they're gonna give their best. Take a guy like Mark Recchi. I love watching him play because he's like a top. He winds himself up and goes a thousand per cent. Same with Kevin Dineen. I love watching a gritty kid like Kevin Dineen. The first time I did a game with the Canadiens Patrick Roy said to me, "You were my favourite Nordique." Things like that keep driving me.

There's a great camaraderie among officials. I was hurt this season, first time, and when I was home the guys called me. Leon Stickle, Gerry Gauthier, Kevin Collins. When my father passed away they all called me. It's a wonderful thing to have that kind of kinship.

Last year when I got my ten-year-service watch I said in my acceptance speech I appreciated it because it was a milestone telling me how far I had come, but it didn't tell me how far I had to go. It meant I was closer to the end than to the beginning. I'm not too psyched up about that. I know I'm getting older and eventually I'm gonna have to take that one last turn around the ice, head to the room, and that will be that. I don't look forward to that day. Until then, like always, I can't afford to have a bad night and I'll accept the challenge. I think it's that challenge that keeps bringing us back.

9

The Boys on the Cover

RON ASSELSTINE BOB HODGES
LEON STICKLE RON FINN

Bryan Lewis called the 1996–97 season "The Year of the Linesman." To prove his point there were four linesmen pictured on the front and back cover of that season's rule book, three on the front and one on the back. On the front were Ron Asselstine, Bob Hodges, and Leon Stickle, all of whom were scheduled to retire at the end of the season. On the back cover was Ron Finn, who was forced to retire during the previous season because of health problems. When he retired, Finn held the record for most games worked and was just twenty short of two thousand regular-season games. The four represented a total of ninety-seven years of on-ice service in the NHL.

The three active linesmen received a form of royal treatment from the league in their final season. They, and their wives, were invited to the All-Star Game in San Jose and they were allowed to pick some spots in their schedule, especially towards the end of the regular season. Some cynics, including the author, thought the NHL was trying to mend a few cracked fences with the officials in light of the 1993 strike and the ill will associated with Andy van Hellemond's retirement. The officials had also been upset when, early in his regime, commissioner Gary Bettman had the names on the back of their sweaters replaced by numbers. Bettman came to the NHL from the National Basketball Association, where officials are numbered but not named. When he instituted the same policy in the NHL, the officials were not pleased. Van Hellemond, the senior man, refused to wear number 1. There is no doubt when numbers replaced names fans lost a personal connection with the officials, especially the younger ones. Be that as it may, the boys on the cover deserved to be there because they were tried-and-true warriors throughout their long and distinguished careers.

Ron Asselstine turned fifty during the 1996–97 season, his twenty-fifth in professional hockey. A big, garrulous man who aptly fits his nickname "Bear," Asselstine spends much of his spare time doing volunteer work for the Children's Wish Foundation. One of his most vivid memories is being struck by Gordie Howe while working as a referee in the WHA. Another is tackling a fan who jumped onto the ice in pursuit of referee Bill McCreary during a game in Boston, January 28, 1989. Asselstine's impression of a linebacker on skates was a reminder that his first goal in life was to be a professional football player.

RON ASSELSTINE

I've lived in Guelph my whole life and as a teenager I was quite a good football player with the Brantford Bisons. We won the Ontario junior championship then went to Montreal to play N.D.G. and they killed us 52–0. I wanted to be a professional football player and in 1967 I got a tryout with the Montreal Alouettes. I thought I was a tough nineteen-year-old but I got my ass kicked by tough old veterans like Tony Pajaczkowski. Montreal has been good to me in my hockey career but it wasn't good to me in my football career.

I quit football right then and there. I might have been the tough guy on the block in Guelph but when you play against married men with families, you're not so tough. I was trying to take a job away from those guys and they were ready to hand me my head on a plate. It's the same thing I try to tell kids about hockey. Kids are stars in junior but they're just ordinary against the big boys. For every guy they might have knocked over in junior there's twenty waiting to cut their head off in the NHL. It's a totally different mentality.

I went home from Montreal dejected and proceeded to eat myself into oblivion. I weighed 235 when I played football and soon I was 280. I got married and kept gaining weight. By the time I was twenty-three years old I weighed 315 pounds and my blood pressure was through the roof. I was working in a factory and playing some part-time industrial-league hockey. I was a bit of a wingnut when I played and one night I got into a brawl and got my jaw broken. When I showed up at work with my eyes black and my jaw wired the boss asked me what I thought I was doing playing hockey. He was involved with hockey and was the one who first asked me if I would be interested in officiating. At that point I weighed 275.

I was pretty intense when I played sports and I didn't like officials. I played then the way I officiate now, with my game face on. I seem to be a pretty decent guy away from the rink but when I go on the ice I get a game face on. Sometimes they call me Dr. Jekyll and Mr. Hyde. I can be kind of miserable on the ice, but that's okay as long as the players know where you're coming from. Anyway, in the summer after I broke my jaw I put on another forty pounds. I guess that was when I finally decided I was obese. I was sort of at a dead end working in the factory and not very happy. We'd been married about a year and my wife was real concerned about my health. My doctor told me if I didn't lose about a hundred pounds I'd be dead by the time I was thirty.

My boss had put a bug in my ear about officiating and I found myself thinking about it. I called Jack Fisher, who was the head of the officials' association in Guelph, and he gave me a chance. That was twenty-eight years ago. As soon as I started doing it I loved it. The weight started coming off and I thought, Why didn't I do this sooner? I started feeling good about myself and the next thing I knew I was working university games. By then I'd lost about sixty pounds.

I went to the OHA's officials' camp. Hugh McLean was running it and he told me I had potential but I'd have to lose about thirty pounds because my ass was four feet wide. He didn't know where I was coming from. I'd just lost sixty pounds and he wanted me to lose another thirty. So I did. I went down to about 225 and I worked the OHA championships that year. The following year I worked the full OHA season and did the lines at the Memorial Cup finals. That was in 1972, the year Cornwall won it. It was in Ottawa, a round-robin format, and there were kids there that got to the NHL like Bob Gainey, Richard Brodeur, Al Sims, Mike Veisor, and John Wensink. Roger Neilson was coaching Peterborough.

The WHA was opening up that year and after the Memorial Cup Vern Buffey offered me a contract. So did the NHL. Buffey offered me $10,000 a year, plus $1,000 for the playoffs, which he guaranteed. That was what three- and four-year guys were making in the NHL. Scotty Morrison offered me around $7,200 with no playoff guarantee. Even though people were saying the WHA didn't have a snowball's chance in hell of lasting, the four-thousand-dollar difference was a lot of money in those days. I asked Scotty what he'd do in my position and he said he'd take the WHA's offer and that really surprised me. I asked him if the WHA went belly-up would he hold it against me and he said no, and he didn't. When the WHA folded in 1979 I went to his camp and fought for a job. When it was over he hired me, so Scotty Morrison is a man of his word.

I had a stint as a referee in the WHA but I'm not cut out to be a referee. It was at a time when some officials had been knocked over by players and manhandled in fights and they weren't suspending anybody. I was refereeing in Houston, Winnipeg was there, and it was mayhem. Winnipeg had skilled players like Hedberg and Nilsson and Hull and Houston was hacking away at them. It was akin to the old Philadelphia Flyers playing the Montreal Canadiens.

At the end of the first period it's 3–0 for Winnipeg, I've got Houston down about ten to one in penalties and I probably could have given them another ten. That was the time when Houston had the Howes, when Gordie was playing with his sons. At the start of the first period the old man hit Bill Lesuk with an elbow. It spun Lesuk's helmet around and he's looking out an airhole. I gave the old man a penalty and he came up to me and said, "These people didn't come here to watch you." He had his stick right across me so I gave him ten. The next thing you know he elbowed me in the ribs, right in the ribs. I tossed him out, gave him the nine of hearts. Now the chairs and bottles start coming down, they're throwing everything, and it's just mayhem for about five minutes. There was a canopy at one end of the rink and I went there with the linesmen because the stuff was just raining down. I'm standing there saying to myself, What am I doing here?

I went into the dressing room and told the linesmen, "Somebody else can do this because I don't want it. I'm not prepared to take this kind of shit to make a living." I told them I was going back to the hotel and have a drink because I'd had enough, and I started to take my skates off.

The two coaches came in, Bill Dineen of Houston and Bobby Kromm of Winnipeg, and they asked me what I was doing. I told Dineen his people were running around trying to hurt the two Swedes and that they almost broke one guy's arm. I told him if that was the way he wanted it, then he could get somebody else and shove the game up his ass.

The next thing you know, Bobby Hull comes in the room. I told him I was going back to the hotel to have a drink, then I was going home. He said, "Ron, listen. We've got a young league here, we've got a building full of people, and we need you out there. If you want to quit, do it tomorrow, but don't quit now. I'm asking you as a personal favour to finish the game." So I went back and finished the game. When it was over the press all came in and I let loose. I told them we had officials who were being verbally and physically abused by players and nothing was being done. I said the league was more concerned with filling the buildings than protecting the officials. As for the Howe family, I said I had the utmost respect for them but I wasn't being paid to babysit $250,000-a-year crybabies.

Naturally it was a big story because Gordie Howe was involved. Bud Poile was executive director of the WHA and when he called I told him exactly what happened. He said, "Relax. Go back to Guelph and stick your head in a snowbank for a week." I thought I was done. They held a meeting in Toronto and I said I didn't want to keep on refereeing, that I wanted to go back to the lines. At the time they needed refs, not linesmen, but finally the referee-in-chief, Bobby Frampton, called and said I could go back as a linesman. It

DIANE SOBOLEWSKI

Paul Stewart is the only ex-NHL player on the league's officiating staff.

DENIS BRODEUR

Penalty coming up, courtesy of Paul Stewart. Stewart's grandfather, Bill Stewart, was both an NHL referee and a National Baseball League umpire.

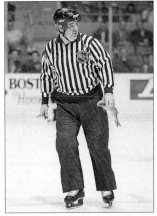

DIANE SOBOLEWSKI

Left and below: Ron Asselstine performing two essential tasks in Hartford: maintaining order and cleaning up debris. The debris, in this case, is a fish. "The Bear" was one of the NHL's best and most popular linesmen.

DIANE SOBOLEWSKI

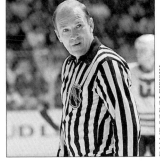

Linesman Bob Hodges overcame several serious injuries during his long NHL career. Hodges retired after the 1997 playoffs at the age of fifty.

DIANE SOBOLEWSKI

DIANE SOBOLEWSKI

Leon Stickle has restored order. Next stop, the penalty box. Stickle was one of the NHL's best and strongest linesmen during his twenty-seven-year career.

NATIONAL HOCKEY LEAGUE

A lot of smiles for the camera prior to a playoff game in the 1980s. Left to right: the late John McCauley, John D'Amico, Ray Scapinello, Dave Newell, Ron Finn, Andy van Hellemond, and NHL vice-president Jim Gregory.

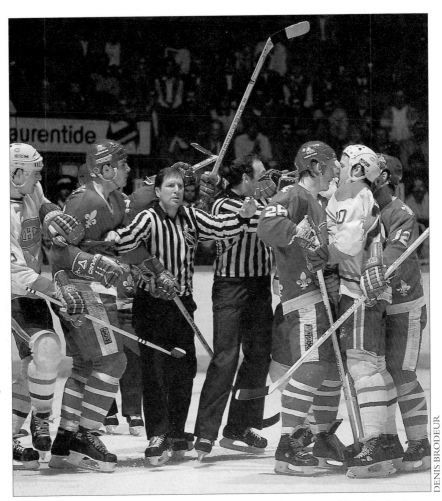

DENIS BRODEUR

Ron Finn could always tell you how many games he appeared in. His final total was 2,271 – including both league and playoff games. But he didn't keep track of how many fights he broke up.

NATIONAL HOCKEY LEAGUE

Terry Gregson was selected to referee the seventh game of the 1994 Stanley Cup finals and the Canada-U.S.A. championship game in the 1996 World Cup.

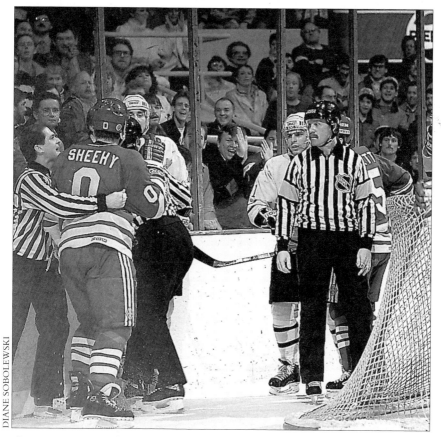

DIANE SOBOLEWSKI

Gregson was one of the first referees to wear a helmet. Here he's deciding if he should make a penalty call during a Whalers-Bruins game in 1988.

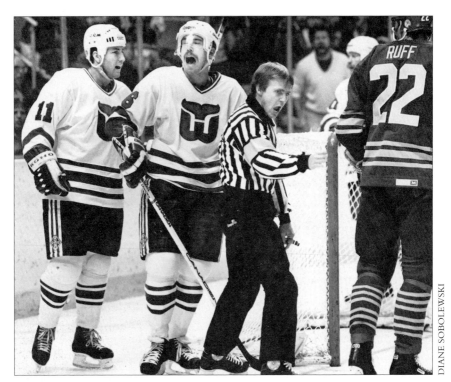

DIANE SOBOLEWSKI

Kerry Fraser making a call early in his NHL career. Obviously, Kevin Dineen and Ray Ferraro of the Hartford Whalers are not in agreement.

Fraser ready to drop the puck between Mark Messier and Vincent Damphousse to begin the first game played in the Montreal Canadiens' new home, the Molson Centre, March 16, 1996.

DENIS BRODEUR

NATIONAL HOCKEY LEAGUE

Gord Broseker worked the lines for the 1996 World Cup final between Canada and the U.S.A., and the 1997 Stanley Cup final between Detroit and Philadelphia. Broseker has worked the most games of any American-born official.

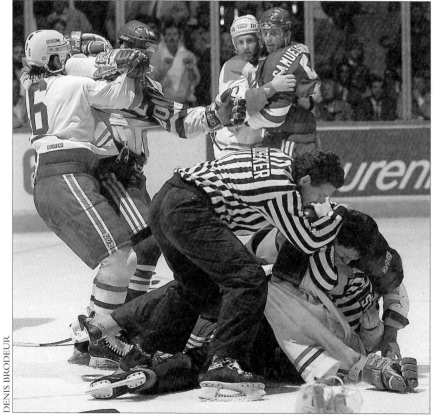

DENIS BRODEUR

Broseker helps sort out another player pile-up.

NATIONAL HOCKEY LEAGUE

NHL officials and supervisors at a training camp in 1996. A few veterans were away working the World Cup Tournament. Bryan Lewis, the director of officiating, is on the left in the front row.

DENIS BRODEUR

Getting together with Paul Stewart. We like to reminisce about the period when both Paul's grandfather (a referee) and my father (a coach) were in the NHL.

takes a very special person to be a referee and I just don't have the make-up. I was man enough to realize it and I've made a living and had some great experiences as a linesman for the past twenty-five years.

My first game in the NHL was in October of '79, in Pittsburgh, with Bruce Hood and Will Norris. But the first games that I considered special were in Maple Leaf Gardens and the Montreal Forum. I had worked at the Gardens when the Toros were in the WHA but it wasn't the same thrill I got in the NHL. I grew up watching Toronto and Montreal on TV and listening to their games on the radio before we had TV. All those great teams and great games. What a place the old Forum was. Every Saturday night was like the Super Bowl with everybody talking hockey, the papers full of it, the buzz around the rink. I'll never forget my first game there, walking down the hall and out onto the ice. I get goose-bumps talking about it even now. I'm a bit of a nostalgic slob anyway.

When that incident occurred in Boston and I tackled the fan, Bill McCreary was the referee and Mark Vines was the other linesman. It was an afternoon game. The Bruins had a good team with Ray Bourque, Steve Kasper, Glen Wesley, the Crowder boys. Andy Moog was in goal. They were playing Winnipeg, who had nothing, but for whatever reason the Bruins don't show up and Winnipeg takes a 4–0 lead. Boston mounts a comeback and late in the third period it's 4–3. Glen Wesley got tangled up with Paul Fenton and Wesley got clipped. It was an accident but Wesley got cut. Terry O'Reilly was coaching Boston and they're going goofy. They want a five-minute major and all that, but there was no call.

The faceoff was in the Winnipeg end and I'm about fifteen to twenty feet down the boards from the bench. The gate is open and O'Reilly is standing there yelling at me. He got my attention but I just waved my hand at him like, shut up and close the door. I turned back and I see this guy running on the ice towards McCreary. Bill's got his back to him and all I can think of is that there's a guy on the ice and he's gonna sock the referee. So off I go after him, and when I caught up to him he was almost at McCreary. I called on some of my old football experience and I just lowered the boom. I got him from the back and we were airborne, right into the end boards. *Crash.*

By then Mark Vines had come over and we proceeded to grab him by his hair, and his legs, and the ass of his pants, and out he went. We fired him right through the door where the Zamboni came out. Of course he got an ambulance chaser and wanted to sue me, and the league, and the Boston Garden, everybody. But it never went anywhere.

I don't know if he did it on a dare, or what, but anybody that comes on a hockey rink has got to be nuts. Remember the time in Quebec when the fan jumped into the Buffalo bench and Rob Ray hung a beating on him? That guy did it on a dare. One of his buddies bet him he wouldn't jump into the Sabres' bench. I was there. Kerry Fraser grabbed me and told me I wasn't going anywhere and I agreed because Ray was doing real good. I tell people, there are forty-three guys out there when a game is on, twenty players on each team and three officials, and we've all earned the right to be there. I earned it with my sweat, blood, and guts. So did the other officials and the guys who are playing.

If you pay fifty or sixty bucks for a seat you can yell and scream all you want, but if you come down on that ice surface you're taking your chances. Of the forty-three guys there may be forty who wouldn't do anything, but there'll be three who might clean your clock. Know something? That day in Boston I thought, here's my chance. I can get back at all the fans who have ever berated an official. I can get it all back in one shot, so I did.

When I refereed I took the game home with me all the time and that's one of the reasons I realized I couldn't live that way. But you do worry when things don't go right. There's many nights I've lain awake thinking, why did I do this, or why didn't I do that? You think about all the things you're taught from the time you get into officiating. Sometimes the system breaks down and we make errors. The other night, in Hartford, Vancouver is there and it's a good game. They're banging and crashing and it's intense. Mogilny gets a breakaway and I go to cover the net because the referee was trapped deep. Sean Burke makes the save and shoots the puck into the corner. It hits me on the leg, bounces out in front of the net, and Vancouver puts it in. One assist for Ron Asselstine. Burke looked at me, I looked at him. I felt terrible. I don't care who wins or loses, but when I become part of the process I don't feel very good about it.

When a fight starts and two players are evenly matched you allow them to fight. We don't jump in right away for our own personal safety. If I stick my nose in while they're still flailing away I might get it broken. I always yell, "Have you had enough? Have you had enough?" You can see. They'll usually look at me, shake their heads, and keep throwing them. Then the fire will go out of their eyes and we'll go in. Nine times out of ten they're played out. You just grab them around the arms and make sure nobody comes over the top and suckers the other guy over your shoulder. The referee never tells us to move in and break it up because between periods I'll tell him to mind his own business. I've told a few, "If you were doing a better job maybe we wouldn't have to break up fights all night." That conversation has gone down. Breaking up fights is a linesman's domain. But if you have a mismatch you have to get in quick. You can't allow a big tough guy to beat up on a smaller player.

I just turned fifty and this is my final season. I'm gonna miss being around young people because when you're working with them it keeps you young, keeps your outlook young. My age is fifty but I don't feel fifty. One time a player was giving it to me and I said, "How old are you?" He said he was twenty, so I said, "You know something? I've got a twenty-two-year-old son at home and if he ever talked to me the way you're talking to me, I'd slap him right in the face."

I still don't tire of seeing a young player score his first goal in the National Hockey League and go berserk because he knows his parents are back home watching. Or when a guy plays a great game. The other night in Montreal Saku Koivu threaded a pass right through a Tampa player's legs. Gerry Gauthier was behind him and he said to me, "Ron, that puck went exactly where he wanted it to go." That's the type of thing I like.

But with it all is the travel, and the aches and pains. My knees are shot. But I'm a lucky guy. I've spent half my lifetime doing something I really love, watching great hockey players, meeting wonderful people. Now there's a new generation of players, executives, and officials and I'm an old warhorse. It's time for me to move on and let the young guys take over. I know when the training camp opens in September, that's when it will hit me. After a life like this you can't help but miss it. Not when you love it as much as I have.

Bob Hodges is one of the few former goaltenders who became an official. Hodges quit playing hockey after junior C and began refereeing minor hockey games in 1968 still wearing his goal skates. Eventually he learned how to get around on regular skates and a couple of years later his work in the OHA impressed Frank Udvari, who hired him to work weekends in the American Hockey League. His full-time job was in a machine shop in Hespeler (now Cambridge), and while the extra money was handy, the workload was a bit much.

BOB HODGES

On Friday mornings I'd punch a clock at 7:00 in the morning and leave at 11:00. I'd go home, kiss my wife goodbye, and go to the airport. In those days I could be flying to Boston, Cleveland, Richmond, Tidewater, any-where. I'd work games Friday, Saturday, and Sunday nights, fly home Monday morning, put in another forty-hour week at the machine shop, and do the same thing the next weekend. During the week I'd work one or two games in the OHA. In those days I had to do that. I was newly married and had a family on the way. That's how things worked.

At the end of that season I had worked fifty-two games in the AHL plus two playoff games. Then it was back to the machine shop, back to reality. That was in 1972. The NHL was adding two more teams, Atlanta and the Islanders, and I knew they would need more officials. The unfortunate part was that I was twenty-eight years old. The machine shop had me on a repetitious job running a lathe and I kept asking myself, Is this what I'm gonna do the rest of my life? One day in July, just before my two weeks' vacation, I asked the boss if I could use his phone and I called Frank Udvari at his house. When he answered I told him who I was and then said, "I need a job." He asked me if I was out of work and I told him no, but I wanted to work full time as an official. I said, "I think I'm good enough." He said he couldn't really answer me because he wasn't the boss, Scotty Morrison was, but he'd look into it.

A couple of weeks later I got a letter inviting me to their training camp. So I saved my two weeks' holiday and went to the camp. There were all these young guys there and some of them were pretty cocky. I'm kind of a low-key guy myself and some nights they'd get the best of me. I worked hard and had a good camp. When it was over Scotty spoke to the group and at the end said, "Okay, everybody have a good year. Now, I want all the rookies to stay behind." There were about twenty rookies and I was the oldest. We're all sitting in the room and they started calling out names, alphabetically. Each guy would go in to see Scotty and you could tell when he came out whether he got a job or not because either he had a big grin on his face or he looked like somebody just gave him a good boot in the ass.

Finally I hear "Hodges." I go in and Scotty says, "Frank told me you did a pretty good job for him last year, but you're twenty-eight years old." I thought, here it comes: thanks a lot but you're too old. Then he says, "We're going to take a chance. We think you can do the job for us. Would you like to be a linesman in the NHL?" I was so shook up I could hardly talk, but I managed to say, "Most definitely." Then came the part I'll never forget. He slipped a piece of paper across the table at me. My contract. When I picked it up he pointed to a line at the bottom and said, "Just sign it, right there." When I started to read it he asked me what I was doing and I told him I don't sign anything I don't read. He keeps telling me to sign it and I keep looking for the dollars and cents and I finally see $8,000. I was making $8,000 in the machine shop. I told Scotty if I was gonna give up being home every day after work as opposed to being on the road for two or three weeks at a time, then I wouldn't sign it. Scotty had a short fuse and he just exploded. "What do you mean you can't sign this? Don't you want the job?" I told him I did, but that was my position. So he took the contract, put a line through the eight, wrote nine, and said, "Will you sign now?" I said, "I certainly will." And I signed my first NHL contract for $9,000. He looked at me and smiled and said, "You and I are gonna have problems. I can see that." And that's how I got started.

I used to watch games on TV and criticize the officials. I never dreamed I'd be on the ice with guys like Art Skov, Neil Armstrong, and John D'Amico. It was a thrill for me. Now that I'm in my last year people are asking me about my most memorable games. One of the toughest was the one in Montreal when the Canadiens and Quebec had the big fight in the playoffs, on Good Friday. I was working with Bruce Hood and John D'Amico. I have a picture of that one on my wall at home that was in *Sports Illustrated*. It shows me holding up Chris Nilan, who pretty well started the whole thing, him and Dale Hunter. We had things calmed down at one point and then Nilan went after Randy Moller and suckered him, opened him up, and that started the whole thing really going. I remember going to the dressing room when we finally got them off and thinking it was a godsend because we'd have time to sort things out and decide who we were gonna throw out. But somebody rang the buzzer for the teams to go back before we had told them who was being thrown out. We weren't ready. The players were skating around and when they started to announce the penalties and all the game misconducts they started to fight again, even before we dropped the puck to start the period.

A lot of people don't realize this but there is no job description in the rule book which says a linesman has to break up a fight. It's just part of our job. In a brawl like that one in Montreal, what you're trying to do is control mayhem. That night I never left Nilan because I knew the type of player he was. I knew Moller wasn't coming back because he was hurt pretty good but Chris kept trying to go from one pile to another. He kept yelling, "Let me go! Let me go!" There were fights here and fights there and John kept running from one brushfire to another and I'm thinking, Why are you doing this? You're gonna put out one and when you leave it's gonna flare up again. Grab somebody, stay with him, and watch what happens.

I won't go charging into a scrum any more because nine times out of ten it's push-shove, push-shove, yelling and swearing. As soon as the linesmen get there they're really gonna get at each other because now, here comes the judge, and they're really gonna look tough. I've told players if you're gonna fight, then drop the gloves. If not, get out of here, and nine times out of ten they'll look at you, like, is this guy serious? And they'll quit because they realize you're not gonna stop them. Mind you, you have to pick your spots. You don't say that to Tie Domi or somebody you know has been hired to be an enforcer. They'd take advantage of that situation, I'm sure.

Things have changed in hockey between players and officials. Back in the '70s, if you had a confrontation with a player there would be a few f-yous back and forth, and that was it. I can remember getting into it with Stan Mikita when I was just starting, and Phil Esposito. Five minutes later it was forgotten. You might see the guy after the game and have a beer with him. The run-in you had wouldn't even be discussed. Now you have to be careful. You're not supposed to swear at the players. Maybe it's because of the TV coverage, the cameras are on you a lot more. But we have to police ourselves because the players will run and squeal on you. It's an emotional game and to relieve the stress you used to tell a guy to go screw himself. It was man to man, and then it was forgotten. Today you might get a phone call – Did you say such-and-such to so-and-so? – and get reprimanded and even fined.

The respect is not there like it used to be and maybe money has a lot to do with it. We've had players make comments like, "You're only making sixty a year. Who do you think you are?" I had a guy one night who had been in the league one year say to me, "You're the best, eh? Yeah, you're the best." You never heard things like that back in the '70s. You never knew a player who had been in the league one year was even on the ice unless he scored a goal because he never opened his mouth. It's different now and it's the money, I'm sure.

Injuries? I don't know if you've got enough tape to put them all down so I'll tell you about the more serious ones, on and off the ice. The worst on the ice happened in Boston. A fight broke out and two guys were going at it pretty good. One of the guys got spun around and he was airborne. I put my hands up to protect myself and his skate caught the back of my hand and tore it open, cut the tendon across the back. I was knocked down and when I went to get up I looked at my hand and all I could see was bone. Dan Canney was the Boston trainer and when he saw what happened he jumped on the ice and took me off as soon as he could. The fight was still going on so the other linesman, Bob Luther, was on his own.

Dan took me to the medical room and as soon as the doctor saw me he said, "Get this man to the hospital. His tendon is severed." Frank Udvari was supervising the game and he came in and I remember him saying to the doctor, "Is he gonna be ready for tomorrow night?" I was supposed to work in Atlanta the next night. The doctor said, "This man isn't going anywhere for about six weeks." Frank looked at my hand, turned white as a sheet, and left the room.

Thank God it happened in Boston because they took me to a great hospital. The surgeon did a helluva job because he put in about fifty stitches and you can hardly see a scar. I woke up in the room and the nurse said, "You must be somebody special." I asked her why and she said, "Because this is the room Bobby Orr had." It had a fireplace, right in the hospital room.

I was in hospital three days and the first visitor I had was Don Cherry. Grapes was coaching the Bruins and his son, Tim, was in the same hospital with a kidney problem. Grapes is there visiting with me and says, "By the way, Hodgie, have you still got your beeper?" In those days we wore beepers for the TV commercials and I always pinned mine on my suspenders. It was still there. Back then the teams owned them. So Don got his beeper back and I always wondered if he was more concerned about me or the beeper. [Laughs] Scotty flew my wife Gail down to Boston so she could come back with me. They told me six weeks but I was back in four. I had to wear a plastic cover on the hand for quite a while, but it's pretty good now.

I've had two back operations. Bob Myers lives about twenty-five minutes from me and one summer I was at his farm helping him hay. I was in the loft throwing the bales up to Bob. Those things weigh about eighty pounds and when I threw one I felt something pop. I went down and couldn't get up. They finally got me into the house and I spent the night there. The next day I couldn't get out of bed. We called Scotty Morrison and he arranged for the Maple Leafs' doctor, Dave Hastings, to look at me and he ended up taking out a disc. That was in late June, or early July, and I wasn't able to go back to work until January.

My back was all right for a while, then I had a second accident. I was in Toronto for an exhibition game and I was on the floor before the game stretching when suddenly it felt like someone had just stuck a knife in my back. There was a big noise, *crack*. John D'Amico was in the room – he was supervising then – and his eyes got big and he said, "What was that?" I told him it was my back and he ran for the doctor. They told me not to work the game but by then I was feeling a bit better so I did it. But the next morning I had no feeling in one leg and I knew I was in trouble. So there I was, back in hospital again. I was there about three weeks and after I got mad at them because nothing seemed to be happening they finally took some tests and then decided to operate. They took about a third of the vertebra out just above where I had had the disc removed and it's been fine ever since. Oh sure, I have back pain every game, but it's something I've had to live with.

Everybody is in better physical shape today, the players and the officials. I mean, you never used to see players riding a bike after a game but now lots of them do. I maintain you can fine-tune yourself a little too much. We've got officials who do it. Before all this conditioning, guys weren't getting hurt as much as they are now. I've never lifted a weight and I don't intend to start now. This year I wrote a letter of commitment telling them I wanted to work one more year because it would be my twenty-fifth. I worked hard in the summer and when I came to camp I had one of the best fitness tests of the whole crew, and I was the oldest. Bryan Lewis used me as an example to some of the younger guys, telling them an old guy like me shouldn't be showing them up. Sure, I've slowed down a bit. It's the old story, you use your head to save your legs. You can cheat a bit and still be in position to make your calls. I'm pretty proud that I'm still doing this at my age. The magic number used to be forty-five. I'll be fifty-three when I retire.

The finals are the ultimate for an official and I've done them three times. We have some guys who are there every year and more power to them. We're rated and sometimes maybe I think the rating system isn't right because I should have been there instead of the other guy. That's human nature. I worked the All-Star Game this year with Ron and Leon because we're retiring and that was a nice gesture. And, unbeknownst to us, they put us on the cover of the rule book. We're going out in a bit of style and I appreciate the way the league has handled this.

I'm prepared for retirement. I'm not gonna have to worry where my next meal is coming from. I've looked after things and I've never really changed my lifestyle from the time Gail and I were married. We have a cottage up north that we bought two summers ago, right on the tip of Algonquin Park. I love to hunt and fish, so I'm kind of looking forward to it. And I won't miss the travelling. Not at all.

"I know eventually you're gonna get to the 1980 thing," said Leon Stickle as I turned on my tape recorder for our chat in the officials' room at the Molson Centre in Montreal. And, of course, I did. Even as he worked through his twenty-seventh, and final, NHL season, the "1980 thing" was, obviously, still on Stickle's mind seventeen years later. In the realm of incidents in an official's career, this one is a ten. It shouldn't have to haunt someone who was as good at his job as Leon Stickle, but it comes with the territory.

I did get to 1980 on tape, eventually, but in print we'll get to it right now. On May 24, 1980, the New York Islanders defeated the Philadelphia Flyers 5–4 to win the Stanley Cup at the Nassau Coliseum. Islander fans remember it as the game Bob Nystrom scored the Cup-winning goal, in overtime. Philadelphia fans remember it as the "Offside

Game," because of an offside that wasn't called by lines-
man Leon Stickle.

LEON STICKLE

Of all the Stanley Cups I worked that series was probably
the toughest, physically and mentally. The teams had no
regard for each other at all. The Islanders were on their way
up and that was the first of their four straight Cups. The
Flyers still had some players left from their Cup-winning
teams in '74 and '75 and that season they set a record by
going thirty-five games without a loss. I remember the
intense divisional games those teams played all season. The
finals were tough, tough, tough hockey. We were dealing
with players like Mel Bridgman, Clark Gillies, Bob Nystrom,
Bobby Clarke. Pat Quinn coached Philadelphia, Al Arbour
was with New York, and the Flyers had completely intimidated New York, in Philly, in game five. Beat them 6–3 and
there was a big fight near the end of the game.

Ron Finn and I worked as a team in that series and we
had the second, fourth, and sixth games. Bob Myers refereed game six and the first period was just unbelievable.
Almost every stoppage in play was called because of something physical. There were all kinds of penalties. [Fifty-
four minutes total.] It was great spectator hockey but very
tough to officiate.

As for the play in question with me, it was in the first
period and the score was tied 1–1. Clark Gillies carried the
puck into the Philadelphia end. He and Bridgman got into a
schmozzle along the boards four or five feet inside the blueline. Gillies dropped the puck back and I turned, for what
was probably a half-second, to watch them. The puck went
out over the blueline. By the time I went from watching
the two players to where the puck was, Butch Goring had

carried it back inside the blueline and was making a pass across the ice to Duane Sutter. He took a shot that hit either the post or the crossbar and went into the net. One quarter-inch the other way and I'm saved.

At the time nobody said a word, no griping from the bench or anything, but by the time I picked the puck up about three Flyers had me kind of half-assed pinned in the net. I knew right then we had a problem. A few minutes before that Denis Potvin had scored the second goal of the game with what might have been a high stick. It wasn't a glorious time.

I did not know the play had been offside until the end of the first period. Frank Udvari was supervising the series and he came down with Scotty Morrison and asked me what I had seen. By then they knew because they had seen all the replays. What was the first line in the book, *Tale of Two Cities*? "It was the best of times, it was the worst of times." I have to accept the fact that I made a mistake. I admitted it immediately to the press and everybody else. You have to go on. The next year they were selling a whistle in Philadelphia that had on it, "I blew it on Long Island," plus my name.

I got on a plane right after the game and flew to Toronto. I had about a ninety-minute drive home and by the time I got there the news had circulated. We live in a small town. Any time I tried to forget it that summer it was always brought up. I do a lot of stuff with the Special Olympics and different charities and I'd go to golf tournaments and somebody would want to talk to me about it. I never really got away from it for another five or six years. I guess people finally got tired of talking about it. I know I got tired hearing about it.

Scotty Morrison didn't assign me to a game in Philadelphia again until the next season was about half over. I arrived at the airport in the morning and I'll never forget the headlines. There had been some kind of an election there the day before but, still, the main headline was: "STICKLE RETURNS TO THE SPECTRUM." They were ready for me. The league had extra security set up in the building. We always used to go upstairs to the lobby before the game to get a coffee but Scotty, and the security people, told me not to go. The other guys could but I was to stay by myself in the room, which I did. Wally Harris was the referee and Ron Asselstine the other linesman.

As I sat in the room by myself I was nervous and wondering what the hell was going to happen. Has somebody out there got a gun? They have very intense fans in Philly. I was told not to answer the door, but when somebody knocked I said, what the heck. A priest, Father Casey, was always coming around in Philly and it was him. When I opened the door I said, "Jesus Christ!" He said, "Not quite, Leon. I just came down to wish you luck."

Finally we skate out and as I circled around the rink they stood up and booed me, section by section, and this was before the wave started. I had grown a moustache the previous summer and on the penalty-box side of the rink they had a big poster of me with the new moustache and it said, "WE STILL KNOW WHO YOU ARE." I have that poster now.

The game started and I was sure it was gonna be the longest three hours of my life. They didn't stop booing for the whole game. I can go along with that. I'd been involved with something they didn't like that had happened against their team. But a minute into the game Asselstine trips going in on an icing and hits the boards. I thought he was knocked out. He wasn't, but he did have a wee nick above his eye. Ron doesn't like the sight of blood, if it's his own. If he wears red underwear he thinks he's bleeding to death. As he's down we're crowding around and nobody wants to stand near me because they figure somebody's gonna come out of the stands and shoot me. I'm saying to Ron, "Get the hell up. I'm gonna get killed standing here." He got up, and the game went on, and there were no incidents. I got through it, and I'm still going.

Believe it or not, I go into Philadelphia now and I'm still the guy that lost the Stanley Cup for them in 1980. It's not just the people who were around at that time. Now it's their children who are yelling at me. There's one guy and you can hear his voice more than anyone else's even if there are nineteen thousand people in the building. He's still after me, even in their new building. If there's anyone in the rink who doesn't know the story, they do by the time this guy's done with me. It's got to the point where, if I don't hear him when I go on the ice in Philadelphia, I wonder if he's sick or if he's got a problem with his family. It's part of the thing now, I guess.

In my research for this book I heard a lot of nice things about Leon Stickle's work from his peers. Stickle was born in Toronto in 1948 but did most of his growing up in nearby Milton. Another aspiring junior hockey player who turned to refereeing around the age of twenty, Stickle was scouted by the ever-present Frank Udvari. After a very brief professional apprenticeship, he joined the NHL for the 1970–71 season.

LEON STICKLE

I've always been a linesman. I had aspirations to referee when I was younger but I was up against the likes of Bill Friday, Ron Wicks, Lloyd Gilmour, John Ashley, and Art Skov. It was gonna be a long road and, besides, I needed the money more as a linesman at the NHL level than at the minor-league level as a referee. After the first couple of years I gave up on the idea of being a referee, especially after I worked playoff games. This is my twenty-seventh season and I'm happy with the career I've had.

I did my first game in Pittsburgh with Ron Ego and Art Skov. I remember thinking if I got through my first game I'd get through the whole year. I don't think I heard the anthem for my heart beating. I got through that night and then flew to Detroit for a game the next night. Now I'm on the ice with players like Gordie Howe and Alex Delvecchio, players I had been admiring on TV for a long time. I found out very quickly that night that it's a lot different watching them on TV and taking abuse from them as an official. Lloyd Gilmour was refereeing and he used to kind of let things dangle. I was breaking up scrums and thinking that, a few months before, I had been doing the same thing only with juniors when Montreal played Regina in the Memorial Cup final. Big difference in a short time.

Bruce Hood and I are both from Milton and he was always one of my boosters. I worked my first playoff game with him and was also with him the first time I worked the last game in the Stanley Cup finals. That was in Boston when Montreal beat the Bruins. I'd worked playoff games but I had never been on the ice when the Cup was actually won. I remember the feeling, leaning against the penalty box in the old Boston Garden seeing the presentation. Bruce was standing beside me and I thought we'd come a long way for a couple of kids from Milton.

Stan Mikita was probably the greatest pure faceoff winner of any centre I saw. I don't know if he had that little special thing that he knew when you were going to drop the puck or if it was just pure skill. I remember the first time I dropped the puck between him and Jean Béliveau. I tried to look cool but inside I couldn't believe that I was on the same ice surface as they were. Béliveau was so classy.

I learned about intimidation of officials when I was a linesman for the first time, in a junior-B game. You always had guys that ranted and raved on the bench. It's still there. I've gone through Scotty Bowman when he was that way as a young coach to a very placid Scotty Bowman now. When he was in St. Louis he was downright irritable. Mike Keenan was tough on officials, and so was Jacques Demers. But Demers was kind of funny tough. You could always say something to Jacques to get a little bit of a laugh out of him. Michel Bergeron was one of the biggest showmen who ever coached in the NHL. I don't have any background in French and lots of times I didn't know what he was saying but he could certainly put on a show. Pat Burns was another showman. He was the same person in Toronto he was in Montreal. He was one of those coaches who went after the officials to try to fire up his players. I think with him there were a couple of times I might have been fired up myself. One thing about Pat, you could pretty well say back to him what he said to you and he would accept it.

Doug MacLean is probably the most vocal coach in the NHL right now, the most intimidating to officials, although maybe not as intimidating as he thinks he is. His team, Florida, had Brian Skrudland as captain. [*He has since been signed by the New York Rangers.*] You can talk to him on the ice, tell him that if his coach doesn't shut up the team's gonna suffer. With other guys you can say the same thing and have a real problem. By the time the message is delivered the whole meaning has changed. The wire service in this league is very fast and very small. I try to think a bit more now about what I say and some nights I have to bite my tongue.

The only time I've been hurt in a fight was in Buffalo. Bob Gainey, believe it or not, was involved and it wasn't much of a fight. But Gainey got flipped and his skate came up and severed the tendons in my hand. Same thing that happened to Bob Hodges. But the worst was when I missed a year of my career. It was on the Island when they played New Jersey. I got caught in the bottom of a pile up with my leg in a precarious position. My knee was wrecked. That was in December and I didn't come back until the following November.

I never hated a bicycle so much. It was a real mind game. Like anyone in the game – officials, players, coaches, broadcasters – I'm programmed. You leave home September 1 and you hope you'll be going all the way to the finals the next June. But there I was, home for Christmas, and New Year's, and Valentine's Day, and Mother's Day. It was just something I wasn't supposed to be doing. After I had the surgery it never entered my mind that I wouldn't want to come back, but I wondered if I could come back. But time heals, and so does your body, which is an amazing thing. Maybe I shouldn't be here but, five or six years later, I still am and I'm enjoying it.

The game today seems to be much more of a panic game than it was when I came in. I think of those Montreal teams in the '70s with their speed, and their skill at passing. Now it's get the puck, and get rid of it. They use the glass to clear on a shorthand situation, which they never did before. The puck is up around your head all night. We've heard about the neutral-zone trap the past few years. I still don't know what the hell a neutral-zone trap is. But I do see goal scorers having to play a more defensive style, which takes away what got them to the NHL. It's still the greatest game in the world, but it's tightened up a lot.

What I'm going to miss most is the guys I work with and the friends I've made on the road. I'm an avid golfer and there's that to look forward to. I wish some of the cities in the league now, in the warm-weather spots, had been there a while ago. I'm fortunate to have been doing something for a long time that I love to do. Right now I'm enjoying each game as it goes. I've had a very nice season.

The action shot on the back cover of the NHL's 1996–97 rule book is of a perspiring, intense-looking Ron Finn with the caption: "Linesman Ron Finn's NHL career spanned a league-record 1,980 regular season games. He worked his first NHL game in 1969 and retired in 1996."

When an official works that long he is bound to suffer injuries. In Ron Finn's case they included a cracked vertebra and breaks in his nose, ribs, teeth, and fingers. He even survived a hold-up attempt when he was in his hotel room in Los Angeles. After Finn slammed the door shut in their faces one of the two would-be thieves fired a bullet from a .357 Magnum through the door. The bullet passed close enough to Finn's hand to bruise his fingers and narrowly missed his head before it lodged in the ceiling. (Two suspects were arrested, charged, and convicted, and sentenced to nine years each.)

None of the above was enough to end Ron Finn's career, but his heart did. He worked his 1,980th game in Winnipeg, February 23, 1996. The next day his doctor told him his career was over. Finn was fifty-five, and the oldest official in the history of the NHL.

RON FINN

When we were being tested before training camp in 1994 I jumped on the bicycle and, after about two minutes, the girl told me I'd better get off before I had a heart attack. My heart was beating too fast for the level I should have been at and she told me I'd never pass the test. They weren't going to let me go to camp but, finally, I did. They took me out of all my exhibition games and told me to keep training. A doctor tested me again and he sent a letter to Bryan Lewis saying that with the kind of heart I have I won't get a true test-reading all the time. Bryan told me, "You're not going on the ice until you pass the test." So I did it again and got something like 82 per cent on the bicycle. I guess I was more relaxed and I passed with flying colours. So one day I failed and the next day I passed. It's like now. One day I can run up and down the stairs fifty thousand times with no problem and the next day I can hardly breathe after I do it once.

I worked that season, which was a short one because of the lockout, but they didn't give me any playoff games. Before the next season I took a stress test. The league didn't know much about what I was doing. It's like a player with an injury who doesn't tell his coach or he'll never get back in the line-up. After the test the doctor told me I had over-loaded my heart and I had a weakness on my left side. I told him I wanted to work, and that was it. He said he would let me, but if I had any trouble on the ice I was to leave right away and go to the hospital. I worked with it but I was having trouble on the ice with my breathing. I thought if I ever had to break up a big fight, forget it. I'd probably just die on the spot.

I went back to the doctor and took another stress test. He said I could keep working, but if the results were the same, or worse, I was coming off the ice. I told him I'd take it easy. I went back after the game in Winnipeg for the results and I was sure they would be the same, or better, because I had felt great when I did the testing. He said, "It isn't. It's worse. The weakness is starting to show up on the right side now. You're off the ice."

I phoned Bryan Lewis and said, "Bryan, I'm at the doctor's office and it doesn't look like I can work any more. Well, let's put it this way, I can't work any more. I have a bad heart and that's all there is to it." I gave the phone to the doctor and he told Bryan that my heart was getting worse and it wasn't going to get any better. And that was the end of it. I ended up doing 1,980 regular-season games and 291 in the playoffs. They had let me choose the game for my two-thousandth and it was going to be St. Louis at Toronto on April 6. But it didn't happen.

Ron Finn's career as a linesman in the National Hockey League is best summed up by a story involving Scotty Bowman, who is a perfectionist in all aspects of hockey. John McCauley, then referee-in-chief, supervised a game in Buffalo when Bowman was coaching the Sabres. Immediately after the game Bowman hustled to the officials' room and asked McCauley to step out into the hall. As soon as McCauley had closed the door behind him Bowman said, "I got him, John! I got him!"

"Got who?" McCauley asked.

"Finn, I got Finn," Bowman replied. "I finally caught Ron Finn making a mistake. I can show you on the tape."

The Sabres had won the game and McCauley told Bowman to calm down, it was no big deal. "I know," said Scotty. "The play didn't mean anything. It's just that I finally caught Finnie making a mistake on an offside call. He was wrong. Ron Finn was wrong. God, I feel good."

RON FINN

My career began when I answered an ad that was in the *Toronto Star*. I had played minor hockey and then in industrial leagues for places I had worked, like Christie's Biscuits. I even won a scoring championship one year. Sheilagh and I were married in 1961 and she persuaded me to leave Christie's and take a job at the post office where the benefits were better. That's where I was when I read the ad in the *Star*, which said the Toronto Hockey League was looking for young, eager individuals to work as referees. They held tryouts at St. Michael's Arena and one of the supervisors, who knew me from the industrial league, asked me how I could expect to enforce rules when I broke all of them when I was a player. He laughed, and then said they'd take me on. That's how it all began.

I moved on from the THL to the OHA and along the way attended Vern Buffey's summer camp for officials. Scotty Morrison was there and invited me to the NHL camp the following week, in Kitchener. This was in 1968. When it was over Scotty explained that there were no openings at the time and, as I was twenty-six years old, I was sure the message was I was too old. I went back to the OHA and the following summer I was working at the post office when Frank Udvari called and offered me a job in the NHL. I was making $5,200 at the post office plus another $1,000 or so officiating. The NHL's offer was $5,000, so if I took it I would be losing money. Our first child, Sean, had just been born and it was a tough decision, considering how much I wanted to be in the NHL. Sheilagh was very supportive, so we took the chance and I signed.

When I got to the training camp I found out the officials were considering a strike. They wanted to form some kind of an association to air their grievances, a major one being the verbal and physical abuse they were getting from players and coaches. The day after I signed my contract they walked out of camp. I told Vern Buffey I was willing to be supportive but he said the veteran officials felt a newcomer like me shouldn't be included and it was okay with them for me to work.

The exhibition season was just starting and I did my first game as a referee in Paris, Ontario. Minnesota was playing and early in the game I signalled a penalty on their big defenceman Moose Vasko. I skated over to the penalty box and he followed me, at a pretty good clip. He was the biggest player in the league and I was sure he was on his way to knock me over. But he skated right past me and went straight into the box. That was a big moment for me, a big confidence-builder, and I lost my nervousness right there.

The strike lasted six days but while it was still on I was a linesman in Ottawa for a game between Boston and St. Louis, September 21, 1969. About halfway through the first period Ted Green and Wayne Maki had a stick-swinging fight that was one of the worst ever in the NHL. Ted swung his stick first and hit Maki on the side of the ear and there was blood. Maki swung back mainly through fright. He was scared as hell, out there against the big, bad Bruins. Green swings at him and Maki must have thought, To hell with you, I'm gonna hit you and run. And that's what he did. He hit him and ran. Green went down, tried to get up, then collapsed. He was paralysed. I can still see his face. That was the worst because I felt I was looking at someone who could have lost his life. Hockey is an intense game played at high speed and I think fighting is a release valve. If Green and Maki had dropped their gloves we'd have broken it up and nobody would have been hurt. But when you get hit with a stick like Ted Green did, that doesn't belong in the game.

[*Green was rushed to hospital and underwent a five-hour brain surgery. He missed the 1969–70 season but returned to play two more years in Boston and seven in the* WHA. *Maki was suspended for thirty days and Green for thirteen games when he returned. Both appeared in an Ottawa court on assault charges but were exonerated. Wayne Maki played four more seasons and died of cancer a few years later.*]

Early in my first season I was in St. Louis and there was a fight I still talk about. The Canadiens were there and John Ferguson fought two of the Plager brothers, Barclay and Bob, and gave them both a thumping. Then Noel Picard came in and Fergie took him on. Picard kept yelling, "Fergie, calm down!" Claude Bechard was the other linesman and Fergie still had the strength to push us off. We finally got him off the ice and to this day I don't know how he had the strength to even skate to the end of the rink. The officials all got fined over that one because we didn't throw Fergie out of the game after his third major. My son plays hockey in Milwaukee and I saw Bob Plager when I was down there recently. I asked him if he remembered the fight with Fergie and he said, "Shit, all I wanted to do was save my brother. So I end up getting in a fight with him and then he fought Picard. It was a great night, wasn't it?"

Those games in Ottawa and St. Louis were right at the beginning of my career. As you might imagine, I was involved in my share of incidents after that. In 1977 there was a brawl in a game between Philadelphia and the Islanders. Gary Dornhoefer and Garry Howatt got into it and Howatt ended up breaking his hand. Moose Dupont charged in and grabbed Howatt and I had hold of Dorny. He pushed me away and did it so hard I fell over backwards and landed on top of Howatt and Dupont, who were on the ice. Ron Wicks was the referee and we all ended up at a hearing in Mr. Campbell's office in Montreal. Dorny got a three-game suspension. With the rules today he couldn't afford to do that to me because you're talking about ten or twenty games. That's a big difference when you think of the money they make now.

The one time I really got mad at a player was in a game in Toronto, in 1989, and it was Dave Manson of Chicago. Two fights had broken out at the same time and Manson was cruising around looking to get involved. I got him off the ice but he charged back on to go after Gary Leeman, and he ran right over me in the process. I was knocked flat and was lucky I wasn't hurt badly; I was sore all over for a long time. When I got up I wanted to take a shot at Manson, go toe to toe. I was out there to keep control and I almost lost control of myself. Andy van Hellemond was the referee. He saw what was happening so he got Manson off the ice and he stayed off that time. I let Manson have it pretty good with some colourful language. It was the only time in my career I almost lost it.

On a different note, I was doing a game in Toronto when a streaker jumped onto the ice. There he was, starkers. I motioned to three police officers who were standing near the penalty box but they didn't move. I went over and said he was their responsibility, not mine. Then I realized, one of the officers was a woman. She didn't budge and neither did I, because that wasn't part of my job description. Her partners finally went on the ice and grabbed the guy.

Fans often like to get in on the act, although that guy in Toronto went a bit far. There are some I call "pounders" who sit at ice level and pound their fists against the glass when you skate by. One night in Pittsburgh there were three of them, all ladies, who made a hell of a noise every time I went near them. Finally I stood right in front of them as often as I could to block their view of the game and they didn't see Mario Lemieux score the winning goal. I must admit I turned around and gave them a big smile.

I worked in Washington in the 1987 playoffs the night the Capitals and the Islanders were in the fourth overtime period when Pat LaFontaine scored to end it. That made it, at the time, the fifth-longest game ever played. It was the longest game ever shown on *Hockey Night in Canada*. Andy van Hellemond was the referee and John D'Amico was the other linesman. It was hot that night and at a time like that you drink a whole bottle of Gatorade yourself between periods to get the fluids back in you. John McCauley was there and he wouldn't let anyone in our room between periods, so we could relax.

When it came to overtime the key word for me was always *focus*. I found if everything had gone smoothly in the three regulation periods, overtime wasn't going to be any different. You got into a routine. Whatever you did in one period you were going to do in the next period because everything was the same, same players, same atmosphere, same everything. That night in Washington was just like that.

The first time I was assigned to a Stanley Cup final was 1979 when Montreal played the Rangers. I was a standby for the first game, in Montreal, and after the first period I treated myself to a couple of those famous Forum hot dogs everyone liked so much. Suddenly I heard an announcement over the P.A., "Ron Finn, please report to the officials' room immediately!" I gulped down my second hot dog and rushed to the room. Matt Pavelich was feeling sick and Scotty Morrison told me I would have to take his place. So I jumped into my equipment and when we came out of the room the TV cameras were pointing at us walking down the hallway. I skated onto the ice and Larry Robinson said to me, "Congratulations, Ron, on your first final series. And by the way, you should probably do up the fly in your pants." I'd been coast to coast on *Hockey Night in Canada*, and my fly was open!

Travel plays a major role in your life when you're an official. I was doing a game in Oakland, December 14, 1973, when I learned our daughter, Tara, had been born. Almost exactly two years later I was in the middle of a game when I learned that Theresa had been born. That time Wally Harris delayed a faceoff and the players all congratulated me. I was in Edmonton, in 1981, working a Canada Cup series when Scotty Morrison informed me my mother had passed away. You miss birthdays and anniversaries and your kid's hockey games, because you're on the road so much. A hockey life can be tough on a family but it runs in ours. One of our sons, Shannon, is playing in the International League and the other, Sean, is a linesman in the American League. He's hoping to get into the NHL. Tara is an usherette at Maple Leaf Gardens and Theresa would go to every game I worked there.

Late in my career I wasn't getting the good teams and the big games. I worked two rounds in the playoffs in '94 and then they didn't use me at all in the playoffs in '95. Younger guys were starting to come up and take the big games and it was getting really disappointing. Bryan Lewis kept saying, "We have to give the younger guys the experience. If they don't get it, they won't know what you know." I said, "I've got the experience. Why don't you use me in the games that are so important? If you want me to go through the whole season being perfect, I won't, because my body won't take it. But if you give me one important game to do, I'll be perfect." They couldn't see that. So there was a clash between management and myself.

I talked to Wally Harris about it and he said, "Ron, what's more important? You want to keep working, don't you? You can fight management but it won't help. They've made their decision. Why don't you just bite the bullet, let management do what they want to do, and go on with life. You can come back and work as many years as you want because we need experienced people like you." So, if I wanted to stay around I had to be quiet.

It really hurt down deep that after all the years, and everything, they wouldn't put me in the playoffs in '95. I was hoping for two or three rounds because all I needed was nine games to do three hundred. Only nine games. I said, how cruel. That's the dark side of hockey. All my life the thing I had always turned to was hockey to save me, put me on the right track. Even back when I had problems in school. That's why I really got upset over not doing the playoffs because they were taking hockey away from me. Now, it's my heart that's doing it, taking away hockey, the one thing I wanted so much.

IO

The Teacher and the Little Guy

TERRY GREGSON   KERRY FRASER

The officials featured so far in this book came from a variety of work backgrounds before settling into a career on the ice. There were jobs in clothing stores, automobile factories, machine shops, and the post office. Don Koharski was a milkman. One of the newer officials in the NHL, Don Van Massenhoven, served in the Ontario Provincial Police for ten years. Three members of his graduating class have lost their lives in the line of duty. During a game in Toronto the Maple Leafs' Tie Domi said to Van Massenhoven, "Why the hell would you quit your job to take all the abuse we give you?" The former OPP officer replied, "Pucks only hurt. Bullets kill."

Denis Morel left teaching to become a referee and so did Terry Gregson. Gregson may have been under pressure at times standing at the blackboard in a high-school classroom, but not as much as when he was refereeing the seventh game of the 1994 Stanley Cup finals, or the deciding

*game in the 1996 World Cup tournament. Terry Gregson
was selected to referee in both those pressure-cookers
because he has become one of the best referees in the game.*

TERRY GREGSON

I don't think anyone is born wanting to be a referee, it just
happens. But we are born, not hatched, as some people
think. I was born and raised in Erin, a small farming community northwest of Toronto. My father ran the minor-
hockey program and had the key to the arena. They had
trouble getting someone to drop the puck at 6:30 in the
morning so I started doing that when I was about twelve. I
was officiating in the Ontario Minor Hockey Association
when I was fifteen. Then I went off to the University of
Western Ontario where I played hockey and officiated on the
side to get a little pocket money. I graduated with a science
degree and went overseas, where I played First Division
hockey and refereed in the Second Division.

I came back from Europe and went to Queen's University
for a year to get my Bachelor of Education. A fellow in
Kingston named Pat Haggerty knew I was interested in
officiating and got me into the OHA doing junior-B and -C
hockey. I started getting a little more serious about it then.

I became a high-school science teacher in St. Catharines
and started doing more games for the OHA. I became a
power-skating instructor and got hooked up with some
referee schools in the summer. Scotty Morrison saw me at
one and asked me if I was interested in making it a career. I
told him I hadn't thought about it. In my second year of
teaching high-school science in St. Catharines he invited
me to their training camp. I told him I'd go and give it an
honest effort and if he could promise me eighty to a hundred
games in the coming season I'd take a year's leave of absence

from my job. He said, "Yeah, I can do that. I can put you in the Western Junior League, the International League, and the Central League." So I took a year's leave of absence and ended up doing eighty-five or ninety games all the way from Brandon, Manitoba, to Billings, Montana, to Albuquerque, New Mexico.

I never went back to teaching. After that first year I got hired under contract. I spent the next two years exclusively in the American and International leagues. In my third year I did eleven NHL games, my fourth year I did twenty-two, then fifty-six in my fifth, and in my sixth year I became a full-time official in the NHL.

My first NHL game was Los Angeles at Hartford, December 19, 1981. I was excited, nervous, and I'd have to say probably unconsciously incompetent. I remember giving Chris Kotsopoulos a major for spearing. The next night I was in Boston and I had to give Wayne Cashman a match penalty for throwing his stick. Two games in two nights and a couple of tough calls like that. I started off with a real bang.

They brought me along slowly. Those years out West and in the American and Central leagues and in the IHL were the formative years for me. My favourite travel story is about the time I flew from Toronto to Regina, on a Thursday, and rented a car. On Friday I drove to Saskatoon, worked a game, and drove back to Regina after the game. I had to be in Brandon to do a game Saturday afternoon, Billings for a game Sunday afternoon, and Calgary for a game Monday night. The trip from Brandon to Billings was through a snowstorm and took nine hours. I was getting paid sixty-five dollars a game, cash, and there were a few nights when I had sixty-five one-dollar bills thrown through the door at me because the home team didn't like my work. So there I was, a guy from the East with a light topcoat and little wee toe rubbers, driving through the snow in Manitoba and Montana to make sixty-five dollars a game and thinking, hmmm, I'm not so sure I made the right decision here.

My longest road trip was back in those days too when I was working in three or four different leagues. Scotty Morrison was doing the assignments and at times he'd lose track of where you were. The long trip lasted forty-two days and I checked into a hotel in Tulsa, Oklahoma, on about day thirty. Back then we had to put our airline tickets, hotels, everything on our own credit cards. I had a two-thousand-dollar limit. So I check in and they cut my card up, right in front of me. I hadn't been home to pay my bill and I owed something like four thousand dollars. There I was in Tulsa, twenty-three years old, with no credit card and no money. They had been mailing my expense cheques to my house but there wasn't anyone home. I was single at the time and the cheques were sitting in the mailbox. The office had to wire me money. After the forty-two-day trip I got home for four days and then left again.

When you work for a while in one league you reach a comfort zone. When you move to the next level, you start all over again. In the NHL you reach a point of acceptance and then you get to be a senior official and they start saying you're too old, you're getting lazy. You've got to re-establish yourself. Those are the inherent challenges. Going through those challenges back in my minor-league days were the most fun. You take a step back in time. No one knew anything about the games except the score.

At each step you were a raw rookie. One of my first games in the International League was Milwaukee at Toledo. The game ended 16–2 for Milwaukee. They emptied the benches three times on me, and this is my second or third game at the pro level. In those days the IHL was pretty wild. After the game the supervisor, Fred Blackburn, said to me,

"You've got a little to learn but I think we can work with you. You didn't get excited." Inside, you're like a duck on water, just churning because you're thinking, Where did I go wrong? What did I do wrong?

I know there was a time when officials were pretty well on their own, but I came from an era of real supervision. We had people working with us in the minor leagues. Then when I shifted to the NHL the focus changed from the minors to working with us in the NHL. Now it's gone back again. They're working more with the younger guys and we're doing more self-evaluation. We get videotapes sent to us. In the minors I spent a lot of time talking with John McCauley. He'd be at a game and then drive with me to the next city and we'd just talk. It wasn't so much about good penalties or bad penalties I had called, it was more about life as an official, preparation, how to handle conversations with the players. Like, if a player comes to me and he's heated up I like to touch him on the elbow or the lower back, or use open hands to try and slow him down a little bit.

In the past, people didn't communicate very well. We had some supervisors who couldn't put into words what they wanted to get across. They came from the age of intimidation. They would yell and scream and kick wastebaskets. Now the supervisors want to know *why*, and you can't just say *because*. There's dialogue. When I first came in, senior guys would kind of look at you and the message was, "I learned by jumping into the fire and you can learn that way too." Now older officials are paired with younger guys on a regular basis. It's good that Bob Hodges and Leon Stickle communicate with the young officials. There is better teaching going on now.

I always relate officials and players to parents and children. The kids want to see how far they can push their parents, and early in my career I let the players push me further than I should have. I remember a Rangers game in New York and I wasn't in control. The game was happening and I was along for the ride. It's like driving a team of horses. You better have the reins tight early or they'll get away on you. That night in New York the players were challenging me and I wasn't meeting the challenge. The score stayed close to the end so things never really got out of hand. It would have been different if it hadn't stayed close. After the game Bob Hodges told me, "You know the rules, and you can do this job. But some night you're gonna have to get mad."

In 1987 I did the first game of the semi-finals between Philly and Montreal. It went into overtime and the Flyers scored. The puck went just over the line and then came right out again. As luck would have it, I was in perfect position so I gave the signal that it was a goal. Larry Robinson was just livid. You know, I'm this young punk who hadn't been around much in the playoffs and I'm awarding a goal that gives Philadelphia the game. I had to fly to Edmonton the next day and when I got there I went straight into the pre-game meeting. One of the supervisors said, "You had a tough call last night but you made the right one. The video-tape proved it." I still remember standing there with Larry Robinson. He was so convinced the puck wasn't in I began to wonder if maybe we could check it out somewhere. But there was no video replay then. It was a case of, I saw it, but did I see it? It turned out I was right but it led to somewhat of a sleepless night, to say the least.

I love playoff hockey. Let's face it, we go through this six-month dance to get there and, when we do, it's the greatest feeling. I know I work much better in the playoffs than I often do in the regular season because there is such a concentrated rush of adrenaline. It's the big show and you're on stage.

In the playoffs nobody wants to take a stupid penalty for instigating, or whatever. When you see a player being interviewed during the playoffs, the first thing out of his mouth is, "We have to play disciplined hockey." And I'm thinking to myself, You know what? It wouldn't hurt you to do that eighty-two games a year.

One of the games I enjoyed the most ever was between Buffalo and New Jersey in the playoffs in '94 when they went into the fourth overtime period. It didn't end until ten to two in the morning. You really want the players to decide a game like that, and that night they did. I had to call only two penalties in the overtime and they were the type Ray Charles would have called. Nobody said a word when I called them. Between periods we lay on the floor and took a lot of liquids because we were getting a bit dehydrated. When it really hit me was the next morning. I drove home after the game because it's only a two-hour drive. The next morning I went to get out of bed and, whoa! was I ever stiff.

I know we get accused of letting the players decide things late in the game or in overtime. It's funny. If you don't call something late in a close game the team that got fouled says you put your whistle away. If you call it the team that gets the penalty says to look at the score. You can't win. I think you have to consider the fairness and safety aspects. If they've played fifty-eight minutes and you had let something worse go you'd better use your head. But if it's flagrant you have to look at it from a fairness standpoint.

The final game in the 1996 World Cup tournament between Canada and the United States was the best hockey game, and the toughest hockey game, I've ever been involved with. It was the best because the players were so focused and it was the toughest, from my perspective, because you wanted to let them compete. But, boy, they were walking a fine line.

However, my best memory of a game would be game seven in the '94 finals, Vancouver at the New York Rangers. When you start out in this business you think, Geez, will I ever get to do a game seven of a Stanley Cup final? The World Cup was a great hockey game, but when it was over everybody moved on to what I would call their real job, winning the Stanley Cup. I remember standing on the ice in game seven when they were playing the national anthems and the place was just nuts. Ray Scapinello and Kevin Collins were the linesmen. Ray said to me, "This is where everybody wants to be," and I thought, he's right. I really enjoyed that game. It was like you were at peace with yourself saying, okay, trust yourself. You got to this point so you must have been doing something right. I refereed the deciding game in '93 when the Canadiens won, in Montreal, and it was the hundredth anniversary of the Stanley Cup being presented. That was a nice thing when you think about it. But doing a seventh game in the finals is pretty tough to top.

There's much more analysis of the game now, whether it be from the media, the spectators, or the teams themselves. Videotape is a great thing, but you know if you make a bad call it's going to be on the screen on the big clock hanging over centre ice about two and a half seconds later. You've got to have mental toughness to go through that and move on. Fifteen years ago if I made a bad call I knew it, and the players knew it, and we moved on. It wasn't on public display.

I can't get over how much is written and said about officiating. Very rarely do I see a TV sportscast in the evening when there isn't something mentioned about officiating and sometimes it's taken out of context. Now, there's talk radio. Everybody's looking for the warts, not the good.

A few years ago I was in Victoria to do game at the L.A. Kings' training camp. Rogie Vachon, the Kings' GM, came into our room and introduced the new hockey writer for the *L.A. Times*. He asked me to chat with him and clue him in a bit on the rules, and then he winked at me. This fellow had never seen a hockey game, live, in his life. He'd only written about basketball. Well, if you read his reports – I mean, this guy had no idea. If somebody got hit with a high stick he wrote a big article about the club in the guy's hands.

Two years ago Philly and Washington had a big punch-up, in Philly, and I had the return match in Washington two nights later. The place was just buzzing because they figured it was gonna be the same thing. The media pumped it for forty-eight hours. As quite often happens, nothing happened. It was just media hype. Let's say there's a game between Montreal and the Islanders and it's a good game, no crazy stuff. The next morning in the *New York Post* there'll be a picture that looks like some guy's about to behead somebody. I say to myself, Is that the same game I saw? No wonder we struggle sometimes.

The hardest part of our job is the mental side and I think we need a little more guidance in that area. I really do. Last year they brought Dr. Peter Jensen to our camp. He works with a lot of Olympic athletes, setting up goals and challenges for the individual. It's a long season, you go from game to game, and you can get stale. You have to have goals to help you stay on track.

These days there's a lot of discussion about "marginal" calls. What is marginal? I'm not really sure. I've asked my bosses and they come up with words like "non-essential." They're really struggling with what is marginal. They say it's something you can get away with, and I find when you start to bring in this type of thing it starts to undermine your trust a little bit. You don't know if you're gonna get supported. I say to my bosses, Don't tell me I made a marginal call, tell me I made a bad call. I can live with that. If I'm gonna get criticized from the officiating department, it should be teaching, not some statement that leaves you hanging. We all look for direction and discipline. If nobody's giving it to you, eventually you think, Are they waiting for me to fall over, or what are we doing here? I just think it's led to some greyness we didn't need.

In 1988 Terry Gregson succeeded Dave Newell as president of the NHL *Referees Association, a position always held by an active official. He stepped down in 1994 but resumed the presidency two years later. (As we spoke, work had begun on a new contract to replace the existing agreement, which was to expire August 31, 1997.)*

For years the average fan was likely unaware the association even existed, but that changed early in the 1993–94 season when the officials went on strike. Suddenly, they were the biggest story in hockey. The league brought in amateur officials from far and wide to take over. There was no doubt these men tried to do as good a job as they possibly could under the circumstances. There was also no doubt their work was not up to NHL *standards. The games went on, but it was not a pretty sight.*

TERRY GREGSON

We ended up going out for seventeen days, which was one of the most stressful times I've ever had. You had fifty people's livelihoods at stake and the decision to go on strike wasn't made easily, that's for sure. Don Meehan was our lead counsel at the time and our executive was me, Andy van Hellemond, Kerry Fraser, and Kevin Collins.

We started negotiations in the summer. That was in a transition period when Mr. Bettman and his group had just taken over and we had to go through some sort of familiarization.

I guess you could call it shadowboxing. We had to walk them through many parts of the old agreement. They had basketball and football backgrounds, which was terrific, but here's a case in point. We have a section in our agreement about injury indemnification. They couldn't understand why we would need an injury clause so we produced a list of how many guys had been injured in our business. It's not like getting hit in the head with a basketball.

We got down to August 31, we're going to training camp, and we don't have an agreement. They wanted us to continue working for another year. We didn't think that would be healthy because people could be angry at each other. We set a date of November 17. If we didn't have an agreement by then we had the right to withhold services. Unfortunately, we got to that point and we did withhold our services. There was a lot of midnight oil burned, a lot of sparring that I felt wasted a lot of time, and that's on the part of both parties. I guess if I learned anything, it's that 95 per cent of a deal is cut in 5 per cent of the time. The strike ended at the Airport Hilton, in Montreal, November 30. It was a battle. Sure, some issues weren't resolved the way we wanted and I'm sure others weren't resolved the way they wanted. Nobody's gonna have a complete victory, no matter how you look at it.

Let's be realistic. It came down to monetary issues, not non-monetary issues. It was never a situation where the league said we didn't deserve more. It was how much. The old document was established in 1988. Between '88 and '93 there was a whirlwind of changes in the NHL. The revenues generated really started to change. We shot for the sky and hoped to land on the roof. They wanted to keep us close to the ground. Did we get a good bump-up in money? Yeah. If you want to take me as an example, my base salary went from $80,000 to $135,000.

We really changed the place of officiating at the professional level. Before, it used to be, here's your paycheque, it's not a big piece of the pie, now go figure out what to do with it. Now we have employee-assistance programs, education programs, severance, good medical benefits, and a better pension. There's a pay scale there that, if people are smart and manage their money properly, they can have a very good and comfortable life. Now, I see a guy like Bob Hodges looking forward to retirement. The strike was, for me, one of the highlights of my career.

The first thing you notice about Kerry Fraser when you see him off the ice is how small he is. You wonder how someone his size can maintain law and order amongst rough, tough hockey players in the NHL who, with the exception of Theoren Fleury, are all bigger than he is. Yet, since 1980, Fraser's banty-rooster-like confidence has served him well. He refereed in the Stanley Cup finals his fifth year in the league, a rapid advancement by today's standards.

The second thing you notice about Kerry Fraser is his trademark hairstyle. There was a time when most NHL officials were easily recognized when they walked down the streets of Toronto or Montreal. Red Storey, Matt Pavelich, John D'Amico, and others from bygone eras were as familiar to fans as most of the players. Fewer teams meant more visits to league cities, and no helmets meant quicker recognition. Today, most officials walk out of an arena after a game and are quickly lost in the crowd. But not Kerry Fraser. His familiar not-a-hair-out-of-place 'do has made him the NHL's most recognizable official. Fraser wore a helmet a few years ago but discarded it fairly quickly, a decision he says had nothing to do with his hair.

Except for three years in the late 1970s, when he worked in the men's clothing business, Kerry Fraser's life has centred on hockey. He was too small to make it as a player and, at first, the people who eventually hired him for the NHL thought he was too small to referee in their league.

KERRY FRASER

I was born in Sarnia, Ontario, in 1952. My father played minor pro hockey and when the original-six teams would come to Sarnia for exhibition games he'd play against them. We have pictures of him playing against Rocket Richard and Gordie Howe. Hockey was a way of life for me and my brother when we were growing up and, of course, I wanted to be a player. I played with limited size, and limited ability, up to the tier-two junior level with the Sarnia Bees. When I wasn't drafted in my final year of junior I was thinking of playing in the minor leagues. I'm 5 feet, 7 and a half inches, and weigh 155 pounds, but in those days I weighed 135. Ted Garvin, who played with my father and was a long-time coach, suggested I get into officiating. He was probably one of the worst referee-baiters ever. He felt the officiating ranks needed former players with a good knowledge of the game, what was a penalty and what wasn't, and understood the frustrations players and coaches go through.

I took his advice and went to a summer refereeing school. That was in 1972 when the WHA was in its inaugural season and both leagues were looking for officials. Frank Udvari showed up and watched me work ten minutes of a game. Frank saw something in those ten minutes I worked and I don't know what the heck it could have been. I didn't know much about officiating but I was a good skater. He invited me to the NHL training camp the next weekend. Scotty Morrison, who isn't very big himself, thought I was too small, but Frank went to bat for me. He put me in the American League and I worked forty-five games as a linesman.

I went back to training camp the following season and, again, on Frank's recommendation they hired me as a referee. I was given a contract for $6,500 with a bonus of ten games in the American or Central League. I got another thousand dollars for each level. It was a foot in the door but, as I'd never refereed much before, I wasn't real comfortable. My first assignment was in the Western Junior League, in Flin Flon. I flew in there on one of those rubber-band prop jobs. I'm sitting in the lobby of the hotel and there was a little old lady working at the switchboard. The phone rings and it's a call from New York, which was probably big news in Flin Flon, and it was for me. It was Frank Udvari calling to wish me well in my first game.

Frank always kept a close watch. In my second year I had tendinitis in my ankles and had to have them frozen before a game in New Westminster. It was the last game of ten in eleven nights and I was so crippled I spent most of the game pulling myself along the boards. I got back home and Frank called and gave me the devil. He said I was nothing but a big baby, young guys have to be tough, and ten games in eleven nights was nothing. It got to the point where I finally said, "Frank, are you telling me I'm fired?" He said, "No, but you'd better knuckle under and get ready for the playoffs." A lot of guys had a love-hate relationship with him, but he knew what it took to make you an official. I owe him a lot.

I did the Memorial Cup finals in 1974, the end of my first year. The Regina Pats won it with players like Clark Gillies and Greg Joly. Bob Turner, who played for the Canadiens when they won five straight Stanley Cups, was their coach.

That experience elevated me, helped me develop my style. I'm small in stature and when I played I wasn't going to be pushed around. I always thought I had to fight the biggest guy on the other team to let them know I wasn't afraid. I think I took some of that gutsiness, or whatever, with me as an official. I could be a little cocky and that was the perception of me when I started.

I did a junior game in Calgary when the home team was losing miserably. They were challenging me all night and I kept giving them penalties. With about two minutes to go the penalty box was full, another goal was scored on them and the fans were throwing things on the ice. The captain came to me and said, "The coach wants to know if you give penalties for thinking because he thinks you're nothing but a blankety-blank asshole." I started to laugh. I looked over at the coach and he cracked a smile. That taught me that, once in a while, you have to lighten up a bit, find some humour in things.

That lesson I learned in Calgary helped me early in my NHL career. I was in Edmonton when the Oilers were young, cocky, and starting to get on a roll. Glen Sather was the coach and he was a needler. I called a penalty Sather didn't like and as I'm getting ready to faceoff my back is to him and I can hear him chirping at me with that squeaky voice of his. I turned around and put my fingers to my lips, like, hush, be quiet. He said, "It wasn't me, it was him," and he pointed to a photographer who was sitting between the two benches. I laughed, he laughed, and the players laughed. The next night I had them again, in Vancouver. Sather never appeared behind the bench until after the national anthem. I was waiting for him and as soon as he arrived I skated over and said, "Glen, are we gonna have any trouble with that photographer tonight?" He said, "No, I left the sonofabitch at home. He can't keep his mouth shut." [Laughs]

I spent three years in the minors. I was also working with a fellow who owned a clothing store back in Sarnia. I'd moved up to the American League and had a good season my third year. I knew they were pleased with me but there was a pecking order when it came to the National League. The staff there was fairly junior and there were a lot of fellows in the minors who had been hired in advance of me. I wanted to get there as quickly as I could but I had to wait my turn. I became somewhat frustrated with that. The opportunity came up to become a partner in the clothing business and build a second store. I went to the officials' training camp, did all the tests, then decided to retire. Scotty Morrison was shocked. Frank Udvari was somewhat disappointed and I guess hurt, but I moved on and we opened a second store. I worked there for three years.

I really missed hockey and officiating. I guess I didn't realize what I had or how enviable my position was. I just threw it away. So, when the four WHA teams were amalgamated into the NHL in 1979, I thought there might be an opportunity to jump in and get there quickly. I sat down with Scotty Morrison, although I was pretty sure I would meet with rejection, and I did. After an hour and a half he told me he couldn't be sure I was serious about it. When our meeting ended I said, "Scotty, I don't want you to think I'm cocky, but the next time you call me, I'm confident you'll be offering me a contract." He laughed and said, "I hope so," and we shook hands.

I had already contacted the International League, so I went there pretty well full time. In mid-December that year I was getting ready to go to a Christmas party when the phone rang. It was Scotty. He said there had been some injuries and a linesman had quit so would I be interested in working for him? I said that would be wonderful if he could arrange things with the International League. He said he'd already done that and he was sending me a sweater, although there hadn't been time to sew my name on the back. My first assignment was in Dallas, in the Central Pro League. Roger Neilson was coaching there. I skated out with no name on my sweater and the players thought I was a nobody coming in, which I was. Early in the game a confrontation took place and one of the players started to chastise me for being a rookie without a name on my sweater. I said, "No-name products are selling well at the grocery store, and you're gonna see this one sell, too."

At the end of that season I was selected to do the finals in each minor pro league, the American, Central, and International, and the next year I was up in the National League. I had reached a level where I was respected by the players and coaches. Orval Tessier was coaching in the American League and during the playoffs I ran into him in Binghamton. He shook my hand and told me what a great job I was doing. A few years later he was coaching the Blackhawks and one night, in Chicago, he got mad at me and broke a stick over the boards and I threw him out. He had to walk across the ice to get to the gate and the people started throwing stuff. Orval went to kick some debris that was in his path and he slipped and fell flat on his ass. He was livid. By then they were throwing everything that wasn't nailed down so I moved to centre ice, under the old clock at the Stadium, figuring that was the safest place to be. It took about fifteen minutes to clean the ice. Two of the Chicago players, Bob Murray and Doug Wilson, came up to me and told me I'd made a good call, that Orval deserved to be tossed. I said, "Guys, I appreciate your support, but I think you'd better get away from me because they've got a bigger target with the three of us standing here." [Laughs]

When I got to the NHL there was that great rivalry between the Canadiens and the Nordiques, the Battle of Quebec. In

'82 John McCauley assigned me to the fifth game of a best-of-five series between the teams. As a young official, that gave me such a lift in confidence. Then, in the '87 playoffs in Montreal I disallowed a goal that Alain Coté scored for Quebec. Paul Gillis had knocked Brian Hayward out of the goal and I ruled interference. All hell broke loose after that. That call was very difficult.

A couple of days later I was back home, in Sarnia, and I heard on the radio that a fan in Quebec, as well as the team, was launching a lawsuit against the NHL and against referee Fraser. I called the league and Jim Gregory said not to worry, that a replay showed I made the right call. I sat at home watching a game six or seven being played and all of a sudden I said to my wife, Kathy, "I'm all done this year." She said, "You've got to be kidding me," and I said, "I'm not kidding. It's over." I was sitting at home with a couple of seventh games going on and there was the threat of the lawsuit, and all the rest of it. I knew I was finished. Sure enough, I got a call from John McCauley telling me I was not working any more playoff games. I had worked the finals the previous two years. His call didn't come as a complete surprise but it was disappointing. I told him it was B.S. and we had a rather heated discussion for a few minutes. It was a difficult time and, to make matters worse, that summer I contracted hepatitis and I missed almost half of the next season.

One last story on the call in Montreal: That summer I received a videotape and a letter in the mail from Serge Savard, who was the general manager of the Canadiens. It was a tape of the incident and in his letter Serge said he knew it was a difficult time for me but he wanted to show me that I had made the right call. The tape was highlighted to show Hayward being dragged out of the net by Gillis. That showed me the class of Serge Savard, and the Montreal organization.

You ask me about other incidents and I have to go back to my first game in the NHL. It was in Denver, Minnesota and the Colorado Rockies, and it was the year they put in a new rule that if a fight broke out other players had to leave the area and if they dropped their gloves they automatically got misconduct penalties. There was a fight early in the game and of course, on instinct, everybody else dropped their gloves and paired off, so they all received misconduct penalties. They had a picture in the paper the next day showing almost as many players in the box as there were on the benches. Ryan Bozak and Jim Christison were the linesmen and we almost had to fight our way out of the building. My first NHL game. The fans were very abusive and one guy wanted to fight. Glen Sharpley was playing for Minnesota and he came over and told us if we needed any help he'd give us a hand. Christison said, "Sharp, I've seen you fight. We're better off by ourselves." [Laughs]

You can have all of the technical coaching and teaching they can give, and know the rules, but when you're in a tough spot a person's integrity, courage, and character carry him through. I did a game in Detroit early in my first year where I called two penalty shots, both against the home team. The second one was with thirteen seconds left in the game and Detroit was leading by one goal. They were playing Vancouver and Harry Neale was coaching the Canucks. Stan Smyl was the player fouled. Normally he would have taken the shot but he was injured on the play. Harry selected Ivan Hlinka, a player from Czechoslovakia, and he scored. Afterwards Harry said, "I told Hlinka that if he didn't score on that penalty shot he could skate right out of the end of the rink and keep going all the way back to Czechoslovakia."

When the goal went in the Detroit bench went nuts. Reed Larson fired a water bottle at me and I had to gong him. Leon

Stickle was with me and we ended up, like in Denver, literally having to fight our way out of the building. They gave us a police escort to get back to the hotel. The next day John McCauley called and said, "I hear you had a tough game last night, big guy. You were right. I'm proud of you for making a gutsy call." That sort of established very early that I wasn't afraid to make tough calls and I've proven that over my career. Some people may have the impression that I look for the controversial call, but I don't enjoy controversy. Believe me, nobody does. But it's there, like with that penalty shot in Detroit and with the call in Montreal in '87. Although they were unpopular I wouldn't have been able to look at myself in the mirror if I hadn't made those calls.

I've seen all kinds of reactions from coaches. Bryan Murray would wave his arms and yell and scream at the officials and we were responding properly with bench penalties. One night when he had one foot on the boards and was yelling at me, I skated over to him and said, very calmly, "Bryan, I'd love to talk to you but you're gonna have to calm down and get your foot off the boards. Then we'll talk." Right away his level of emotion went from ranting lunatic to almost my level of conversation. We had a discussion, I told him why I made the call and, after saying he didn't agree with me, he thanked me and the game went on.

Michel Bergeron and I had a bit of history, not the least of which was my call in Montreal in '87 when he was coaching Quebec. He moved to New York with the Rangers when Phil Esposito was the general manager. One night, in New York, I had just called a penalty against the Rangers and I heard abusive language coming from the area of their bench. I looked over and saw it was Esposito who was swearing at me. I gave the Rangers a bench minor because he was a member of the hockey club and was readily identifiable in the bench area. Bergeron demanded an explanation so I went over and gave it to him. As I was skating away he said, "My wife doesn't like you either. She's sitting in the third row. Why don't you give her a bench minor, too?"

Al Arbour–coached teams on the Island were the epitome of discipline in my years in the league. I can remember having them against Edmonton when the Islanders were leading by one goal late in the game. I could hear the players on the New York bench telling themselves and the guys on the ice, don't take a penalty. With Gretzky and all the fire power the Oilers had, their best chance would be a power play. A player was going around Denis Potvin and Potvin put his stick across his chest and started to chug a little bit. But you could see what Potvin was thinking, that the guy was gonna go down and try to draw a penalty. So with great presence of mind he pulled his stick away and forced the player to go too wide for him to take a shot. That, to me, is what discipline is all about. Of course, when Al Arbour spoke to me, or yelled at me, I had a lot of time for him because it would twig in my mind that maybe he had a legitimate complaint.

One of the most talked-about calls I have ever made was one of the easiest, in the '93 finals, when Marty McSorley got caught with an illegal stick. It was cut and dried, it really was. L.A. had won the first game in Montreal and they were a goal up late in the second game. For any player to go into the third period in a Stanley Cup final with an illegal stick was, to my mind, absolutely asinine. The stick was so illegal, I mean, I just looked at it and said, Holy smokes, we won't need the gauge for this one. But we went through the motions and measured it. It was a brilliant coaching move by Jacques Demers the way it turned out because Montreal tied the game on the power play and won in overtime. So instead of L.A. going home with a 2–0 lead, the series was tied, and they didn't win another game.

I tried wearing a helmet for a half-season but gave it up, and it has nothing to do with my hair, or vanity. I just wasn't comfortable with it. I felt a sense of false security from a safety standpoint and from a reaction standpoint. You develop an awareness of what the players are doing, or are going to do, their speed and their reactions. With the helmet I lost a bit of that, no question. I learned early that, being small in stature, I have to always be in position to see the play. I can't see around those big guys, and I can't see over them.

So, my hair is still out there for everyone to see and I get needled about it all the time. After a playoff game, in Buffalo, a lady asked if she could speak to me and I thought she was going to give me the devil. I said sure and she said, "I have a real difficult time with my hair. It's unmanageable. I want to know what kind of hairspray you use because your hair never moves." I laughed and gave her the name of the product and she said she'd go out and buy some the next morning.

I got hit with a high stick in the '96 playoffs, in Denver, and was cut on the scalp. I was at the bench getting patched up and one of the players had a smart remark for me, so I said, "This doesn't happen very often. The hairspray normally stops the stick from going in."

11

The Record-Holders

GORD BROSEKER RAY SCAPINELLO

Veteran linesman Gord Broseker holds an unofficial National Hockey League record he is justifiably proud of. Broseker, a native of Baltimore, Maryland, was the first American to be on the ice in 1,000 NHL games. When this book was being written he was past 1,600, and counting.

Gord Broseker has officiated in the Stanley Cup finals and, along with Terry Gregson and Ray Scapinello, worked the dramatic championship game between Canada and the U.S.A. in the 1996 World Cup. The Brosekers of Baltimore were into sports in a big way. The father, Joe, refereed hockey in the United States, at times with his teenage son Gord working the lines alongside him. But, despite his father's involvement in hockey, young Gord's ambition was to be a major-league baseball player.

GORD BROSEKER

I was a catcher. Tools of ignorance. I signed with the Washington Senators and then they moved to Texas. I played five years, then ran into contract problems. I had worked the lines for my dad in the East Coast Hockey League when I was fourteen years old, when they'd be short in places like Charlotte, Greensboro, and Roanoke. When I was playing baseball I had piddled around with officiating in the winter, doing kids' games and this and that. After the 1972 baseball season I came home. The American Hockey League had put teams in Richmond and Norfolk, and my dad said they were looking for linesmen in those places. He said, "They've got a weekend camp coming up in Hershey. Why don't you just go?" So I went, and they hired me.

Dan McLeod was running the camp and he said he knew I was aspiring to be a baseball player so they would likely give me only a half-dozen or so games. When I got my first set of assignments I had twelve games. I ended up doing ninety that season. Because of my contract problems with the Texas Rangers I sat out that year in baseball. The Baltimore Orioles were interested in signing me, but in August Scotty Morrison called and invited me to the NHL training camp. The same thing happened. I went, and they hired me. I've been with them ever since.

The first time I worked in the Boston Garden I went down on one knee and made a call, offside Boston, and the next thing I know I feel pressure on my throat. It was Wayne Cashman's stick. He said, "Kid, the next time you make a call like that I'll shove this thing right down your throat!" I said, "Well, you might do that sometime, but not tonight, because you're outta here. You're done." And I threw him out. But I was scared because I thought he was gonna do it right there. After the game Frank Udvari came into our room and said, "Kid, it's a good thing you threw him out because if you didn't do it, I was gonna fire you. I want officials who have balls." I said, "I may have balls, but I have to tell you, in all fairness, I was scared shitless."

I've run into Cash lots of times since. A couple of years ago I played golf with him in Tampa when he was assistant coach with the Lightning. We were partners and I screwed up. He said something to me and I said, "I suppose you're gonna shove that golf club down my throat. Well, let me tell you one thing, you're older now, and I'm a lot bigger." [Laughs]

With so many players, like a Wayne Cashman, it's all emotion. A couple of weeks ago I did an afternoon game in Philly and I was talking with Ron Hextall, just shooting the breeze about things that had happened in the past. As you know, he's been in trouble more than once. He told me, "Gord, I'm so intense that, when a game is over, if you asked me about certain things I did or said, I probably couldn't remember. I just react." I told him that, when you think about it, that's a little scary. He said, "It's nothing personal against the officials or the other team. It's just me. I'm just intense."

When the Kansas City Scouts were in the league I was there one night working the lines with Jim Christison. Chicago was there. In the first period Chicago goes across the line and Jim calls an offside. Ivan Boldirev had been carrying the puck and he said to Jim, "Who was offside?" Jim said, "No one. I blew the call." Ivan was a classy guy and he said that was okay. In the next period Chicago goes across the line, Boldirev is carrying the puck again, and I go down on one knee and blow the whistle for an offside. Ivan stops and says, "Come on, Gord. Who was offside that time?" I said, "Same guy that was offside at the other end in the first period." He says, "Same guy? Like, nobody. Geez, are you guys ever consistent tonight."

I worked the game in New Jersey when Koho had his run-in with Jim Schoenfeld and I was supposed to work the next one too, the one where we refused to work. That thing coming off the ice, the doughnut business, happened so quick it was hard to really digest it. I guess it was fortunate there was a camera there to help get it all sorted out. It was an ugly situation. I always say the best thing about all that was that I got fired three times but rehired four times. As long as they rehired me more times than they fired me, that was okay. John McCauley, God rest his soul, was kinda left hanging out to dry. They couldn't find the president, John Ziegler.

The next game, we were all dressed and ready to work. John McCauley came in and said, "Do you know if you refuse to work it's grounds for termination?" We said we knew that. There was me, Dave Newell, and Ray Scapinello. Then he told us that Schoenfeld was gonna be allowed to coach after the league had suspended him. That's when we got dressed and walked out. John said, "I just want to let you know, all you fellows are fired." We went to Toronto for a meeting with our association. The league came back and said they were gonna reinstate us and then Ziegler got into it, from wherever he was, and said he wasn't rehiring us so we were fired again. It almost got funny. Jim Gregory would come in and say, "You're fired again." Then he'd come back and say, "You're hired again." I think they knew damn well they weren't gonna fire us. I was supposed to work again if there had been a sixth game in the series between Detroit and Edmonton but it ended in five. That was the semi-finals and I wasn't working the finals that year.

Brawls? I've had my share. My first NHL game was an exhibition, New York Rangers at Philadelphia. The officials were Andy van Hellemond, Matt Pavelich, and me. We had about 350 minutes in penalties. What an eye-opener for a rookie doing his first game. There was another exhibition game I did in Philly when they played Montreal. I was there with Bruce Hood and Leon Stickle and the game never finished. With about a minute or so to go the benches emptied and Bruce finally said, "That's it. Game over." If Fred Shero and Scotty Bowman hadn't come on the ice to tell their players to stop they'd still be fighting.

If you check the record book, the game that's listed, "Most penalty minutes" was between Boston and Minnesota, in Boston. I was there with Dave Newell and Kevin Collins. The three of us still call it the "Boston Massacre." The game started at 7:30 and ended at 12:20 the next morning. [*The game, played on February 26, 1981, is in the record book as follows: "MOST PENALTY MINUTES, BOTH TEAMS, ONE GAME: 406. . . . MOST PENALTY MINUTES, ONE TEAM, ONE GAME: 211, Minnesota North Stars. . . . MOST PENALTIES, BOTH TEAMS, ONE PERIOD: 67. . . . MOST PENALTIES, ONE TEAM, ONE PERIOD: 34, Minnesota North Stars." The final totals were: 38 minor penalties, 26 major penalties, 9 ten-minute misconducts, and 9 game misconducts.*]

I was skating around before the opening faceoff and a player for Minnesota, Tommy Younghans, said to me, "Gord, did you work out at the Y today?" I told him I hadn't because Kevin and I had been in Washington the night before and we had just flown in. He said, "Well, you should have." I asked him why and he said, "You'll find out." Glen Sonmor was coaching Minnesota and I don't think they had ever beaten Boston. Bobby Smith and Steve Kasper were the starting centremen. Newell dropped the puck and Smith jumped Kasper. After we broke that up I said to Dave, "Way to go, Newly. You've lost control already." [Laughs] It just went on from there. The first period was unreal. At one point we had thrown out Craig Hartsburg and Brad McCrimmon and they got into a fight in the hallway. Kevin and I charged off the ice to break it up. They were fighting outside the door to our dressing room. There was a guy named Herbie who looked after our room in Boston, and I yelled at him to unlock the door. Hartsburg wouldn't quit, wouldn't leave, so I threw him into our room, into the officials' room, if you can believe it, and we locked him in. You should have heard him kicking the door and screaming. Then I thought, hey, that wasn't a very smart thing to do because all our clothes are in there. But he didn't do anything. Afterwards, when he talked about that particular part of it, Dave Newell said, "There were about six fights on the ice and I couldn't find my linesmen. Even they bailed out on me."

I'll tell you what I think about fighting versus no fighting. I did a game this season in Tampa between the Lightning and Colorado. There was nothing but scrums. Players like Claude Lemieux and Dino Ciccarelli were yipping and yapping constantly. The game lasted three hours and nothing really went on except a lot of f-yous. Phil Esposito came in after the game and said, "How are we ever gonna stop this stuff?" I said, "You know why we had a game like that? Because they wouldn't run the risk of being thrown out for starting a fight." And Phil agreed with me. Before, guys fought. They didn't yip and yap. They dropped their gloves, had a fight, and went to the penalty box. Now, you start a fight and your team has to kill a penalty, plus you get suspended. The only way the players can vent their frustrations is by yapping. We really don't have penalties that can curtail what went on that night in Tampa. You can't call an unsportsmanlike minor every time somebody mouths off. You'd ruin the game. We've become real stringent with fighting rules and I really think it's brought other things in, like stickwork and more scrums. Each scrum takes three or four minutes, and look at how long some of the games are.

Last year I was doing a game in Pittsburgh and the Penguins were taking their time getting set for a faceoff on a power play. I said to Ron Francis, "Ronnie, get in here. Let's go." He moved in and said, "Take a look at what's happening right now. Mario is talking to Leroux in French. Jagr is talking to Nedved in Czech. Gord, please talk to me in English."

There's a lot of talking going on right now in our league. Centremen will try to intimidate younger officials verbally. I find that young kids who come out of junior and the minors into the National League have no respect for officiating but we usually put them in their place real quick. It's an easy fix. You go to one of the veterans, say someone like Mark Recchi, and you say, "I don't know who this kid is, but you better tell him how things work up here. If you don't, I will, and if I do it your team is gonna get hurt because I'm calling a penalty." It usually works. The older guys are real good about that.

I've been very fortunate. I've worked finals, I've worked All-Star games, I've worked seventh games in playoff series, but by far the most intense game I've ever officiated in was game three of the World Cup, Canada against the States. It was just unbelievable. I don't really know if there are words to describe the emotion, the intensity, the pressure, on the part of everyone. We were all into it, players, coaches, officials.

Our whole world changes at playoff time. We do things a lot differently. We have curfews, we don't work back-to-back games. There is so much more TV coverage than there was when I started. Now there's a dozen or so cameras at every game. If you're right, wrong, or indifferent, everything you do is under a magnifying glass. These days every team has a coach upstairs who has a telephone to the bench and he's watching the replays. I've had it happen where, after a play when you've chosen to blow the whistle or not blow it, a player comes up and says, "Our coach upstairs just saw the replay and you missed that one." That doesn't bother me. As long as you have confidence in what you do they can do whatever they want.

I don't think the players today have much compassion. When I first came up, when a player got hurt there was concern, even if he was an opponent. Now a guy can get hurt and you'll hear somebody on the other team say something like, "Come on, get up, you big blankety-blank suck."

Right now I'm forty-six and I still thoroughly enjoy the game. I love getting ready for the game, going to the rink, feeling the atmosphere. My biggest problem is the travel, and I don't travel nearly as much as the referees. I'm very fortunate living where I do, in Richmond, Virginia. I get to do a lot of games in Florida. I feel sorry for those poor buggers out West who are always travelling between Vancouver, Edmonton, and Calgary when it's maybe twenty below. My heart goes out to them. What gets me is packing my bags, going to the airport, getting on planes. But once I get to a city, settle in, and know I'm going to do a game, I love it. Every game is a challenge.

On January 2, 1997, the Phoenix Coyotes played the Chicago Blackhawks at the United Center, in Chicago. The referee was Paul Stewart and the linesmen were Ray Scapinello and Mark Paré. Phoenix won the game 4–2. As is usually the case, no special attention was paid the linesmen by the players, fans, media, or the National Hockey League itself. The game started, the game ended, and everyone went home without knowing they had just been in on some hockey history. The moment referee Stewart dropped the puck to start the game it meant Ray Scapinello had set a record for being on the ice in more regular-season NHL games than anyone in the history of the league. It was his 1,981st game, and it broke Ron Finn's record. On February 26, in Toronto, Scapinello reached 2,000. That time, they did have a small ceremony. Scapinello, one of the smallest officials ever to work in the NHL, also holds the record for most playoff appearances, 329. Gordie Howe has the record for most regular-season games as a player, 1,767, while Mark Messier is the playoff leader with 236.

Among those who ignored Scapinello's record-setting appearance in Chicago was the record-setter himself. Along with everyone else at the United Center that night, Ray Scapinello had no idea it was his 1,981st game.

RAY SCAPINELLO

What happened was, I came home from that road trip and my future assignments were in the mail that was piled up on my office desk. They had a game highlighted as being number 2,000, Washington at Toronto. I said to my wife, Maureen, "I guess I'd better look at the calendar." I counted back and found out when I had set the record. They really didn't have to do anything. Nobody has to give you a dinner, or a ring. Your longevity is enough and I don't think it will ever be caught. When I was starting out it was nothing to do eighty or ninety games in a regular schedule. Now, we're contracted to do eighty but most of us end up with sixty-five or seventy. And they're hiring guys a little older too. What I'm proud of the most is that, in twenty-six seasons, I've never missed a hockey game.

I was twenty-five years old when I signed my first contract with the NHL. I played senior hockey but the team I was with in my home town, the Guelph Regals, folded. I was working in the production control department at Canadian General Electric and frustrated that I didn't have anything to do with hockey. Bill McCreary's father-in-law, Mel McPhee, was involved locally and asked me if I wanted to be an official. I thought it was a great idea and started doing kids' games. The National Hockey League was the furthest thing from my mind. I was just happy to be around hockey again. Then I got into the OHA and everything just snowballed from there.

I went to the NHL's rookie camp. They would bring in forty or fifty officials and invite six or seven to their main camp. The first year I was there I didn't get invited but I went back the next year and did get invited. I wasn't hired, but in the middle of the next season Frank Udvari called and asked me if I would work the lines in the American League on weekends. My boss at General Electric was very understanding and allowed me to do it, even if it meant that sometimes I couldn't get back to work on Monday until the afternoon. The year after that I was hired by the NHL. Talk about being in the right place at the right time. I'm sure there are hundreds of officials just as good, or just as bad, as I am who were never afforded the opportunity.

When I was hired I thought I was going to have to move to Dallas or Fort Worth to work in the Central Hockey League. The standard joke around the NHL staff is that I've always been a momma's boy because when I left my parents' house in Guelph I moved right across the street. Bryan Lewis says he's sure I've built a tunnel from my house to theirs. Anyway, right after I was hired, one of the American League officials quit so Scotty Morrison said I could stay in Guelph and do American League games. In my first year under contract I did forty American League games and forty NHL games. That was in '71–72, and I've never done a minor-league game since.

My first NHL game was Minnesota at Buffalo and it went really smooth. I basically don't remember what happened to me yesterday because I try not to live in the past, but my next two games are still very clear in my mind. The second was Chicago at Buffalo. The Sabres were leading 2–1 and Chicago was carrying the puck up the ice and a Buffalo defenceman started to go off on a change. When he saw the rush coming he stayed on the ice. The player who was going to take his place had jumped on, but then he jumped off. Me, being a little over-officious, called a penalty against Buffalo for too many men on the ice. At the time I thought it was a wonderful call but, in reality, it was an awful call. The guy was only about one foot onto the ice when he jumped back on the bench. Punch Imlach was coaching Buffalo and he was so angry he refused to put a man in the penalty box. Art Skov was the referee and he warned Imlach three times. Finally he gave him a bench minor penalty and Buffalo was two men short. Bobby Hull scored two goals on the power play and Chicago ended up winning 5–2.

I was flying out to Oakland the next day and when I got to the airport I bought a paper. The headline on the sports page was: "HULL AND SCAPINELLO BEAT SABRES." I was mortified. One of the quotes was from Punch Imlach. He said, "I don't know who that number 36 is but they must have 36 officials. If his number was one higher he'd be out of the league." I was number 36 and all the way out to Oakland I was just shaking. I figured that, when I landed, there would be a message for me saying, "Go home, young man, you're no good," but there wasn't. The next night in Oakland, their coach, Vic Stasiuk, tried to kick down our door after the game to get at me because he felt an offside goal had been scored. At that point I just couldn't take it. I was a basket case and was sure I couldn't handle the NHL. Bruce Hood was the referee and he told me, "Don't worry about stuff like that. Someday I'll show you my scrapbook. It happens to all of us."

When I started out I was a sensitive guy on the blueline, but I had to change. A sensitive guy can't survive in this league because he'll never get respect. I'm dating myself here, but I remember doing a game in the old Detroit Olympia working with John D'Amico. I was near the red line and the play was going over the blueline. From where I saw it I thought the play was offside by a mile but John waved it good and the goalie had to make a great save. I looked around and nobody was even going near John D'Amico. Not one player said a word to him. I remember it like it was yesterday, saying to myself, "God, I wonder if I'll ever get that kind of respect." At that time they were always on my case, saying things like, "Wake up, you little prick. Who are you, anyway?" You had to take all that stuff and you'd wonder if you'd ever achieve the respectability John D'Amico had. Now, I think I have.

I have good rapport with the players and I've been quite successful in the business. I've worked the Stanley Cup finals sixteen times in the last eighteen years. The finals are never picked by seniority. It's strictly by performance and I'm really proud of that. When you work the finals it means you are considered one of the four best linesmen in the world. I'll tell you, standing at centre ice and hearing the national anthem being played the first game you work in a final series, you get goosebumps. Unfortunately, not every linesman will have that experience, nor every referee, but it's really something. When I was picked to do game seven between the Rangers and Vancouver in '94, that was a real highlight.

Another was working the third game of the World Cup. Oh man, what a night that was. Bryan Lewis was in our room before the game. It was important to Bryan because he's the head of the officiating department and he wants us to do a good job because it makes him look good, right? I was lacing my skates and he said to me, "Are you ready for this game?" I looked up and said, "I won't even answer that question," and continued lacing up my skates. It was incredible hockey. They were hacking and slashing and during a commercial break I said to Terry Gregson, "I think we've lost control of this game. These guys are nuts out here." Every player was a National Leaguer and the pressure and intensity were incredible. I think it was the greatest game I've ever been involved in as an official.

You really appreciate players in a game like that, and at other times too. In the 1992 finals between Pittsburgh and Chicago, Jaromir Jagr got the puck inside the Chicago blue-line and it was like he was taking on the entire Chicago team and just toying with them. I was standing at the blue-line with my hands on my knees watching this guy and it was really something. It seemed like he went around everybody wearing a Chicago uniform and he scored a marvellous goal.

Guy Lafleur was another one, a real class guy. I remember doing a game when he was pulled down on a breakaway and everybody was thinking it was going to be a penalty-shot call. Ron Wicks was the referee and he chose to call nothing and suddenly there were four Canadiens all over Wicks arguing about the non-call. I looked over at the Montreal bench and there was Lafleur, sort of dusting himself off and sitting down. He didn't bat an eye. Such a gentleman. Another was Jean Ratelle. If he told you he felt you missed an offside there was a good chance you missed it. He never said anything unless he was pretty sure.

People always ask how a guy my size breaks up the fights and I tell them that when you're 5'7" it's not easy. [Laughs] But seriously, when you step in to break it up the object is to tie up their arms so they can't throw any more punches. Mind you, you could be John D'Amico or Ron Asselstine, if there's a big guy like Barry Beck in the fight he's gonna break away and keep whaling. I'll watch the heavyweights and let them fight. Then I'll say, "Are you guys done?" and more than likely they are and they'll break away. I can count on two fingers the number of times I've seen a so-called heavyweight fighter hit a guy when he's down. They have a job to do, just like you and I.

I was manhandled once, by Stu Grimson, in a game in Chicago. He wasn't angry at me, he just wanted to get at some guy, but he waltzed me around pretty good. We can't be thrown around like he did to me. We decided on a ten-game suspension. I didn't like to do it because ten games is a big chunk out of the schedule, and if a guy's not a marquee player, after ten games somebody could have taken his job. That's the only time I've ever done anything like that, but it had to be done.

Breaking up fights is a minuscule part of our job. We make our living on precision line calls, our judgement, our rapport with the players, and being able to defuse situations. Skating ability is a must for a linesman because it puts you in a position to make an accurate call. I've never counted the number of decisions and non-decisions you have to make in an evening, the number of times they go over the bluelines, and the red line, whether it's an offside pass or an icing. If the play is in the corner you can't relax and say they're not coming your way, because as soon as you say that, they come your way. The game is so fast. If you look somewhere you're not supposed to, that's when you miss an offside. It happens in the blink of an eye.

Linesmen have much more responsibility now. We can call major penalties, if there's a man in the crease, if the goal's displaced. There's a zillion things you've got to be focused on. You're on automatic pilot, you just react. If you stop to think about something and then react to it, four other things have happened. It's all night long, and you don't get a break.

I don't worry about a hockey game until the puck is dropped at 7:35. I've lost a lot of my hair now but I would have lost it years ago if I worried all day that I might miss an offside that night. Take the Stanley Cup finals. An offside goal could cost people millions of dollars. It could be the difference between being eliminated or going on to a sixth or seventh game. The pressure is tremendous on referees and linesmen. I don't think people realize that.

Anybody good at anything makes it look easy. Andy van Hellemond made refereeing look easy. A junior-A referee could be sitting at home watching a game on TV that was being officiated by Andy van Hellemond, Bob Hodges, and Leon Stickle. Say it's Montreal and Toronto, and they're going up and down, nobody's slashing, and the game is moving along smoothly. The junior-A referee watching at home will say, "I can do that." But he can't do that. That showed when we were on strike. The game he's watching is going smoothly because the officials are Andy van Hellemond, Bob Hodges, and Leon Stickle.

I don't like attention, like the ceremony for my two-thousandth game. Ron Asselstine phoned my wife and asked her what she was going to do for it and Maureen said, "Nothing. Ray doesn't want me to do anything for it." I just like to do my job, get off the ice, grab a couple of pucks from that game to give to the kids in the neighbourhood, and move on to my next assignment. A guy from ESPN was at our camp doing interviews and he asked me, "What would you like the people to know about you?" I said, "I'm a family man, married eighteen years with a sixteen-year-old son. I don't have a favourite team, and I don't care who wins or loses. I'm just an ordinary guy trying to do a good job."

I'm not trying to blow smoke at you, but I love my lifestyle. I used to go on two-week road trips. Now they're five, six, or seven days and then I might be home for four or five days. It's a great feeling to come home to Guelph on Monday and know you don't have to answer to anybody until 7:35 Thursday evening, in Buffalo. My home time is my quality time, and now I'm getting a lot more of it.

I'm fifty years old and I don't know how much longer is left for me. I guess Bryan Lewis is gonna have to tell me that. I feel great, my health is good, and, as I told you, I've never missed a game since I started. I'd love to go on. I forget who said it, but someone once told me, "Find a job you love and you'll never have to work a day in your life." I found that job.

When the Detroit Red Wings and the Philadelphia Flyers opened the 1997 Stanley Cup finals in Philadelphia, Ray Scapinello was one of the linesmen. That made it seventeen finals in the last nineteen years for Scapinello, quite an achievement.

The final series brought a quick and peaceful conclusion to what had been a turbulent season for the officials as the Red Wings easily swept the Flyers in four games. There wasn't a fight in the series and, despite fears that it might happen, the Stanley Cup–winning goal was recorded without the referee having to make a phone call "upstairs."

Acknowledgements

The idea for this book came to me in a hotel room in San Jose, California, early in March 1996. Two nights later I ran into Andy van Hellemond after a game he refereed and I broadcast, in Anaheim, and I asked him what he thought about it. Andy's instant enthusiasm convinced me then and there to carry on. I want to thank Andy and all the officials I interviewed, past and present, who so willingly gave their time to make this book possible. They reinforced my opinion that hockey people are great people.

From the outset I received full co-operation from the NHL's director of officiating, Bryan Lewis, and his staff. In particular I want to thank Jackie Rinaldi, who patiently and efficiently handled my many questions and requests.

Ron Finn kindly gave me permission to use material from his 1993 book, *On the Lines*, written with David Boyd. Broadcaster Ron MacLean, who does a lot of refereeing when he's not in front of a camera, provided encouragement, ideas, and contacts.

Denis Brodeur and Diane Sobolewski supplied the majority of the photographs. Carole Robertson transcribed the many hours of recorded interviews. Ted Blackman, sports director of CJAD Radio in Montreal, allowed me to miss a couple of Canadiens road trips late in the 1996–97 season so I could cope with approaching deadlines.

I was fortunate that McClelland & Stewart again assigned Jonathan Webb as my editor and Peter Buck as my copy editor. Jonathan was the referee-in-chief who ruled with a firm and skilful hand right from the opening faceoff. Peter worked the lines, whistling down any factual offsides. I thank them both.

Finally, while hockey games cannot be played without officials, I cannot write books without the love and support of my personal officiating crew, Wilma, Nancy Anne, and Doug.

Index